THE LAMB AMONG THE BEASTS

THE LAMB AMONG THE BEASTS

A CHRISTOLOGICAL
COMMENTARY
ON THE REVELATION
OF JOHN THAT UNLOCKS
THE MEANING
OF ITS MANY NUMBERS

ROY C. NADEN

REVIEW AND HERALD® PUBLISHING ASSOCIATION
HAGERSTOWN, MD 21740

The author assumes full responsibility for the accuracy of all facts and quotations as cited in this book.

This book was
Edited by Richard W. Coffen
Interior design by Patricia S. Wegh
Cover design by Matthew Pierce
Lamb illustration by Jerry Dadds
Typeset: 12/14 Century Old Style

PRINTED IN U.S.A.

99 98 97 96   5 4 3 2 1

R&H Cataloging Service
Naden, Roy C
    The lamb among the beasts.

    1. Bible. N. T. Revelation—Commentaries.
2. Bible. N. T. Revelation—Study and teaching.
I. Title.

                228

ISBN 0-8280-0983-X

Dedication

Dedicated
to Jennifer
for her constant
encouragement
and unfailing
insights

Contents

Outline of the Revelation of Jesus

The **resurrected Jesus** promises, "I will return" (Rev. 1)

The **stellar Jesus** supports His churches (Rev. 2, 3)

The **enthroned Jesus** worshiped by all of heaven (Rev. 4, 5)

The **proclaimed Jesus** despite great opposition (Rev. 6)

The **shepherd Jesus** with the redeemed in heaven (Rev. 7)

The **attacked Jesus** in conflict with Satan (Rev. 8, 9)

The **angelic Jesus** commissions the church (Rev. 10)

The **witnessed Jesus** presented by the church (Rev. 11)

The **lamb Jesus** in great conflict with Satan (Rev. 12)

The **mimicked Jesus** in a parade of opposition (Rev. 13)

The **reaping Jesus** commissions three angels (Rev. 14)

The **wrath-filled Jesus** judges Babylon (Rev. 15-18)

The **bridegroom Jesus** with His bride in heaven (Rev. 19)

The **victorious Jesus** destroys Satan and his followers (Rev. 20)

The **re-creating Jesus** with the redeemed forever (Rev. 21)

Introduction

This commentary is written from the historicist point of view. Despite assertions in a 1993 dissertation by Dr. Kai Arasola, printed under the title *The End of Historicism,* many Protestant scholars continue to espouse historicism as the most appropriate lens through which to view John's visions. But this commentary also seeks to note the importance of viewing the work from the point of view of the original readers at the end of the first century, as well as recognizing its devotional relevance for readers on the threshold of the twenty-first century.

I was first introduced to the symbols of Revelation as a child. In my mind I can still see, on spotlighted auditorium stages, cutouts and charts of dragons and monsters as impassioned evangelists proclaimed the prophecies. In time I also began to preach from the Apocalypse, and have continued to do so for 40 years. But during those decades, my perspective on this book has changed radically from fascination with the future to security in a past—the cross of Jesus.

Twenty-five years ago I wrote *Spotlight on Revelation.* Fifteen years ago I expanded those thoughts in *Today's Life.* Four years later I completely revised the material and published it under the title *Revelation.* But the present work represents a different emphasis. It seeks first to be Christological, which, I have come to believe, was John's primary emphasis (one of the hazards of ongoing publication).

Jesus is the central theme of the entire Bible. First, He is the focus of all the crucial Old Testament prophecies. As the learned bishop of Lincoln, England, once put it: "All God's promises and prophecies to the Jews, all their priesthoods, sacrifices, Temple, and sacraments, preached Christ" (Christopher Wordsworth, *The Holy Bible With Notes,* vol. 1, p. xxiii). And after His first coming, all revelation continued to center on Him, from Matthew to the last book in the sacred canon.

But those of us who continue to believe in the historicist tradition sometimes become so fascinated by time lines, dates, historical outlines, and eschatological nightmares, such as economic boycotts and death decrees, that we miss the central point of the book. That is, we see so clearly the faces of all who are against Christ that we miss the reassuring presence of He who alone can guide us to the eternal Sabbath rest.

Considering the vast amount that has been written about the Apocalypse, one needs to consider thoughtfully what contribution, if any, might be made to such a body of literature, and for whom. The audience for which this book has been prepared is clearly designated. It is written for college students and laypeople who have an interest in apocalyptic writings. And two reasons have led me to write. First is the fact that little has been written on Revelation with the stated objective of exploring Christocentricity. The second reason is that no work of which I am aware has approached the book with a hermeneutic that includes a major emphasis on the vast use of numbers in Revelation.

As I wrote this work I attempted to be theologically precise, but at the same time to approach theological discussion and terminology so that it will not discourage college students and laypeople. So if your interests are the result of years of study of the Johannine corpus, this book will be nothing more than an introduction, and you probably will be interested only in the first two chapters, which deal with hermeneutics.

Some points of view you may find different. In some cases a new position is suggested, because recent scholarship has shown the inappropriateness of an early point of view (for example, a nineteenth-century dating of the fifth and sixth trumpets). But in the main, any newness is merely a matter of emphasis. Truth is not new, but very old, and for the Christian it comes directly from the Founder, Jesus Christ. As Jude puts it: "I felt I had to write and urge you to contend for *the faith that was once for all entrusted* to the saints" (Jude 3). As we shall see in the presentation of the hermeneutic on which this volume is based, the Apocalypse is grounded solidly on the words of Jesus. To stay with Him is to be on safe ground, but to wander from Him is to digress into dangerous territory. So above all, this book on the Apocalypse is designed to help us see and hear Jesus, and in this way find security in Him. In this setting newness is more the better understanding of well-known themes.

One additional note about historicism. The facts of church history, especially details of the claims and acts of the Papacy during the Middle Ages, have been researched and presented in numberless Protestant works. Because these details are so widely reported, I intentionally do not repeat this material in length. Not because it is untrue or an incorrect interpretation, but because my purpose is to help readers see Jesus in all the Apocalypse. The length of the manuscript does have practical limits. One cannot do everything in a work this size, and Christology is my main emphasis.

I know that no reader will agree with every position presented in this book. That is to be expected. But I hope that readers may be inspired to study the Apocalypse themselves and in that process become more intimate worshipers of the Lamb, following Him always.

As is the case with most manuscripts, many people have made significant contributions. Most of the typing was handled by Lynda du Preez, ably assisted by Carolyn Wilson, Nancy Richardson, Cathy McDaniel, Doris Stonas, Anita Anzures, Lori Hubbard, and Allyn Craig. Suzy de Oliveira and Debi Robertson were responsible for the manuscript as a whole. I am deeply indebted to the entire team.

Discussions with colleagues are an important part of the process of writing. In particular, Drs. Kenneth Strand and Jon Paulien were both good listeners and good advisors. Drs. Richard Fredericks and Colin House, two of my former students, did me the favor of a thoughtful and insightful critique of the manuscript. And the final manuscript was reviewed by Dr. Hans K. LaRondelle, who himself has written insightfully on the Apocalypse. I especially thank him for the time he devoted to reading and commenting. And to those whose comments appear on the back jacket, both here in the United States and in Europe: Alger Keough, Z. Lyke, Dragutin Martak, Lee J. Gugliotto, and Ulf Gustavsson, I also offer great appreciation for the time taken and suggestions made. And last of all my editor, Richard W. Coffen, examined the manuscript meticulously and helped to clarify the text for its intended readers.

All these reviewers gave excellent input. But I am sure that their good advice has not been adequately incorporated despite my best efforts. So the manuscript's shortcomings are my responsibility, not theirs. And in the final analysis, no book *about* Scripture is the final word. The Holy Spirit guides any who seek Him as they read the Word itself. ●

Outline

1. The context of apocalyptic literature
   Revelation: the biblical example of apocalyptic writing
   common in John's day

2. Structure of Revelation
   Two halves
   Chiasm
   Seven-part arrangement
   The major sevens
   > Churches
   > Seals
   > Trumpets
   > Bowls
   Repetition, expansion, eschatology

3. Primary symbol
   The lamb

THE LION-LAMB PARADOX

The study of John's Apocalypse is one of the most difficult and, at the same time, one of the most exciting opportunities for a Christian. I still recall my first readings of the book of Revelation and the alternate exhilaration and despair I experienced studying the vivid pictures. An understanding of some of the visions seemed beyond my comprehension.

One cannot read far in the book without sensing intuitively that the usual tools for understanding are inadequate. What do you make of a passage that talks about a creature that was, and is not, but is, and that has seven heads, which are not really heads but mountains, while its horns are kings? A woman rides the creature, but she is floating on water, which symbolizes people, but is really a city! This is the fascinating world of apocalyptic.

In this chapter we attempt to place the book of Revelation in the setting of John's time, discuss the sources on which much of the writing is dependent, and analyze the coordinating symbol of the book, which becomes the first interpretive clue to our understanding.

THE CONTEXT OF APOCALYPTIC LITERATURE

The years that led up to Jesus' birth were difficult for Israel. The guidance of living prophets had ceased, and as the world waited for the Messiah, Israel busied itself with writing and ritual that did little to prepare her to recognize the Messiah when He came. They had the writings of the Old Testament prophets and knew where He would be born and the general period in which He would come, but thoughts of national grandeur blinded them so that they failed to recognize Jesus when He came in such humble circumstances.

Throughout Jesus' public ministry the scribes kept asking Him for a sign, despite the miracles He performed throughout the Holy Land. Ignoring prophecies constantly fulfilled in His daily life, the religious teachers kept asking where He came from. After He had given a masterful presentation of the meaning of the heart of the law, learned scribes shook their heads and asked for documentation of His authority. And at the end of His three and a half years of public ministry, during which evidences of His divinity had multiplied astoundingly, the Jewish leaders called for His execution and went home to keep the Sabbath.

The spiritual declension of the two centuries preceding Jesus' birth and the religious chaos of the first century A.D. were often stirred by the writings of the apocalypticists. Their works all centered on the coming of the Messiah to elevate Israel as the head of all nations, and they couched their messages in fiery language that roused nationalistic pride.

William Barclay has noted several characteristics of these writings. They emphasized:

1. The coming of the Messiah in avenging power and glory.
2. Elijah's return to announce the Messiah's coming.
3. The entire world terrified and shattered.
4. All human relationships disrupted.
5. The destruction (or conversion) of the Gentiles.
6. The resurrection of the dead.
7. Ultimate peace and fertility throughout nature, including vineyards producing bunches each of 1,000 grapes.
8. A new kingdom, with Israel and Judah reunited in an eternity of holiness and righteousness *(The Revelation of John,* vol. 1, pp. 7-13).

Some of the more graphic examples of works in this genre include 4 Ezra, Enoch, Apocalyptic Baruch, the Testaments of the Twelve Patriarchs, and the Sibylline Oracles. Apart from the content described by Barclay, these works shared a common style. They employed dramatic descriptions with numerous symbols. Thus, when John wrote his Apocalypse, he did not invent a new form, but rather wrote in a well-known vogue.

When modern readers open the pages of the Bible's last book, they must keep in mind that this style of literature is quite different from any other complete New Testament book and that it follows a style widely known in John's day, works with which both he and his readers were familiar.

Think of apocalyptic as a kind of verbal "impressionism." What Renoir is to art, apocalyptic is to literature. You will see many graphic colors. At first reading they may seem to be without form. But when you catch the perspective, the picture will stand out boldly. And just as an artist would not explain the significance of every brushstroke, so we are not always able to attach significance to every word, because some appear to be only for dramatic effect.

This ought not to disturb us: the same is true of other parts of Scripture. When Jesus told stories, He did not mean for us to give each word equal weight. Some of the words are just part of the setting in which a major truth is taught. A whole chapter of the Gospel of Luke is devoted to telling the story of the prodigal son. Although we can find several minor lessons in this parable, Jesus seems to be illustrating one major truth: We can come to the heavenly Father just as we are; we do not change to come to Him, but we come to Him to be changed. In the same way in John's Apocalypse, we read picture stories that illustrate at least one major truth, and we may not find significance in every detail.

THE STRUCTURE OF REVELATION

Although it may not appear obvious at first reading, Revelation has an intricate structure, and understanding this structure helps us grasp the message of the book. One reason the structure is not as obvious as John intended is because of the insertion of chapters and verses, which sometimes interrupt the continuous reading of his theme. Only centuries after the writing of the book were these artificial divisions incorporated.[1] They help us identify the sentences of the text, but they sometimes interrupt the flow of a passage. For example, chapters 2 and 3 are one vision, as are chapters 5, 6, and 10, 11.

The first and most basic aspect of the structure is that Revelation is divided into two halves—chapters 1 through 12:10 being historical and 12:11 through 22, which are eschatological.[2]

Then too, a dominant feature of some Hebrew writing is its chiastic structure. According to this ingenious approach, the introductory theme is repeated in the climax, the second theme is repeated in the second last part of the work, the third theme is repeated in the third last, etc.

Some scholars have shown a chiastic structure in every major section of the Apocalypse, as well as the entire book itself.[3] Kenneth Strand has identified a clear chiasm. The recognition of a chiastic structure is a helpful interpretive clue to which we will often refer. The chiastic structure recognized in this work is as follows:

CHIASMUS OF THE BOOK OF REVELATION

Historical   Eschatological

The Central Words

Victory Through the Lamb
Rev. 12:10, 11

Satan Cast Down

Initially, Rev. 12:7   Finally, Rev. 12:13

Church in the Wilderness

Flees, Rev. 12:6   Preserved, Rev. 12:14

The Woman's Seed

Son, Rev. 12:1-5   Church, Rev. 12:17

Worship

God, Rev. 11   Beast, Rev. 13

Gospel to the World

Directed, Rev. 10   Completed, Rev. 14

Judgment

Provisional, Rev. 8, 9   Final, Rev. 15, 16

Decisions of the Judgment

Vindication, Rev. 7   Vengeance, Rev. 17

The Gospel

Proclaimed and opposed, Rev. 6   Opposers rejected,
                                          Rev. 18

The Throne

Lamb/Lion, Rev. 4, 5   Lion/Lamb, Rev. 19

The Church

On earth, Rev. 2, 3   In heaven, Rev. 20, 21

Second Coming

Promised, Rev. 1   Realized, Rev. 22

Another approach to the understanding of the book is to recognize the 54 sets of sevens in Revelation. This has led several commentators to divide the book into seven sections,[4] for example:

1. The seven letters to the seven churches
2. The seven seals
3. The seven trumpets
4. The seven mystical figures—woman, dragon, Man-child, beast from sea, beast from land, Lamb, and Son of man on the cloud
5. The seven bowls (or plagues)
6. The doom of Christ's foes
7. The consummation

This work follows an even simpler outline based on Jesus' words in Matthew 24, 25.[5] That structure is:

Introduction—the seven churches
Section 1—the seven seals
Section 2—the seven trumpets
Section 3—the seven bowls
The final appeals

A simple structure based on the four major sevens—churches, seals, trumpets, and bowls—reminds us of an important precedent in an Old Testament apocalypse on which John drew more heavily than on any other Old Testament book. When God revealed to Daniel the story of the world as it relates to the story of the church, He imparted it in four major visions: Daniel 2; 7; 8, 9; 10-12. As you read these four prophetic visions, you find an illustration of the hermeneutic of *repetition, expansion,* and *eschatology.* Each successive vision covers the same basic history, but from a slightly different perspective, and with the focus shifting more and more toward the *eschaton.* For example, Daniel 2 spends more time describing Babylon than any of the other three world kingdoms. Daniel 7 shifts the emphasis to the fourth kingdom, the little horn, and the judgment that inaugurates the kingdom of glory. Daniel 8 and 9 maintain a similar emphasis but spotlight the cross. Daniel 10 through 12 have less to say about the early kingdoms and reserve the most important comment for the moment when Michael stands up for His people and closes the age of sin.

The same approach is obvious in John's Revelation. The first main presentation, the seven churches, gives a somewhat equal glimpse of all the periods between the First and Second Advents. The next sevenfold presentation, the seals, moves rapidly over the first four periods and reserves its longest comments for the fifth and sixth. The third septet, the trumpets, also moves rapidly over the first four and gives an expanded view of the fifth and sixth. In the last major seven, the bowls, the focus is exclusively on the final moments of time before the Second Advent shatters Satan's reign. In other words, Revelation follows, to a significant degree, the approach of the prophetic passages of Daniel.

Considering Daniel's visions, we can see that an outline of the book of Revelation based on the four major sevens is not imposed on the text, but is implicit in it.[6] This principle will guide us in our examination of the text. We will seek to see in what ways each major historical presentation builds on what precedes it.

To this point we have discussed the apocalyptic literature in vogue in John's day and used by him under the inspiration of the Holy Spirit. Then we set down several approaches to understand the structure of the book and identified the particular approach followed in this present work. This leads to another fundamental consideration: What holds the book together? What is the coordinating principle or symbol? To these questions we would answer without hesitation, *the Lamb of God*.

THE BOOK'S MOST IMPORTANT SYMBOL, THE LAMB

Twenty-eight times in Revelation we read about the Lamb. The first overt reference is in chapter 5, but it is introduced with increasing frequency in later chapters, until we read seven references to the Lamb in chapters 21 and 22 alone.

John could not have presented a more arresting symbol for Jewish readers. For more than 1,000 years the lamb had been the central focus of their worship services. The offering of a perfect male lamb on the altar of burnt offering twice a day (so punctually, so predictably, that there was never a time when a lamb was not burning on the altar day or night) had brought the Jews a verbal shorthand. They called this sacrifice *the daily*. The full import of John the Baptist's cry "Look, the Lamb of God, who takes away the sin of the world!" (John 1:29)[7] can be understood only in the context of Jewish sacrificial practice.

Interestingly, considering what he would later write in his Apocalypse, only John mentions this introduction by the Baptist, and he records it twice. Evidently it happened both on the day of Jesus' baptism and the next day as well (see John 1:36). Thus the introduction to his Gospel and the Apocalypse bear the same symbolic imprint. John would have us all "behold the Lamb of God" because only He takes away our personal sins.

Driving home this point in his opening remarks, John speaks about the shed blood of our Redeemer. As Richard Fredericks has noted: "The sixth verse at the heart of the opening doxology is the key to the book. Notice the order of the phrases. First, Jesus loves us—before any action or change by us. Christ loves us just as we are. Second, He has freed us from our sins. The verb is in the past perfect tense; our freedom from sin is already an accomplished fact. Sin's grip was broken not by us, but by Him. *He* has freed us. Finally, how did He free us? By His blood! It was in His death that Christ freed all men. Not even His holy life could have released us from the bondage of the law's awful sentence of death. No matter how holy another might be whom we love or how diligently we might strive to be like Him, we are debtors and criminals before a holy and just, but merciless, law. This changed at the cross; mercy and justice met, righteousness and peace kissed, man's prison door opened as his execution was carried out on Christ. God remained just and yet the justifier of the ungodly" ("The 'Lamb' in the Book of Revelation," [term paper, Andrews University, 1980], p. 3).

The lamb had great significance in the Exodus experience. The night before Israel's emancipation, the blood of a lamb was used as a symbol of the Messiah's protecting blood. When the lamb had been slain and its blood sprinkled on the doorposts of the house, the angel of death passed over and left behind no grim reminder of God's judgment against the enemies of His people. That Exodus theme of God's power to deliver and His equal power to judge His enemies occurs throughout the Old and New Testaments, and Jesus is the ultimate focus of such imagery. In speaking of Israel's escape to the Promised Land, Paul notes that "they drank from the spiritual rock that accompanied them, and that rock was Christ" (1 Cor. 10:4).

Isaiah beautifully utilizes the lamb symbolism: "We all, like sheep, have gone astray, each of us has turned to his own way; and the Lord has laid on him the iniquity of us all. He was oppressed and afflicted, yet he did not open his mouth; he was led like a lamb to the slaughter, and as a sheep before her shearers is silent, so he did not open his mouth" (Isa. 53:6, 7).

Throughout the book this symbol of Jesus keeps our eyes focused on our only Source of redemption. In the opening verse of the book, John tells us that His purpose is to reveal Jesus, and remaining faithful to that purpose, he expects his readers to understand the book that way. However, at times through the course of history it has not always been easy to see the all-powerful Christ. During times of personal discouragement we may wonder where He is and why it seems He does not hear. The millions of martyrs of all ages echo our personal perplexity. John places on their lips the words "How long, Sovereign Lord, holy and true, until you judge the inhabitants of the earth and avenge our blood?" He continues, stating that "each of them was given a white robe, and they were told to wait a little longer, until the number of their fellow servants and brothers who were to be killed as they had been was completed" (Rev. 6:10, 11).

In Revelation John takes us across the sweep of history several times, beginning with the events of the first centuries and ending with earth's closing scenes. But each time he gives a different perspective or point of view. One time we see history from the Shepherd's viewpoint (the churches), another time from the point of view of the flock (the seals), and still another from the view of the attacking enemy (the trumpets). We have to change our focus constantly to understand what we are reading. But Jesus the Lamb is a consistent symbol. Thus the only relief in the otherwise nefarious events of Revelation 13 is to see the portrait of the Lamb (verse 8), and in chapter 17, where John describes a scarlet clothed woman riding a multiheaded, multihorned beast, we are also pointed to the Lamb (verse 14).

How does John intend us to interpret the ever-present symbol of the Lamb? Norman Hillyar suggested at least six roles for Jesus the Lamb: Redeemer, the Object of our worship, Conqueror, Judge, Shepherd, and Bridegroom ("The Lamb in the Apocalypse," *Evangelical Quarterly,* October-December 1967, pp. 232-236).

The Redeemer image is drawn from Jewish history. When a family fell on hard times, it might be forced to sell some of its land, but God introduced a plan whereby none of the tribes would permanently lose the territory given them at the time of the original occupation. The celebration of the jubilee each fiftieth year provided for the automatic return of all land to its original family owners.[8] However, if land had been sold, a relative could buy it back and return it to the original owner before the jubilee. This transaction was called a "redemption of property," and our use of the words *redemption* and *redeemer* are based on that history.

John pictures Jesus as a Lamb looking "as if it had been slain" (Rev. 5:6). But in a wonderful paradox He is further described in the same passage as "the Lion of the tribe of Judah, the Root of David" (verse 5). In the lamb we see a gentle, tender, vulnerable, submissive Jesus; in the lion, the bold, aggressive, fearless, protecting Conqueror. Jesus the Lamb/Lion has paid the redemption price. Each of us as individuals needed to be purchased back to the family of Jesus, to have the debt canceled, to have the price of our sins paid, to accept the substitution of Jesus in death. He is the Redeemer in the full Old Testament meaning. We can now claim His death as if it were ours, His righteousness as if it were our own, His perfection as if we had lived it, His enthronement as if we were seated today with Him in heaven (see Eph. 2:6). In the Redeemer/Lamb we have everything. We have no reason ever to doubt or fear or feel insecure again. We are His purchased, secure possession, and everlasting life is ours now (see John 3:36).

The Lamb is also to be the *object of our worship,* and the songs of praise surrounding the initial presentation of the Lamb symbol carry us to the ultimate of human praise. "You are worthy to take the scroll and to open its seals, because you were slain, and with your blood you purchased men for God from every tribe and language and people and nation. . . . Worthy is the Lamb, who was slain, to receive power and wealth and wisdom and strength and honor and glory and praise! . . . To him who sits on the throne and to the Lamb be praise and honor and glory and power, for ever and ever!" (Rev. 5:9-13).

The third figure is *the Lamb as conqueror*. Later we will note how the beast imitates the Lamb in every possible way. Just as the Lamb has horns of power, so does the beast. Just as the Lamb rules in every nation, kindred, tongue, and people, so does the beast. But when the beast comes against the Lamb, the Lamb is clearly revealed to be the ruler of all the universe, King of kings and Lord of lords. For the "ten horns you saw are ten kings. . . . They give their power and authority to the beast. They will make war against the Lamb, but the Lamb will overcome them" (Rev. 17:12-14).

Fourth, we see *the Lamb as judge*. The only judgment we see in the book of Revelation is on the enemies of God's people. Our Lamb vindicates us, His people, so we are forever at peace in a faith relationship with Him. But He must finally pour His judgments on those who refuse to accept His death to atone for their sins. The cry we hear as the Lamb opens the fifth seal is "How long . . . until you judge the inhabitants of the earth and avenge our blood?" (Rev. 6:10). In the Apocalypse the combined work of judging and avenging go together as one work *for* God's elect and *against* their enemies, as John confirms in Revelation 18:20.

Fifth, we see *the Lamb as a shepherd*. In the setting of the initial presentation of Jesus as the Lamb, John extends the metaphor of the lamb to include Christ as shepherd. (In a similar way the Bible portrays Christ as both judge and advocate.) Describing the ultimate gathering around the throne of God, John writes: "For the Lamb at the center of the throne will be their shepherd; he will lead them to springs of living water" (Rev. 7:17). Who could better understand the needs of sheep than the Lamb who is also the Shepherd? He guides you in this life and guides you into eternity.

The final aspect of the Lamb symbol is *the Lamb as bridegroom.* Revelation 19 is devoted to a description of the wedding celebration in which Jesus and His church finally meet in heaven as bride and groom. The bridegroom symbol speaks intimately to most of us. Few experiences in a lifetime compare with the excitement of a wedding celebration. When bride and groom meet, they pledge to each other a lifetime of togetherness, each seeking the happiness and fulfillment of the other.[9] Jesus offers us a relationship even more intimate than that.

This multifaceted symbol of the Lamb is crucial to our understanding of the visions of the Bible's last book. And with this integrating symbol clearly established, we are ready to begin the task of formulating a hermeneutic, a system of interpretation by which we seek to see Jesus the Lamb in every chapter of the Apocalypse. ●

---

[1] When and by whom the chapters were first introduced is not known with certainty. Some authorities credit the archbishop of Canterbury, Stephen Langton. Others credit Hugo a Santo Caro, a Spanish cardinal. Both lived in the thirteenth century. Langton, a Sorbonne doctor, became a cardinal in 1206 and archbishop of Canterbury in 1207. He had a leadership role in the movement that climaxed in the writing of the Magna Charta in 1215. The division of the biblical text into verses came three centuries later as a result of the work of Robert Stephanus. By inserting verse divisions, he enhanced the usefulness of the 1551 edition of his Greek-Latin dual-text Bible. Another contribution for which he is well known is the preparation between 1538 and 1540 of a Latin version of the Scriptures, which was "in reality the foundation of the official Roman Vulgate, adopted at the Council of Trent, April 8, 1546" (I. M. Price, *The Ancestry of Our English Bible*, p. 171; see also Geddes MacGregor's *The Bible in the Making*, p. 103).

[2] Scholars are not agreed on the dividing line between the historical and the eschatological sections of the book. Some place it later than chapter 11. See chapter 12 of this work for a fuller elaboration.

[3] Thomas Austin has developed a chiasm of 26 sections.

[4] For example, F. W. Farrar, W. J. Erdman, W. Hendrickson, and others.

[5] This feature is discussed in greater detail in the next chapter.

[6] Chapter 2 of this work presents the major argument for this understanding of the structure.

[7] "Lamb" is *amnos* in Greek here and *arnion* in Revelation. The latter has the meaning of a young lamb or lambkin.

[8] Although the Pentateuch commands the observance of the jubilee, we find no solid evidence in either Scripture or other historical sources that the Israelites followed these instructions.

[9] John's first readers, however, would have pictured a scene very much like the one Jesus described in the parable of the wise and foolish virgins.

Outline

1. Four most common interpretive approaches:
   Preterism
   Historicism
   Futurism
   Idealism

2. Hundreds of Old Testament allusions
   Daniel the most frequently quoted

3. Continuous references to the Second Coming

4. Five major interpretive principles:
   Anticipate language to be symbolic
   References to Old Testament places and people are
      to be understood as symbolic and worldwide
      when brought into the New Testament.
   Numerals 3, 4, 7, 10, and 12 understood *first*
      as qualitative.
   Revelation is based on Matthew 24 and 25, which are
      rooted in Daniel.
   The cross is central to everything John writes.

CHAPTER TWO

KEYS FOR THE DOORS

I f you have read any expository works on Revelation, you know that interpretations vary widely. Hardly two scholars seem to agree on the book's basic message, let alone its scores of symbols. The reason for the extraordinary difference of opinion is that few writers agree on a hermeneutic by which to interpret the book, or they utilize no hermeneutic at all.

Hermeneutics is the branch of theology that deals with principles of biblical understanding. When you develop a hermeneutic, you establish a set of principles for a particular theological task. To put that another way, you collect a "ring of interpretive keys" by which to open the doors of the Bible's chapters.

No task is more important than this one, because once we establish a hermeneutic we have to stay with it in every circumstance. It is like mountain climbing. After three days' journey from the base camp, you cannot change guides. The decision about a guide must be made before you leave camp, and you live with that choice until the climb is over. The same applies in the exhilarating climb we make up the slopes of Revelation. Rightly understood, the vision from its pinnacle is far grander and more life-sustaining than the view from the pinnacle of Everest. Thus we should resist the temptation to go straight to the commentary and skip the hermeneutic. If we master the hermeneutic, it will prepare us for the rest of life to interpret and understand the book.

SCHOOLS OF INTERPRETATION

Four main schools of thought guide interpreters' approaches to this, the crown of Scripture: preterism, historicism, futurism, and idealism.

Preterist interpreters (such as Swete and Beckwith) view Revelation as concerned with John's day, with addressing the people and events unfolding in the Roman world of the late first and early second centuries.

Historicist interpreters (such as Morris, Hendriksen, Clarke, and Barnes) generally emphasize the historical facts that form a continuous story of the world from John's day to the Second Coming. The chapters are seen as history written in advance and therefore "prophetic" from John's point of view, and the further removed in time from John's day, the more "prophecy" we will see fulfilled, until the last scenes are fulfilled at the *eschaton* (end of time).

Futurist interpreters (which include dispensationalists) see no application to John's day or the following centuries, but view all meaning in the book of Revelation as focusing almost exclusively on the very last days.

Idealist interpreters (such as Milligan and Minear) see the fiery language applying to themselves and their struggles, successes, hopes, and fears. For the idealists, John's chief concern was ordinary people, and each Christian finds in the Apocalypse a guidebook for a personal walk with Jesus.

The hermeneutic followed in this present volume is rooted in historicism. But it recognizes the literalness of the seven communities named in Revelation 2 and 3. Therefore, the messages to these churches could legitimately be applied to members of those specific faith communities who read the words addressed to them, but additionally the messages contain personal applications for today's Christians.

BASED ON THE OLD TESTAMENT

Chapter 1 pointed out that the genre of literature known as apocalyptic was common for a few centuries. Probably John utilized some of those extrabiblical writings, but far more frequently he incorporated canonical sources. While he does not quote the Old Testament directly, the original passages are obvious, and our reference to these original sources is an important key.

To illustrate, we find John describing a particular angel placing a seal on the foreheads of a special group of people whom he calls the 144,000. The imagery is drawn loosely from both 4 Esdras and Ezekiel 9 (where God was about to send judgment on Jerusalem and indicated the way He would identify those who were faithful to Him). Each of the loyal ones would have a *tau,* the last letter of the Hebrew alphabet, engraved on the forehead. Through Old Testament and noncanonical apocalyptic precedents, the New Testament meaning is suggested.

When John describes the throne room, he mentions four living creatures with the likenesses of a lion, an ox, an eagle, and a human. This imagery is also drawn from Ezekiel. The apocalyptic horses seen galloping from the unsealed scroll are taken from Zechariah 6.

Then too, some symbols, in a single word, conjure up colorful images—Babylon, Jerusalem, Balaam, Jezebel. In all, according to Merrill C. Tenney *(Interpreting Revelation*, pp. 101, 104), John draws on the Old Testament 348 times in his 22 chapters, including 53 borrowings from John's apocalyptic twin, Daniel. This means that the most important Old Testament source is Daniel. The prophecies of each must be studied together. For example, the story of the three worthies sentenced to death because they refused to worship the image erected by royal decree is the interpretative key to the vision of the followers of the Lamb, who in earth's last days will be sentenced to death because they refuse to worship the image of the beast. And just as the worthies went into the fiery furnace and stood with the Son of man, who brought them life, hope, and security, so in the last days those who enter the final trial will stand with Jesus, the Lamb, and find in Him their life and hope and security.

JESUS IS RETURNING

The Apocalypse is also saturated with the sense of the imminence of Jesus' return. The book is emotionally charged with eschatology, and John never lets us forget the impending climax of history. The old proverb "The key lies at the door" certainly applies to Revelation. The opening verse tells us that we are about to read "what must soon take place" (Rev. 1:1). Then within a few lines we read: "Look, he is coming with the clouds, and every eye will see him, even those who pierced him; and all the peoples of the earth will mourn because of him" (verse 7). Because of the chiastic structure, we expect the book to end on this same theme. And it does. In the final verses we read: "Behold, I am coming soon!" and "Yes, I am coming soon" (Rev. 22:12, 20).

So far in these first two chapters we have noted six introductory factors important to understanding the Apocalypse:

1. The book is the canonical exhibit of a symbolic kind of writing common in John's day.

2. In addition to the fiery, colorful language, different from most other biblical books, Revelation reveals a complex chiastic structure, a structure common in Hebrew writing, as well as a four-part structure based on the major sevens of the book.

3. One symbol that helps draw the seemingly disparate visions and details together is the Lamb of God, "who loves us and has freed us from our sins by his blood" (Rev. 1:5).[1] In the darkest passage, when Satan's work and character are unraveled in all their contemptible cunning, still the Lamb is present, and those who worship Him are ever secure in His victory.

4. Expositions of Revelation are based commonly on preterism, historicism, futurism, or idealism. This work adopts historicism as its primary interpretive framework, but sees in some chapters different levels of meaning in which there is a contemporary, local application; a prophetic view; and a very personal experiential meaning as well.

5. The book is riddled with Old Testament allusions, especially from Daniel.

6. The Apocalypse is written with a sense of the imminent return of the Lord Jesus.

FIVE PRINCIPLES OF INTERPRETATION

With those six introductory tiles secured in the mosaic of our understanding of the book, we now state the five primary principles of interpretation we will follow:

1. We anticipate the language to be symbolic.

2. That which was literal and local in the Old Testament when brought into the New is to be understood as spiritual and worldwide.

3. The numbers of the book, especially 3, 4, 7, 10, and 12, are to be understood first as symbols of qualities rather than quantities.

4. Revelation is John's apocalyptic expansion of Jesus' last address to the disciples—usually referred to as the Olivet address, recorded in Matthew 24 and 25, Mark 13, and Luke 21—which in turn has roots in the words of Daniel 9.

5. The cross is central to everything that John writes.

We anticipate the language to be symbolic. Those of us who grew up in Christian homes and listened to the great stories of both the Old and New Testaments tended to assume that the Bible contains only narratives. Later we discovered other kinds of writing in Scripture, including the teaching of the Epistles, the pungency of the wisdom literature, and the lyricism of the poetic books. And maybe last of all we discovered the apocalyptic literature of the Old and New Testaments, in which truth is expressed in dramatic symbols. Extensive apocalyptic writing is found in Isaiah, Ezekiel, and Daniel in the Old Testament, and climaxes with the last 22 chapters of Scripture.

In his prologue John sets the stage for what is to follow. In recounting the circumstances under which he received his visions, he announces: "On the Lord's Day I was in the Spirit, and I heard behind me a loud voice *like* a trumpet" (Rev. 1:10). In Revelation John uses two Greek words, *hōs* and *homoios*, more than a score of times, and the English equivalent is simply "like." The water is *like* crystal, we say. It is not crystal, but it looks that way. A dog is like a fox, that is, its slyness reminds us of a fox. In the same way, John gropes for similes and ideas that convey even dimly the thoughts Jesus opened to his understanding. We cannot hope to "see" all that John saw based on the terse descriptions, but the pictures are vivid enough to encourage us to search for the meanings.

In summary, we must anticipate graphic, symbolic presentations rather than straightforward, literal presentations, as is the case with most other books of the Bible.

References to Old Testament local places and people are to be understood as symbolic and worldwide when introduced into the New Testament. No one faced a more daunting task than the apostles of the first century in deciding what to do with the Old Testament corpus. Their orientation had always been literal and national, centered on Jerusalem and law. They could go to the genealogical records and trace them back from generation to generation to father Abraham, to whom the original promises of a great nation had been made. Israelites were never to forget the families to which they belonged.

The thrice-yearly pilgrimages to Jerusalem for the annual festivals were the celebrations around which all life revolved. The Temple at Jerusalem, with its endless ritual, while confounded by tradition, was still the heart of all that was essentially Jewish. To go to Jerusalem, climb the hill of Zion, and see the gilded roof of the sanctuary filled all Jews with pride. Their delight is hard to illustrate in any culture—except perhaps the sight of Mecca for a Muslim.

To decide what to do with all the elements of that national pride after the arrival of the Messiah took decades of prayerful consideration. The Jerusalem Council, recorded in Acts 15, made great strides in the right direction, but it was only a beginning. And for decades Christians of Jewish heritage continued to evaluate how to relate to their culture.

Paul, of all the apostles, seems to have grasped the situation more quickly and more clearly than any of his contemporaries. In both Romans and Galatians he expounds the new situation and delineates how Christians should relate to it. In Romans, after presenting the story of father Abraham, Paul turns to consider the plight of his Jewish brethren. He moans: "I have great sorrow and unceasing anguish in my heart" (Rom. 9:2) over the Jewish question. He would accept his own damnation if it could bring Israel to accept the Messiah (verse 3). He then recounts some of the advantages they enjoyed: "Theirs is the adoption as sons; theirs the divine glory, the covenants, the receiving of the law, the temple worship and *the promises*" (verse 4).

The heart of the question was the issue of *the promises*. How would the promises God made to father Abraham be fulfilled? He made them to literal Israel in the person of their father Abraham before the nation even existed, before Abraham even had a son to call his own flesh and blood. Paul hastens to give God's explanation: "It is not as though God's word had failed. For not all who are descended from Israel are Israel. Nor because they are his descendants are they all Abraham's children" (verses 6-8).

Paul emphasizes that the promises cannot fail, because God's word can never fail. However, those who benefit from the promises will be those who accept Jesus as Messiah, that is, spiritual Israel. They are to be "counted" as Abraham's descendants. The argument is parallel to justification presented in Romans chapters 4 through 7. When we confess our sins, we are immediately forgiven and "counted" as if we had not sinned.

Paul spells it out even further in Galatians. "You are all sons of God through faith in Christ Jesus, for all of you who were baptized into Christ have clothed yourselves with Christ. There is neither Jew nor Greek, slave nor free, male nor female, for you are all one in Christ Jesus. If you belong to Christ, then you are Abraham's seed, and heirs according to the promise" (Gal. 3:26-29).

The promises made to literal Jews will be received by spiritual Jews. Literal descent is replaced by spiritual descent. That is, those who believe as Abraham believed and receive Christ's righteousness as a gift by grace through faith are counted as Abraham's real descendants and will receive the promises made to him and Israel.

When we read Revelation we find that literal Old Testament places become symbols of worldwide realities and that Old Testament individuals become symbols of widespread experiences. For example, John builds on the experience of Babylon, that literal, local city probably built on or near the ruins of the Tower of Babel. This becomes a vivid symbol of the rejection of God's promises. Those builders did not believe the rainbow promise that glowed after every rain, and they acted on that disbelief in their attempt to build a tower to reach heaven. They wanted to find righteousness and everlasting life through their own works. But God confounded their language, and their human-centered, creature-worshiping experiment ended in chaos and confusion. In John's final work that literal local city is transformed into a spiritual worldwide kingdom, the dominion of Satan. We will meet many such examples as we make our journey through Revelation.

In summary, New Testament references to Old Testament places or people usually illustrate spiritual truths that can be seen anywhere in the world, key elements in the great conflict between Christ and Satan that will be resolved only in the final judgment of the wicked and the vindication of the family of the Lamb.

The numbers of the book are to be understood first as symbols of qualities rather than quantities. It is extremely difficult for the Occidental mind to enter into the mind set of an Oriental or Middle Easterner. But to Eastern people numbers were and are symbols of qualities. Our Western suspicion or denial of the mystical makes it difficult to appreciate this approach. Initially, John did not address his book to those who live in the West, but wrote to Asian Christians, those living in the land we know today as Turkey.

As J. Massyngberde Ford has observed, the symbolic use of numbers flourished during the centuries of apocalyptic writings then went into decline after the writing of the Apocalypse *(Revelation, Anchor Bible,* vol. 38, pp. 11, 12). In reference to the apocalyptic use of numbers, Christopher Wordsworth has observed that they do "not express a *quantity,* but a *quality" (The New Testament of Our Lord and Savior Jesus Christ in the Original Greek,* vol. 2, p. 221).

The history of the symbolic use of numbers began long before the intertestamental period. The Greeks used numbers symbolically as we notice in such works as Plato's *Republic.* For example, Socrates said: "Three times three . . . is the arithmetical distance between the tyrant and true pleasure" *(Great Dialogues of Plato,* p. 388). And in another extraordinarily complex passage, Socrates spoke of multiplying small numbers by 100 in relation to one's birth: "Three and four wedded with five and cubed produce two harmonies, one square, so many times a hundred, an oblong" *(ibid.,* p. 344).

Earlier still, in the sixth century B.C., Pythagoras (of theorem fame) interpreted the universe through numbers. As Martin Walsh has observed: "The philosophy of the Pythagorean school was predominantly a mathematico-metaphysical philosophy. . . . The order and harmony of the universe is explainable in terms of numbers. Numbers constitute the essences of things" *(A History of Philosophy*, p. 7).

There also appears to be a biblical tradition of using numbers symbolically, as evidenced by the divergent life spans ascribed to the patriarchs in Genesis chapters 5 and 11b in the Masoretic, Septuagint, and Samaritan Pentateuch texts. For example, a round 100 years is added to each of the lives of a series of the antediluvians in the Septuagint, as compared with the Samaritan and Masoretic texts.[2]

More than a century ago William Milligan made an impressive statement about the qualitative meaning of the numbers of the Apocalypse: "The numbers of the Apocalypse are no doubt symbolical, but the symbolism has always a *definite* meaning. They express ideas, but the ideas are distinct. They may belong to a region of thought different from that with which arithmetical numbers are concerned, but within that region we cannot change the numerical value of the numbers used without at the same time changing the thought. Substitute the number eight for the number seven, or, in like manner, four for three or twelve for ten, and the idea which the writer intended to express by the number actually employed by him immediately disappears" *(The Revelation of St. John*, pp. 202, 203).[3]

The number 13, which Westerners seem to understand symbolically, is seen by many as an omen of bad luck. As a result, rarely do you find a building with a thirteenth floor or a row or seat in an auditorium or plane numbered 13. We see similar illustrations in other cultures. In Japan a newly married couple would not accept a hotel room with the number 4, because to them this number symbolizes death.

In the Apocalypse, numbers play an incredibly important role. The fact that there are more than 50 sevens in the book could hardly be accidental. The number 7 is the most frequent number used in John's book. But 3, 4, 10, and 12 also are prominent symbols.

One's first reading of Revelation does not reveal the wide use of the actual numbers 3, 4, 7, 10, and 12, since the usage is often subtle. Sometimes the numbers are couched in the text as sets rather than simple numbers. At other times they are hidden in larger numbers that need to be broken down to subsets. For example, the 1,600 of Revelation 14 can be reduced to two numbers—4 and 10: 4 x 4 x 10 x 10. When you combine all the usages (overt numbers, large numbers broken into smaller numbers, and sets of items), the numbers 3, 4, 7, 10, and 12 are found everywhere. Wherever a number is used in a symbolic sense in this work, it is written as a figure rather than as a word.

A comment that is sometimes heard in the discussion of the qualitative significance of numbers is that it sounds contrived. And the fact is that Bible writers, including John, did "contrive," or discipline themselves, with extraordinary skill to present their messages in a genre appreciated by their original readers. The contrivance is similar to poets who, with their own set of skills, can choose to impose on themselves the discipline of writing their thoughts in meter and rhyme. One of the few scholars who has explored in-depth the number phenomenon is M.J.J. Mencken.

The number 7. Throughout the Old Testament the number 7 spelled rest after labor or conflict. It is obviously based on Genesis 1 and 2, which explain that God worked for six days, rested on the seventh, and by resting created the weekly Sabbath.

The Sabbath has always been a sign that a believer honors the Creator. But after sin the Sabbath acquired another significance as well. It continued as a symbol of God's creative power, a sign of the completed work of Creation, but for each believer it also became a sign of God's great act of grace, the removal of guilt, and the experience of the peace and holiness of God. Thus Moses could write: "You must observe my Sabbaths. This will be a sign between me and you for the generations to come, so you may know that I am the Lord, *who makes you holy*" (Ex. 31:13).

The New Testament continues in the same vein. For the believer who enters into relationship with God, the Sabbath spells rest after conflict with sin. Jesus pleads: "Come to me, all you who are weary and burdened, and I will give you rest" (Matt. 11:28; see also Heb. 4). Jesus has always offered us rest after our labors for self-righteousness and our failed conflicts with temptation.

From the first week of this world's creation, the number 7 has celebrated the rest after labor offered by the Creator. Since the Fall it has also celebrated the rest from sin offered by the Redeemer.

In Revelation all the primary 7s—churches, seals, trumpets, and bowls—take us through history into the eternal promised rest of heaven in the presence of our Saviour the Lamb. Thus 7 can be seen as apocalyptic shorthand for "rest in Jesus." This does not mean that the seventh element in the major sevens *is* the promised rest. Rather, the seventh element usually climaxes in eternal Sabbath rest.[4]

The number 12. The number 12 has a significance that is as obvious as the number 7. The book of Genesis reveals the importance of this number in its earliest chapters. Moses selected just 12 antediluvian patriarchs, beginning with God the Father and ending with Shem; just 12 postdiluvian patriarchs from Arphaxad to Jacob; and exactly 12 sons of Jacob, who became the patriarchs of the 12 tribes of the Old Testament.

The number 12 signified the nation, the kingdom of God, or as Milligan has expressed it, the number of the people of God (p. 365). E. W. Hengstenberg has seen the symbol as the signature of the church *(The Revelation of St. John,* vol. 1, p. 360). In the days of Jesus, a group of 12 apostles associated with Jesus throughout His brief three and a half years of public activity, and with these 12 began the New Testament church. That number 12 was so important *qualitatively* that after the death of Judas the apostles solemnly elected a replacement. The kingdom number 12 needed to be preserved to make a "kingdom statement" in those primitive days of the Christian church. We will find extensive use of the number 12 in the kingdom chapters: Revelation 7, 21, and 22.

Greek culture emphasized the same symbolism. Homer recounts that when Odysseus finally returned to the island of Ithaka, the reestablishment of his island kingdom came when he successfully shot an arrow through the holes in the backs of 12 axes set one behind another.

The number 10. The number 10 needs little comment. We think of a baby born with all 10 fingers and toes as "complete" and "whole." And who has not used those fingers to count from 1 to 10? When God wished to make a "complete" statement of His will for us, He couched it in the Ten Commandments. J. Massyngberde Ford has asserted that in apocalyptic literature this number symbolizes completeness or wholeness (p. 395).

Socrates used 10 (and its square, 100) similarly. He said: "Each had paid satisfaction to all persons that he had wronged, and for each offense in turn ten times . . . so as to make the payment for each wrong tenfold," that is, completely *(Great Dialogues of Plato, p.* 416).

The number 4. It appears that the number 4 acquired a qualitative significance in earliest times. To control territory on all four points of the compass spelled "universal" control or dominion. Before people thought of the earth as round, they spoke of the four corners of the earth, meaning everywhere, universal coverage. The Old Testament's use of the number 4 points to an understanding of the number in John's Apocalypse.

Isaiah exclaims: "He will assemble the scattered people of Judah from the four quarters of the earth" (Isa. 11:12). Chronicles uses 4 in connection with the compass points: "The gatekeepers were on the four sides: east west, north and south" (1 Chron. 9:24). Zechariah uses the number 4 when describing the spirits of the "Lord of the whole world" (Zech. 6:5). The Bible's opening verses describe the river of the Garden of Eden that flowed in four streams—presumably to water the whole earth (Gen. 2:10). Baal's prophets appeared to so fully possess the land of Israel that they were described as 4 x 10 x 10 (1 Kings 18:19). And when Elisha on Carmel declared his intent of taking back the whole land in the name of God, he poured four barrels of water over the offering (verse 33). The Old Testament uses the number 4 some 250 times, often with the sense of illustrating that which is universal.

During the twelfth, thirteenth, and fourteenth centuries the myth of the Holy Grail found its way all across Europe and included some interesting uses of the number 4: four youths, 400 knights and ladies, and the four faces of the fire. According to Robert A. Johnson, the number 4 was simply a symbol of totality *(He,* p. 51) and is an illustration of the understanding of antiquity.

In the Apocalypse John uses the number 4 as a symbol of totality or universality. Sometimes the numbers are prominent, as for example: "I saw four angels standing at the four corners of the earth, holding back the four winds of the earth" (Rev. 7:1).[5]

Subtle uses of the number 4 are more common, however. When describing the final, universal crescendo of evil against good, John paints the picture in the form of a quartet. He writes: "Nor did they repent of their murders, their magic arts, their sexual immorality or their thefts" (Rev. 9:21). The focus is not exclusively on those four particular sins, as if these are the ultimate demonstrations of evil. The fourfold designation is a symbolic description of universal sinfulness among the lost.

Guilty Babylon is lulled into satanic stupor by the seductive music of a group of four: harpists, musicians, flutists, and trumpeters (Rev. 18:22). The weapons of the fourth horseman are four: sword, famine, pestilence, and wild beasts (Rev. 6:8). God's final judgment is so universal that it is described as happening at a specific hour, in a particular day, within a particular month, in a specific year (Rev. 9:15). When God is about to pour His judgments on the world, it is announced with thunders, rumblings, lightnings, and an earthquake (Rev. 16:18). Satan reaches out through the beast to every tribe, people, tongue, and nation, as the Lamb reaches out to every tribe, people, tongue, and nation through the church (Rev. 13:7; 10:11). The list of 4s grows quickly as soon as you become aware of this apocalyptic symbol.

The number 3. From the early centuries of the Christian church, the number 3 has been associated with the triune God, the Trinity. And the Trinity always spells oneness, the mystical "three in one," and thus symbolizes unity. The Members of the Godhead are suggested in Genesis 1, and the Holy Spirit is named. The New Testament identifies Jesus as the active agent in Creation (see John 1:10).

John opens his Apocalypse by sewing into the fabric of the opening six verses a series of three 3s symbolizing the Godhead united to redeem the world, not willing that any should perish. The singing of the angels—"Holy, Holy, Holy" (Rev. 4:8)—is not thoughtless repetition, but the symbol of heaven's unity. However, there is not just one trio united in effort in this universe; there are two. The opposition to the united Godhead is a united trio of beast, dragon, and false prophet. And out of their mouths come three evil spirits like frogs (Rev. 16:13). But the united Godhead is far stronger than the united opposition, which ultimately will fall at the Lamb's feet and acknowledge Him (Rev. 11:13).

Consistently throughout the chapters of the Apocalypse we will seek to apply this fundamental hermeneutic regarding numbers. These numbers are primarily symbols of these qualities: 3, unity; 4, universality; 7, rest; 10, completeness; and 12, the kingdom.

Revelation is a symbolic presentation of Jesus' Olivet address and is based on the writings of Daniel. The Synoptic Gospels—Matthew, Mark, and Luke—all contain the Olivet address in which Jesus detailed the course of future history for the church, the major problems it would encounter, and its ultimate triumph. Interestingly, the Gospel of John does not contain a word of Jesus' treatise. Yet as we analyze the sermon and the Apocalypse, we see that John reserved his account of the Olivet address for presentation in the transcendent symbols of the book of Revelation.

To discover the connection, we analyze the Olivet address. The sermon has an attention-arresting introduction, three main points, and an extended conclusion with several emotionally charged illustrations designed to bring each hearer to decision.

The introduction begins at the Temple in Jerusalem, where Jesus lamented that the people He had come to save had rejected Him. As He walked by the Temple built by Herod, He observed that it would soon be shattered; not a single block of marble would be left standing. Later as they walked through the east gate across the Kidron Valley and over to the Mount of Olives, the disciples plucked up the courage to ask when the destruction would come and what would be the indicators of its destruction and the end of the world. *They linked these two events together, believing that no other event but the end of the world could possibly bring about the destruction of the city.*

Jesus then proceeded to answer their questions. However, He responded to the two questions with only one answer. They thought they had asked one question, and He did not enlighten them that the destruction of Jerusalem and the end of the world would be separated by at least two millennia. But the signs of the one were the signs of the other, and the fall of the one became a symbol of the fall of the other. Jerusalem, in its death throes, is a stark picture of the "Jerusalem of this world" at the moment the seven last plagues fall.

In *the first part* of His sermon Jesus noted that the end time was still future. He did this by listing the general indicators of that approaching period, including famine, pestilence, earthquakes, wars, and spiritual declension. Then He named the ultimate indicator of the imminent end: the preaching of the gospel in all the world. When that transpires, the end will come (Matt. 24:3-14).

The second part of the address touches the issues of physical attacks and spiritual corruption. Both factors were to be experienced prior to the fall of Jerusalem and again at the end of the world.

Warning of physical attack, Jesus described those who would need to flee to the mountains without time to take anything from their houses, and He admonished them to pray "that your flight will not take place in winter or on the Sabbath" (verses 16, 17, 20).

Next Jesus described the corruption of teaching and belief. The corruption from "false Christs and false prophets" would be most persuasive through "great signs and miracles to deceive even the elect" (verse 24).

In *the third part* of Jesus' presentation we read of history's culmination—His return to bring vengeance on nonaccepters and immortality to the accepters (verses 30, 31).

Then follows *an extended appeal* with several illustrations: Noah, the 10 bridesmaids, the parable of the talents, and the separation of the sheep and the goats. This is Jesus' fervent appeal to be an accepter and to live in relationship with Him in preparation for eternal life.

Before we observe how this structure is used in the Apocalypse, we should step back in time to find the roots of the Olivet discourse. Jesus plainly stated where we should look. He named Daniel as the source and identified the passage as the one that speaks of the "abomination that causes desolation" (verse 15). Those comments send us to Daniel 9, the Messianic heart of Old Testament prophecy, and a few other passages scattered in Daniel 7 through 12.

The *introduction* to Daniel 9 directs our attention to the throne room of the sanctuary in heaven, the place to which Daniel addressed his prayer, the place from which the angel Gabriel had been dispatched to talk with Daniel. Thus the introduction of Jesus' sermon and the opening verses of Daniel 9 are parallel in that both have a sanctuary/temple orientation.

The climax of *the first part* of Jesus' sermon is the preaching of the gospel in all the world. That gospel is rooted in the death of the Lamb at Calvary. The central focus of Daniel 9 is also on this gospel event. We read: "He will confirm a covenant with many for one 'seven.' In the middle of the 'seven' he will put an end to sacrifice and offering" (Dan. 9:27).[6] And again: "the Anointed One will be cut off and will have nothing" (verse 26). Only one event could bring to a halt all the rituals and sacrifices of Old Testament times, and that would be the event to which these sacrifices and rituals pointed, the Calvary event. In these verses Daniel emphasizes the supreme event that climaxes the first point of Jesus' Olivet presentation.

In *His second point* Jesus describes attacks from without and corruption from within. Daniel makes the same points when he writes of the time when some will "destroy the city and the sanctuary. The end will come like a flood: War will continue until the end, and desolations have been decreed" (verse 26). War against "the city" is plain to understand. It symbolized the physical attacks both against Jerusalem by Titus and against the church by a succession of Satan-inspired persecutors. But what is the meaning of an attack on the sanctuary?

War against the sanctuary is the symbol of an attack on the ministry of Jesus, who once died for our sins and then ascended to the throne in the heavenly sanctuary to minister the benefits of that sacrifice.

In Moses' sanctuary everything symbolized Jesus. The lamb on the altar of burnt offering, the cleansing laver, the guidance of the lampstand, the nourishment of the bread, the incense of prayer, as well as the colors, tapestries, annual festivals, and individual offerings—all preached Christ. Thus a symbolic attack on the sanctuary indicates an attack on the gospel, and without that good news about the Lamb, there is no truth worth believing, no hope worth holding, no faith worth sharing. Substitute saviors and substitute systems for atonement have been the mark of false religion in every age.

The third point Jesus makes concerning vengeance on the rejecters is rooted in Daniel's words: "On a wing of the temple he will set up an abomination that causes desolation, until the end that is decreed is poured out on him" (verse 27). At His return Jesus will bring judgment on those who have tried to destroy His truth and His people.

It is important to emphasize that Matthew 24 is built on Daniel's prophetic chapters, particularly chapter 9. The three main issues in both are (1) the primacy of the gospel, (2) attacks against God's people and God's truth, and (3) the final judgment on the wicked. On Olivet Jesus greatly enlarged the "abomination of desolation" passages using the same three points.

Now, to this point we have noted a similar structure in the words at the heart of Gabriel's words to Daniel recorded in Daniel 9 and in the Olivet address. Finally, we note that the book of Revelation has a similar structure. As we do, we quote the words of two commentators who have observed the connections between Daniel, Matthew 24 and 25, and Revelation.

William Moorehead has marveled: "It is not too much to say that the Apocalypse is the expansion, with marvelous additions, of the Olivet prophecy and the book of Daniel" *(Outline Studies in the New Testament*, p. 19).

Philip Carrington, referring to the Olivet address, adds: "Jesus was a prophet," and we "possess some prophecies of Jesus about the future. These prophecies form the basis of St. John's Apocalypse" *(The Meaning of the Revelation*, p. 54).

In the following paragraphs we note similarities between the contents of Daniel 9, Matthew 23 and 24, and the book of Revelation based on its fundamental structure of seven churches, seals, trumpets, and bowls.

The Introduction. John's book opens with a vision of the resurrected Christ described in sanctuary imagery: lampstands, priestly attire, the daily sacrifice of the lamb, the fire of the altar of burnt offering, the brass laver, the water for washing, the brilliance of the glory of God hovering above the mercy seat, and the angels embroidered on the curtains of the holy place and the Most Holy Place. The vision of the seven churches grows out of this sanctuary setting. And it was while walking by the Temple in Jerusalem that the disciples had asked the questions about that sanctuary, which led to the entire Olivet sermon. Thus Daniel 9, the Olivet sermon, and the Apocalypse all begin at the sanctuary.

The First Point. The seven seals are filled with the same material as the first part of Jesus' address. Both are filled with descriptions of war, famines, pestilences, earthquakes, betrayal, hatred, and the preaching of the gospel.[7] Especially with respect to the primacy of the gospel, Daniel 9, Matthew 24:6-14, and the horse of the first seal all have a common theme.

The Second Point. When we compare the second part of Jesus' Olivet material with the content of the seven trumpets, again we find important links. Both detail attacks from without and corruption from within. Attacks from without shattered the Roman Empire and scattered the early church, and this is symbolized by fire, blood, and the scorching of the earth. Attacks from within brought a devastating adulteration of the gospel and are symbolized by the corruption of the waters of truth and the eclipsing of the Sun of Righteousness. Attacks come in the symbols of locusts and horses, and woe betide those who do "not have the seal of God on their foreheads" (Rev. 9:4)! Clearly a common theme runs through Daniel 9, Matthew 24:15-28, and the trumpets.

The Third Point. There is a clear connection between the judgments on the wicked announced in Daniel 9, Matthew 24:30, and the seven bowls.

Conclusion. Finally, the powerful stories and images that conclude Jesus' address find counterparts in the powerful stories and images of Revelation 18 through 22.

We have discussed very briefly the structural links between Daniel 9, Matthew 24 and 25, and the Apocalypse because this is an important interpretive key to much that follows. For us to stray far from the clear intent of Jesus' sermon to His disciples will mean we have strayed far from the meaning John intended.

In the symbol of the Lamb we find that the cross is at the heart of the Apocalypse. In the previous chapter, we noted that the Lamb is the most important symbol in the book of Revelation. And the Lamb is first introduced to us "looking as if it had been slain" (Rev. 5:6). The imagery of the daily sacrifice is the symbolic portrayal of the cross. It is not the first suggestion of the cross in John's book, however. That was painted in the first chapter: "To him who loves us and has freed us from our sins by his blood . . ." (Rev. 1:5). And to emphasize that God's response to the sin problem was not an afterthought, John later assures us that Jesus was "the Lamb that was slain from the creation of the world" (Rev. 13:8).

In the detailed chiastic structure of the book (see page 21) the central words of the book take us to the foot of the cross to gaze at our Redeemer. Like a grand hallelujah, a "loud voice in heaven" proclaims to all the universe that salvation is secure, that the kingdom of God is secure, and that the overthrow of Satan has been accomplished. Hope is therefore given to all the world, and victory is assured "by the blood of the Lamb" (Rev. 12:10, 11).

The fifth of these five elements in our hermeneutic will be our guiding star in some of the most difficult chapters of the Apocalypse.

In summary, this is the hermeneutic we will strive to follow throughout this volume:

1. We anticipate that most of what we read is couched in symbols and is not meant to be understood literally.

2. References to Old Testament events and people in the Middle East are to be understood as symbolic of worldwide issues and events.

3. We interpret numbers qualitatively, seeing in

> 3 a symbol of unity,
> 4 a symbol of universality,
> 7 a symbol of rest after labor,
> 10 a symbol of completeness,
> 12 a symbol of the kingdom of God.

Sometimes the numbers are used quantitatively as well.

4. In establishing the basic meaning of the broad outlines of the Apocalypse, we use Matthew 24 and 25 and Daniel 9 as a guide, be-

lieving that Matthew 24 and 25 are patterned on Daniel and that the entire book of Revelation is an outworking of the Old and New Testament presentations.

5. In the central symbol of "the Lamb that was slain from the creation of the world," we see the cross of Jesus as the foundation of everything John has to say. That is, we will always seek *first* a Christological view of the visions. ●

---

[1] The Lamb is not mentioned until chapter 5, but the reference to blood in Rev. 1:5 anticipates the later multiple references.

[2] See Colin House's 1988 Ph.D. dissertation, Andrews University, "The Successive, Corresponding Epochal Arrangement of the 'Chronologies' of Genesis 5 and 11b in the Three Textual Traditions: LXXA, SP, and MT." House offers an intriguing solution to the divergent numerical schemes by showing that the three sets of numbers can be understood as three precise paradigms, each with the exact same number of years before and after the Flood. Furthermore, as each scheme was developed, it was made to climax with an event of immense importance to Israel at that time—for example, the death of Joseph and the destruction of Jerusalem. Students interested in the serious study of numbers in Scripture (not to be confused with numerology) might wish to refer to *Numerical Literary Techniques*, by M.J.J. Mencken.

[3] You can find an additional comment on the significance of specific numbers in chapter 19 of this book, in a discussion about the numeral 1,000.

[4] See also Milligan, *Revelation of St. John*, pp. 34-92, for a discussion of the usage of 7, 4, and 3.

[5] The clear inference is that four angels on earth's four corners could contain any strife universally.

[6] Note the 7 orientation. It begins in Daniel 9 and finds its full apocalyptic expression in the 7s freely scattered through the pages of Revelation.

[7] In an unpublished manuscript dated December 1989, Jon Paulien noted an impressive list of subjects common to both the Olivet sermon and the seals, including the gospel, war, famine, pestilence, persecution, tribulation, vengeance, heavenly signs, tribes mourn, and Son of man comes, sends angels, and gathers the elect.

OUTLINE

1. Introducing the Apocalypse as a whole
   About Jesus
   Filled with the theme of judgment
   Points to the Second Coming
   Written by the disciple John
   Written to seven congregations in New Testament Asia

2. Introducing the seven churches and their letters:
   Sequence has significance
   Each letter follows a similar structure

3. Revelation 1

CHAPTER THREE

SEE JESUS

As we read the opening verses of the book of Revelation, we discover the central Person of the book, the central purpose of the book, the human author, the first readers, and the basic method employed to convey the message. Each of these issues is important to our understanding.

INTRODUCING THE BOOK

About Jesus. In Greek as in English, the introductory phrase "the revelation of Jesus Christ" (Rev. 1:1) has more than one meaning. First, it identifies Jesus as the divine author of the book, a fact that is reinforced in the next verse, where John tells us he "testifies to . . . the testimony of Jesus Christ" (verse 2). But it also places the spotlight on our wonderful Jesus, who through many symbols and titles, is the focus from beginning to end. This book is about Jesus. He is the central figure, the champion of the downtrodden faithful, carrying a sword to smite the oppressors of His people. He is the one who walks among the lampstands, sits on the throne, accepts the adoring praise of the angelic host, opens the seals, feeds His flock, banishes Satan from Paradise, comes to receive His own, and leads them to their eternal home in the New Jerusalem.

As we observed in the first chapter, the most compelling symbol for Jesus throughout Revelation is a lamb. His atonement at Calvary has already paid the price of our sins, and He waits for us to confess them and receive the forgiveness that banishes guilt and brightens our lives.

Revelation 1:5-7 summarizes the book. Jesus is declared to be "the faithful witness, the first-born from the dead, and the ruler of the kings of the earth" (verse 5).[1] During His three and a half years of public ministry, Jesus gave ultimate witness to God's love for us all. As the first begotten from the dead, He shattered the seemingly eternal night of death. And He will return as our king, bringing vindication for the redeemed and judgment on those who have rejected His offers of mercy. In that day those who have not wept over their sins in confession will do so in the sorrow of a lost eternity.

A book of judgment. In John's book, five extensive visions describe the Lord Jesus (chapters 1; 4, 5; 7; 15; 19). Chapter 1 is exceptionally graphic. We find in it allusions to the sanctuary and to the high priest as already noted. But one of the important allusions is to the theme of judgment, something that becomes more and more dominant as the Apocalypse unfolds.[2] John draws on Daniel's description of the Son of man seated in judgment to paint the picture: "As I looked, thrones were set in place, and the Ancient of Days took his seat. His clothing was as white as snow; the hair of his head was white like wool. His throne was flaming with fire, and its wheels were all ablaze. A river of fire was flowing, coming out from before him. Thousands upon thousands attended him; ten thousand times ten thousand stood before him. The court was seated, and the books were opened. . . . In my vision at night I looked, and there before me was one like a son of man, coming with the clouds of heaven" (Dan. 7:9-13).

Revelation's themes are often drawn directly from Daniel, as we have already noted and as this passage illustrates. *Son of man* is an expression used of Jesus more than 80 times in the New Testament, and it often carries the association of judgment. But the judgment notion in the words of Daniel just quoted and throughout Revelation is always concurrent with Old Testament usage. The judges of the Old Testament were the deliverers of God's people. Individuals like

Samson and Gideon, the two giants of the book of Judges, were commissioned by God "to judge" by delivering His people and putting down the oppressors. What encouragement when we think of the Judge and judgment from this perspective! He judges *for* each believer and *against* each rejecter. We have every reason to feel absolutely secure about God's judgment as long as we are part of His family by faith in the Lord Jesus Christ. We find this theme emphasized more and more as we progress through the Apocalypse.

Looking for His coming. Another central purpose of the book is also clearly spelled out in the opening verses. It is to unveil "what must soon take place" (Rev. 1:1). For the Christian, all history is directly related to two events: Jesus' death and His return when He will receive His people and judge the wicked. All history between these two events makes sense only by constant reference to both. Thus all history, viewed correctly, is "His-story."

The plotting of the paths of the planets remained a mystery for centuries because astronomers imagined that all stars had a circular trajectory around a single hub. Only when the elliptical path was discovered, with its two centers, did the mystery dissolve. And thus it is with Revelation. This is a book about two events, one past and one future, both events accomplished by our Saviour.

Written by John. The human author of the book was a first-century Christian named John. Until the eighteenth century it was generally accepted that this John also wrote the Gospel of that name and the three small letters of John. During the nineteenth century some scholars emphasized the great differences in style and language between the Apocalypse and the other works, and so suggested a different author with the name John. While there is no internal evidence that Revelation's John and the Lord's disciple are one and the same person, the evidence of the expansion of the Olivet sermon, omitted only from John's Gospel, strongly suggests a common authorship for all five New Testament books.

Leon Morris has mused: "It is often argued that John was a very common name, and that therefore we have no real reason for ascribing Revelation the same author as the Gospel. Whatever be the truth about the use of this name among the Jews, the fact is that we do not have a great number of Christian Johns to choose from. We have no certain knowledge of any Christian John of this period other than the disciple, and John Mark" *(The Revelation of St. John*, pp. 32, 33).

Written to seven churches. To identify the original readers also helps us understand the book as a whole. They were the members of the Christian congregations in the cities of Ephesus, Smyrna, Pergamos, Thyatira, Sardis, Philadelphia, and Laodicea (Rev. 1:11). As Tenney wisely pointed out: "The seven churches must be taken initially as literal. Whatever they may represent, they are essentially different groups located in actual historical cities, with marked individual characteristics. Ramsey has pointed out that the historical facts which archaeological research has brought to light about these cities have a bearing on the interpretation of the text, since the Lord appeals to the churches in terms that they would understand best in the light of their local history" *(Interpreting Revelation*, pp. 45, 46).

INTRODUCING THE SEVEN CHURCHES

The letters to the seven churches are exceptionally precious. Nowhere but here do we have a verbatim account of Jesus' words. All the accounts of the sayings and sermons of Jesus in the Gospels are brief and probably incomplete. But these seven letters were written by John directly from Jesus, full and complete. They were addressed originally to specific congregations in particular cities, not to Christians living some 20 centuries later. Thus they have an immediacy and localness about them. They are filled with encouragement, promises, and warnings against inappropriate courses of action at that time and in those places. However, it is also obvious that every Christian in history has been able to find in these letters a rich source of devotional inspiration.

But beyond the local and devotional applications we find a third level of meaning: the historicist's interpretation. We see symbolized in each letter a period of history and an indication of developments that would "soon take place" (Rev. 1:1). For this reason, the order in which these seven cities are mentioned has significance. They are named in the order in which John would have visited the cities if he had traveled from Patmos to the nearest major port by boat, then by the major roads of Roman times.

Ephesus was the harbor to which he would have come from Patmos. He then would have proceeded up the coast road to Izmir (Smyrna), north to Pergamos, southeast through three more towns, ending in Laodicea. This natural progression illustrates the seven periods of history from the First Advent to the Second. In this case, geography suggests history. The symbolism of identifying just seven congregations, rather than six or eight or some other number, has already been discussed. There were more than seven congregations in Asia. For example, Colossae stood close to Laodicea, but it is not mentioned. Evidently Jesus wrote these letters to present a broad outline of history between the First and Second Advents based on the characteristics of these seven.

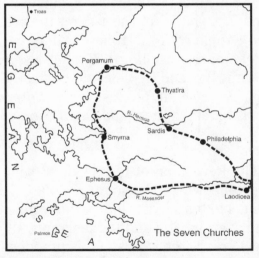

The Seven Churches

Each of these seven names has a specific meaning, as was common with names in Bible times. Those denotations provide an interesting pattern and clue to the interpretation of each letter as a whole, as we shall later see. Following the name is a description of Jesus drawn from the portrait of Revelation 1. Next Jesus speaks about the commendable aspects of the church's life and encourages the members in this, followed by some straight talk about problem areas of life and advice on how to overcome them.

The seven promises, taken in sequence, trace the completeness of God's plan to restore all that was lost by sin. The moment Adam and Eve sinned, they lost access to the tree of life. In the first promise the fruit of that tree is restored. Without access to that tree, humanity was doomed to die; thus the second promise is the "crown of life." Expelled from the Garden of Eden, Adam and Eve were forced to battle the stubborn soil for food and sustenance. The third promise is the manna of God for nourishment and delight. As they left the garden, the dominion once given to Adam and Eve waned and faltered. Thus the fourth promise is the restoration of their dominion. When sin entered, they felt naked and awkwardly tried to cover themselves. The fifth promise is the clothing of righteousness made available through the merits of Jesus' sacrifice. Expelled from the garden, they could no longer daily meet with Jesus; no longer could they approach Him face-to-face. The sixth promise assures the overcomer of a permanent place in the temple with the King of kings. In Eden they had not only the privilege of approaching Jesus but also enjoyed an intimate relationship with Him, and He delegated responsibilities to them—joys all lost by sin. The seventh promise is a restoration of intimacy and responsibility as together Jesus and His redeemed sit on the throne.

REVELATION 1

"The Revelation of Jesus Christ, which God gave him to show to his servants what must soon take place. He made it known by sending his angel to his servant John, who testifies to everything he saw—that is, the word of God and the testimony of Jesus Christ. Blessed is the one who reads the words of this prophecy, and blessed are those who hear it and take to heart what is written in it, because the time is near" (Rev. 1:1-3).

Here John identifies the various Persons involved in this unveiling or revelation. Jesus is named first, and with Him, God the Father. They planned this "uncovering" of circumstances and events for the benefit of the Christian community. They commissioned an angel to fly from heaven to earth to share it with the beloved disciple John, who declared that he faithfully recorded it all (each word of the "testimony" or "witness" as would occur in a court of law).

This communiqué alerts the Christian churches to events soon to overtake them. John then records that a blessing would be bestowed on those who took the time to read, understand, and put into practice the counsel they read in the book. This is the first of seven beatitudes scattered through the chapters. Most of them come near the end of the book, in the second part, the eschatological section, detailing the events of the very end of time.[3]

"John, to the seven churches in the province of Asia:

"Grace and peace to you from him who is, and who was, and who is to come, and from the seven spirits before his throne, and from Jesus Christ, who is the faithful witness, the firstborn from the dead, and the ruler of the kings of the earth.

"To him who loves us and has freed us from our sins by his blood, and has made us to be a kingdom and priests to serve his God and Father—to him be glory and power for ever and ever! Amen.

"Look, he is coming with the clouds, and every eye will see him, even those who pierced him; and all the peoples of the earth will mourn because of him. So shall it be! Amen.

"'I am the Alpha and the Omega,' says the Lord God, 'who is, and who was, and who is to come, the Almighty'" (verses 4-8).

The symbolic use of numbers begins in the opening verses with a series of 3s. God is presented in a threefold time frame: is, was, and is to come. The second three is found in the naming of the members of the Godhead: "His God and Father" (verse 6); "Jesus Christ, who is the faithful witness" (verse 5); and "the seven Spirits before his throne" (verse 4). The last reference is one of the first uses of the number 7 and is applied to the Holy Spirit because by His ministry we are brought into the "rest" of God.

John notes that the church has become a kingdom (verse 6). The kingdom nature of the church had been a primary thrust in all that Jesus had done and said on earth. It began with John the Baptist's cry "Repent, for the kingdom of heaven is near" (Matt. 3:2), and continued as Jesus took up the same message and declared shortly after: "Repent, for the kingdom of heaven is near" (4:17).

The Sermon on the Mount has been accurately characterized as the constitution of this kingdom. Dialogue during Jesus' trial and crucifixion focused on this notion of the kingdom. Had Jesus come to establish a kingdom? What was the nature of that kingdom? Understandably, Rome's representatives in Palestine never understood the spiritual nature of God's kingdom on earth.

Coupled with the kingdom concept, detailed in the last two chapters of the Apocalypse, is the declaration that those who have become members of this kingdom are all priests, because He "has made us to be a kingdom and priests to serve his God and Father" (Rev. 1:6).

The early church soon lost the truthfulness of this statement when a priestly caste came to prominence, denying the place and ministry of members in the kingdom of grace. Hierarchical priests became the dispensers of blessings and the teachers who alone could interpret the words of God. This development marked the beginning of a new bondage of the church and ushered in the Dark Ages. Only in the light of the Reformation would the cry again be heard: righteousness by faith alone; the Bible is our sole rule of faith and practice; and the priesthood of *all* believers.

"I, John, your brother and companion in the suffering and kingdom and patient endurance that are ours in Jesus, was on the island of Patmos because of the word of God and the testimony of Jesus. On the Lord's Day I was in the Spirit, and I heard behind me a loud voice like a trumpet, which said, 'Write on a scroll what you see and send it to the seven churches: to Ephesus, Smyrna, Pergamum, Thyatira, Sardis, Philadelphia and Laodicea'" (verses 9-11).

This is the beginning of the first vision, and how appropriate that it should be a vision of Jesus. John begins by telling us the circumstances under which this vision came to him. He had been exiled to the island of Patmos, some 50 miles off the coast of Asia Minor. Many scholars think that John's banishment came during the reign of Domitian (A.D. 81-96). A later commentator, Victorinus, wrote in the third century: "When John said these things he was in the island of Patmos condemned to labor in the mines by Caesar Domitian."

Following Domitian's death by an assassin's knife, Nerva came to the throne and released all those banished by his predecessor. Thus John is believed to have returned just before his death to Ephesus, where the church members buried him.

The day on which this vision opened before his eyes is stated to be the *Lord's day.* The mention of the weekly Sabbath, a 7, has deep significance. The visions unveiling the future were intended to bring peace and rest to those who would suffer horrifying attacks through the centuries. The 7 orientation of the first vision upheld before them the truth that those who keep the faith will be part of the eternal kingdom in an unending Sabbath of peace.

"I turned around to see the voice that was speaking to me. And when I turned I saw seven golden lampstands, and among the lampstands was someone 'like a son of man,' dressed in a robe reaching down to his feet and with a golden sash around his chest. His head and hair were white like wool, as white as snow, and his eyes were like blazing fire. His feet were like bronze glowing in a furnace, and his voice was like the sound of rushing waters. In his right hand he held seven stars, and out of his mouth came a sharp double-edged sword. His face was like the sun shining in all its brilliance.

"When I saw him, I fell at his feet as though dead. Then he placed his right hand on me and said: 'Do not be afraid. I am the First and the Last. I am the Living One; I was dead, and behold I am alive for ever and ever! And I hold the keys of death and Hades.

"'Write, therefore, what you have seen, what is now and what will take place later. The mystery of the seven stars that you saw in my right hand and of the seven golden lampstands is this: The seven stars are the angels of the seven churches, and the seven lampstands are the seven churches'" (verses 12-20).

The description in these verses is drawn from the Old Testament. The *lampstands* draw our thoughts to the sanctuary built by Moses, a reflection of the heavenly sanctuary (see Ex. 25:31-39; Heb. 8:1-5). The phrase *Son of man* is found in the judgment scene of Daniel 7. The long *robe* reminds us of kings, priests, and prophets (see Ex. 28:4; Zech. 3:4), and He is our prophet, priest, and king. The description of *hair* comes from Daniel (see Dan. 7:9), as does the reference to the *fiery eyes* (Dan. 10:6). The *brass* reminds us of the altar on which the priest offered the daily sacrifice. The *thunderous voice* takes us back to the giving of law at Sinai, when the mountain rocked at the voice of God (Ex. 19:18). The symbol of a *sword* from Jesus' mouth is drawn from Isaiah (Isa. 11:4), and *the brilliance* of His countenance conjures up the entire Sinai experience, when Moses had to step into a cleft in the rock protected by the Lord's hand while He passed by in glory. For some time after that once-in-the-ages revelation, Moses had to wear a veil so that the reflected glory would not frighten the Israelites.

Revelation 1 ends with the resurrected Christ proclaiming that He holds in His hands the keys of death and of the grave.

We live constantly under the threat of death. The victims of auto, rail, and plane accidents; the victims of disease whose pale faces we see and whose weak voices we hear; the mourners at gravesides; the constant processions entering and exiting funeral parlors; suicidal teenagers; nameless little children struck down in wars around the world—all convince us that Jesus is our only hope.

When you lose a friend in death, when you lose your family in death, it comes home at last that no one can escape. The experience called life is like a terminal disease. But Jesus has passed through death into life and left behind the glow of hope in the dark recesses of the tomb. "I am alive for ever and ever. And I hold the keys of death" (Rev. 1:18). You have nothing to fear as long as your trust is centered in Him. Because He lives, we can live too. Jesus said: "I tell you the truth, whoever hears my word and believes him who sent me has eternal life and will not be condemned; he has crossed over from death to life" (John 5:24).

This is the introduction of the victorious book called Revelation. ●

---

[1] Note the threefold title, signifying the unity of the Godhead regarding our salvation.

[2] See Richard Fredericks, "A Sequential Study of Revelation 1-14 Emphasizing the Judgment Motif," 1987 unpublished doctoral dissertation, Andrews University.

[3] See Rev. 14:13; 16:15; 19:9; 20:6; 22:7; 22:14.

Outline

1. Description of ancient Ephesus

2. The letter to Ephesus—a desirable church

3. The letter to Smyrna—a persecuted church

4. The letter to Pergamos—a raised-up church

CHAPTER FOUR

VISITING THREE CHURCHES

O ne evening in my daughter's home I picked up a travel magazine and scanned the opening article, which described the seven most magical cities in the world. Predictably, Paris, London, Hong Kong, and New York were included in this coveted category.

If you had lived near the close of the first century and been asked to identify the most magical cities in the world, a small and equally predictable list of names would have come immediately to mind. Rome, no doubt, would have stood at the head of the list. But where did the rich and famous Romans go for their vacations? They headed east by ship to the glittering city of Ephesus. Here the dubious pleasures of sin were waiting to be enjoyed.

EPHESUS—A DESIRABLE CHURCH

"Why Ephesus?" one might ask. It certainly did not boast the best harbor of Asia. Smyrna, to the north, had a natural, far more desirable harbor. The harbor at Ephesus constantly silted up, and today the original dock area is six miles inland from the Aegean Sea. Pergamos, to the north, had a famous medical center. Laodicea boasted a great banking complex. Sardis offered a mountain fortress for security. But Ephesus outshone them all with its many prosperous trades (especially prostitution), its renowned library, and the world-famous temple of Artemis. The temple occupied a place equivalent to the cities of refuge of the Old Testament. Any criminal who could reach the temple had the right of asylum. This drew an unwelcome criminal element into town.

The Parthenon in Athens would have been dwarfed by Diana's temple, which stood 65 feet high, and its floor measured more than 400 feet long and more than 200 feet wide. One hundred seventeen (by another count 127) pillars supported the roof, the inner 36 being overlaid with relief carvings and maybe gold. Today nothing remains of this wonder of the ancient world because in A.D. 262 the Goths destroyed it (the fifth reconstruction of the temple) when they conquered the city. (Some 600 years earlier, on the night that Alexander the Great was born, a fire had destroyed the fourth construction of the temple. It was lighted by a narcissistic Greek, Herostratus, in an attempt to immortalize his own name.)

Perhaps the most cherished personal memory of Ephesus is, according to tradition, that John took Jesus' mother, Mary, with him from Jerusalem, and both settled in Ephesus, where he became the senior pastor of the congregations of the area, including the seven churches we are about to discuss in detail. According to tradition, when Mary died she was buried in Ephesus.

Jesus' message. We will learn that while two of the churches were in such poor spiritual condition that Jesus had nothing good to say about them, two of the churches were so deeply committed that He had only good to say about them. The other three received from their Lord a mixture of praise and concern.

"To the angel of the church in Ephesus write:

"These are the words of him who holds the seven stars in his right hand and walks among the seven golden lampstands: I know your deeds, your hard work and your perseverance. I know that you cannot tolerate wicked men, that you have tested those who claim to be apostles but are not, and have found them false. You have persevered and have endured hardship for my name, and have not grown weary.

"Yet I hold this against you: You have forsaken your first love. Remember the height from which you have fallen! Repent and do the things you did at first. If you do not repent, I will come to you and re-move your lampstand from its place. But you have this in your favor: You hate the practices of the Nicolaitans, which I also hate.

"He who has an ear, let him hear what the Spirit says to the churches. To him who overcomes, I will give the right to eat from the tree of life, which is in the paradise of God" (Rev. 2:1-7).

The name *Ephesus* probably means "desirable," and the church es-tablished by the apostle in such unpromising circumstances must have gone to extraordinary lengths to live its faith. This was a church of which Jesus could be proud. Among other things, the members had learned to practice perseverance. But there was a downside, and Jesus lamented that they had lost their first love. It was not that the Christian Ephesians had renounced their faith, or become immoral, or begun to worship at the temple of Artemis (she was also called Diana). The issue was far more subtle. What sometimes happens to young lovers had happened to these young Christians—a gradual, imperceptible drifting apart and a lessening of passion for the Lord.

The counsel Jesus had for the members in the church at Ephesus began with a reference to their first love when they had devoted such energy to the kingdom of God, and He urged them to "do the things you did at first" (verse 5), that is, deeds of service.

Then as a second word of praise, Jesus commented that He was pleased they hated the Nicolaitans' deeds as He did. Nothing in Scripture tells us about this movement or who the founder may have been, but the meaning of the name may hold some clues.

"In the letter to Pergamum the Nicolaitans and those who hold the teaching of Balaam are closely connected. They were, in fact, one and the same. There is a play on words here. The name *Nicolaus*, the founder of the Nicolaitans, could be derived from two Greek words, *nikan*, which means *to conquer*, and *laos*, which means *the people*. *Balaam* can be derived from two Hebrew words, *bela* which means *to conquer* and *ha'am*, which means *the people*. These two names, then, are the same name, Nicolaus being the Greek form of it, and Balaam the Hebrew form; and both names can describe an evil, but influential, teacher who has won an evil victory over the people, and subjugated them to poisonous heresy" (Barclay, *The Revelation of John*, vol. 1, p. 81).

Two main heresies have plagued the church since its inception. One is the blight of *antinomianism*, being against the law (the probable heresy of Nicolaus). The other is *legalism*, seeking salvation by obedience to the law. In many passages of the New Testament, writers express rabid opposition to the law. Paul could write that Christ is "the end of the law" (Rom. 10:4), but Jesus went on record that He had not come to do away with the law; in fact, He urged His hearers not even to think such a thought (Matt. 5:17). At first reading, these appear to be mixed messages.

There are dangers in extremes. God's law has an important role to play: to identify sin and to make plain His will, the high ideal He has for each of us. But our weakness and our inherited sinful natures constantly cast a shadow over our lives. No one in history has ever lived a life of sinless perfection except the Lord Jesus. We seek perfection while knowing full well that never, with a sinful nature in a sinful world, can we attain the perfection of Jesus. Thus the joy of our salvation is found not only in the substitution of the *death* of Jesus, which He suffered in our place, but in the perfection of Jesus' *life,* which is substituted for our imperfect lives. As a result, we are counted as being perfect, perfect in Him.

We may dream of the day when we will be like Him—perfect in life, perfect in thought, perfect in motive. But not in this life. God requires 100 percent perfection. Even if we were able to live a *day* in perfection, that would not commend us to God. He requires a *life* of perfection, and unfortunately all of us are well established in a life of sinfulness by the time we make our initial commitment to Him. So no human being can ever offer God a perfect life.

Then how do Christians relate to this dilemma? On one extreme are those who declare their freedom to live as they please. This is libertinism and is foreign to Christianity. The other extreme is legalism, in which individuals seek perfection by obedience.

The balanced position is the teaching of Scripture. We are free from the law for righteousness, as Paul reminds us (Rom. 10:4), free from the deeds of the law as a method of salvation, but the law remains to remind us of the way God wants us to live. Genuine Christians seek by the Spirit's power to obey as an evidence of commitment and constantly to grow into the likeness of the Master.

Lampstand of Ephesus. In this vision Jesus symbolizes the seven congregations as seven lampstands, reminiscent of the seven-branched candlestick that stood in the first room of the sanctuary. When Titus sacked Jerusalem in A.D. 70, his soldiers stole the lampstand (known as the *menorah*) before they torched the Temple. The Romans memorialized this insult to the Jews in a stone relief on the inside of an arch commemorating the exploits of the general. In the Arch of Titus, just across from the Coliseum, this depiction of the lampstand can still be seen. It is the single extant indication of the size of this item of furniture, because the Bible is silent on the point. The lampstand is still a symbol of all that is Jewish.

With that information as background, imagine the emotional impact of Jesus' words: "Remember the height from which you have fallen! Repent and do the things you did at first. If you do not repent, I will come to you and *remove your lampstand* from its place" (Rev. 2:5).

The letter ends with the promise that every overcomer will eat the fruit of the tree of life, which stands in the midst of Paradise.

The third level of application. The local significance of Jesus' letter to the church at Ephesus and its personal application to any of us who find our first love waning has already been addressed. But the third level of application needs to be detailed.

Ephesus the desirable fittingly symbolizes the Christian church in the first century, the seven decades after its inception by Jesus. During this desirable period the words and acts of Jesus were presented and repeated firsthand times without number. Tens of thousands were converted and shared the good news in expectation of His imminent return.

The period between Pentecost, when the real fruit of Jesus' ministry began to be harvested, and the close of the first century, when the last of those who had known Jesus personally would probably have died, can accurately be called the Ephesian period of church history.

And John, the last of the disciples to die, probably the youngest of the original 12 and the only one who did not die a violent death, is a classic example of one who maintained his first love.

SMYRNA—A PERSECUTED CHURCH

"To the angel of the church in Smyrna write:

"These are the words of him who is the First and the Last, who died and came to life again. I know your afflictions and your poverty—yet you are rich! I know the slander of those who say they are Jews and are not, but are a synagogue of Satan. Do not be afraid of what you are about to suffer. I tell you, the devil will put some of you in prison to test you, and you will suffer persecution for ten days. Be faithful, even to the point of death, and I will give you the crown of life.

"He who has an ear, let him hear what the Spirit says to the churches. He who overcomes will not be hurt at all by the second death" (Rev. 2:8-11).

Jesus' message. Jesus addressed the second letter to the angel of the congregation in Smyrna, modern Izmir, the third-largest city in Turkey today.

Smyrna, thought to mean "crushed" or "myrrh" (the etymology remains uncertain), seemed a world away from that thought during the first century. Even today in Izmir it is an impressive sight to look over the area from the top of Mount Pagos. During the days of John the cluster of temples and buildings on the hill were referred to as "the Crown of Smyrna." Orator Aristides later described it as a flower of beauty such as earth and sun had never shown to humanity.

Smyrna's chief asset came in the form of a natural, fully protected harbor that had the remarkable facility of a narrow entrance, reminiscent of the protected harbor of Sydney, Australia. In time of war the city fathers placed a chain across the water to keep out unwelcome visitors!

Smyrna is one of the few exhibits of cities that did not just grow spontaneously. Around 200 B.C. Lysimachus fulfilled a bold dream and rebuilt the city, which had been destroyed around 600 B.C. by Alyattes II of Lydia, as a completely planned metropolis. Paved straight streets dissected each other, imposing buildings crowned the hills, the harbor saw constant flotillas of ships laden with merchandise, and overland trade routes from the Hermus Valley converged on it. Smyrna, which had been all but dead, came to life.

During the first century A.D. a large Jewish population came to live in the city. This caused religious conflicts because many of the Christian population had formerly been Jews, and Judaism now actively promoted Christian persecution.

The most famous martyr of the city was Polycarp, a disciple of John's. He died in A.D. 155, during the annual games. Soldiers were ordered to search for him, and a slave under torture revealed the saint's whereabouts. When the soldiers came to arrest Polycarp, he insisted on providing food for them and requested a final hour of prayer alone while they ate. The soldiers had no desire to see the old man perish and pleaded with him to renounce his beliefs. But Polycarp refused to name Caesar as Lord.

The proconsul gave the saintly leader the choice of life by making a sacrifice to Caesar or death in flames. Polycarp had already made his choice, because shortly before his arrest he had dreamed that he saw his pillow catch fire. When he awoke, he told his friends he would shortly die, burned alive.

So while the crowd at the games watched, the soldiers built the fire and lit the faggots, and Polycarp became a martyr in the cause of Christ. A Christian church still stands to his memory in Izmir, a lonely exhibit to the good news in a land now only 1 percent Christian.

No criticism. Smyrna is one of the two churches that received no condemnation, only praise, from Jesus. The message is brief and full of encouragement. Jesus speaks of Himself as the first and the last, the sum of all, the one who was dead and had come back to life. For this persecuted church, the resurrection glowed brightly. And the expression of being dead but coming to life recalled the story of their dying city rebuilt by Lysimachus.

Jesus acknowledged their tribulation, Jewish antagonism, suffering, imprisonment, and poverty in the eyes of the world; then He added parenthetically: "Yet you are rich!" (verse 9). And they were rich in the eternal sense, even though not in the temporal sense—rich in faith, rich in security, rich in love.

Jesus then warned that the church would suffer tribulation for 10 days. This is the first use of the number 10 in the Apocalypse. Qualitatively it signaled a persecution so intense, so complete, that the church would wonder if any would survive. The persecution that began in the days of the apostles continued into the fourth century and the days of Emperor Constantine.

To a church steadfastly staring death in the face came the promise "He who overcomes will not be hurt at all by the second death" (verse 11). The experience of Polycarp became a parable for the entire congregation.

Third level of application. Along with the local and experiential applications comes also the third application. Smyrna represents the second period of church history, the period of persecution for the church throughout the Roman world during the second and third centuries.

PERGAMOS—A RAISED-UP CHURCH

"To the angel of the church in Pergamum write:

"These are the words of him who has the sharp, double-edged sword. I know where you live—where Satan has his throne. Yet you remain true to my name. You did not renounce your faith in me, even in the days of Antipas, my faithful witness, who was put to death in your city—where Satan lives.

"Nevertheless, I have a few things against you: You have people there who hold to the teaching of Balaam, who taught Balak to entice the Israelites to sin by eating food sacrificed to idols and by committing sexual immorality. Likewise you also have those who hold to the teaching of the Nicolaitans. Repent therefore! Otherwise, I will soon come to you and will fight against them with the sword of my mouth.

"He who has an ear, let him hear what the Spirit says to the churches. To him who overcomes, I will give some of the hidden manna. I will also give him a white stone with a new name written on it, known only to him who receives it" (Rev. 2:12-17).

Famous city. Pergamos, or Pergamum (several forms of the city name were used), had its own claim to fame. Built some 15 miles inland, it could boast no harbor. No main trade routes brought merchandise from distant areas. But despite this, Pergamos had stature through the distinction of being a capital city, and when John wrote, it had basked in that glory for four centuries.

The area is quite flat, but growing out of this plain is a rocky spur more than 1,000 feet high. On its flattened top the city had been built. Thus, the possible meaning of the name *Pergamos*—"raised up" or "acropolis."

Several aspects of life in Pergamos are significant to the modern Bible student. As an administrative center for Rome, the worship of Caesar figured prominently here. In the Roman world of so many diverse cultures and races, cohesion and unity had been difficult to achieve.

Gradually leadership sensed that the empire's spirit could best be symbolized in its leader, Caesar. The emperors themselves did not promote the idea of being worshiped as gods—at least not at first—but it became the law of the empire that once a year each citizen would burn incense and repeat the words "Caesar is Lord." This constituted a political act of allegiance to the civil government. The Romans never tried to make this an exclusive religious act because the citizens worshiped any gods they chose. But Christians balked at using the word "Lord" for anyone other than the Lord Jesus.

In Pergamos the act of allegiance was performed in the setting of the worship of Asclepias, the god of healing, to whom the local community often referred as *Asclepias the Savior (or Healer)*. This god took the form of a serpent—a fact preserved in modern times by the symbol of the medical profession. On the plain at the foot of the hill on which the city proper stood, a large hospital had been established, attracting people from all across the Roman world.

Galen, born in Pergamos, became the most famous local physician, second in reputation only to the towering figure of Hippocrates. An insightful understanding of the psychosomatic cause of some disease led the doctors to wheel patients through underground tunnels. As the patients were moved, they heard voices, presumed to be from the gods, telling them that they were getting well. (The voices came from the assistants of the physicians placed strategically at above-ground openings.) But the fame of the hospital and the cures it claimed established an enviable reputation.

Jesus' message. Jesus describes Himself at the beginning of the letter as the one with the sharp two-edged sword. In Roman times governors were separated into two categories: those who had the right of the sword and those who did not. The right of the sword gave a governor the authority to pronounce the sentence of death and have it carried out. The proconsul of Pergamos had the right of the sword, and this placed Christians in a precarious position. At the mere signal of his finger, the proconsul could execute a Christian. But the letter opens by reminding the members of the congregation in Pergamos that there is Another who also holds the right of the sword against His opposition.

The praise that Jesus extended to the believers in Pergamos begins with the encouragement that He understands the great difficulty of living in a city "where Satan has his throne" (verse 13). This probably refers to the capital's center of Caesar worship, yet the believers witnessed despite this threat.

Jesus names Antipas as one of the more prominent martyrs, but we know nothing about him except through a later reference by Tertullian, who said the martyr met his death by being slowly roasted in a brass bull. Jesus said that Antipas was "my faithful witness." The Greek word *martys* later came to include the meaning of martyrdom, but the root meaning is "witness." Unfortunately, Christian witnessing often led to martyrdom, and thus during the early centuries of church persecution came the blending of these two meanings.

Then follows the critique. This church, living where the Christians could see Satan's throne, needed a reformation of life and practice. They had become tainted by Balaam's teachings. In the letter to Ephesus we saw that this could be equated with the teaching of the Nicolaitans—a serious libertine approach to the Christian life in which the standards of the Christian faith were either ignored or ridiculed. Balaam led Israel into immorality and idolatry, and the name represents those individuals who want to live for Christ but ignore Him at the same time, attempting to gain the security of a relationship with

Jesus and the pleasure of sin at the same time. But one cannot mix these two. As Jesus said: "He who is not with me is against me" (Matt. 12:30). To try to live in two worlds simultaneously is to miss both.

Jesus' counsel tied in with the introduction of this letter and the *ius gladii*, "the right of the sword." He said: "Repent therefore! Otherwise, I will soon come to you and will fight against them with the sword of my mouth" (Rev. 2:16). Jesus will never force our wills. But one day He will come quickly, like the Roman proconsul of Pergamos, to execute his judgment "with the sword of [His] mouth."

Then He concludes with the promise of a love feast in which He will provide food in the form of manna. And at this feast each will be given a white stone. In Roman courts two stones were used to indicate judgments, a black stone for condemnation and a white stone for acquittal. Those who come to Christ receive immediate acquittal—they are saved and so have eternal life, which no person can ever take away from them (John 5:24).

And a new name? God took the old Abram and made the new Abraham, the old Sarai and made the new Sarah, the old Jacob and made the new Israel. So God takes each of us and, through the transformation wrought by His Spirit, makes us new creatures, bestowing on each of us His family name, Christian.

Third level of application. Beyond the local and experiential meanings of the letter to Pergamos, the city represents the third major period of church history, the fourth and fifth centuries, during which a spirit of compromise (the Balaam spirit) came into the church. As a result, the high spirituality of the previous period almost completely evaporated. A faithful remnant "went up into the mountain," so to speak, withdrawing to *Pergamos*, "raised up." But in general, the church fell into apostasy. Virtually all the false doctrines that have plagued Christendom for the past 14 centuries can be traced directly to changes during these two centuries. Such a church needed to heed the words from the mouth of the ever-loving Christ. ●

OUTLINE

1. The letter to Thyatira—a sacrifice church

2. The letter to Sardis—a remnant church

3. The letter to Philadelphia—a loving church

4. The letter to Laodicea—a lukewarm church

CHAPTER FIVE

Visiting Another Four Churches

W hen you travel across this country or overseas, not every village and city strikes you as outstanding. Sometimes you have to stop over in a place that is quite ordinary, with little to commend it. Not every city in France is a Paris, and the cities mentioned in Revelation 2 and 3 were far from equal in interest. After the flair of Ephesus, the grandeur of Smyrna, and the imperial drama of Pergamos, Thyatira seems like a poverty-stricken relative. When I visited Thyatira I could not help feeling disappointed.

THYATIRA—A SACRIFICE CHURCH

"To the angel of the church in Thyatira write:

"These are the words of the Son of God, whose eyes are like blazing fire and whose feet are like burnished bronze. I know your deeds, your love and faith, your service and perseverance, and that you are now doing more than you did at first.

"Nevertheless, I have this against you: You tolerate that woman Jezebel, who calls herself a prophetess. By her teaching she misleads my servants into sexual immorality and the eating of food sacrificed to idols. I have given her time to repent of her immorality, but she is unwilling.

"So I will cast her on a bed of suffering, and I will make those who commit adultery with her suffer intensely, unless they repent of her ways. I will strike her children dead. Then all the churches will know that I am he who searches hearts and minds, and I will repay each of you according to your deeds. Now I say to the rest of you in Thyatira, to you who do not hold to her teaching and have not learned Satan's so-called deep secrets (I will not impose any other burden on you): Only hold on to what you have until I come.

"To him who overcomes and does my will to the end, I will give authority over the nations—he will rule them with an iron scepter; he will dash them to pieces like pottery—just as I have received authority from my Father. I will also give him the morning star. He who has an ear, let him hear what the Spirit says to the churches" (Rev. 2:18-29).

An unexceptional city. Although this fourth city received the longest letter of the seven, it is the city about which we know the least. Virtually nothing of antiquity remains, and there are no redeeming hills or mountains and no beckoning rivers. Originally the area housed a garrison of soldiers with orders to be alert for any attacks against Pergamos. But with no natural defenses, this seemed a difficult responsibility.

Thyatira (perhaps meaning "sacrifice") had only one advantage: it had been established on an important trade route, and its citizens became deeply involved in merchandizing—a fact illustrated in Acts where we read of a merchant named Lydia who traded in purple cloth. The trade route promoted manufacture, and this in turn led to the organization of trade guilds or cooperatives common in New Testament and medieval times. To refuse to join a guild would be even more serious than refusing to join a trade union back in the mid-twentieth century.

Barclay suggested that these trade guilds posed two problems for Christians. The first would be weekly communal meals, often in the temple of a local deity. Sacrifices made to such gods, they believed, brought favors and success. Christians fresh from paganism found such occasions repulsive. Second would be the drunkenness and immorality associated with temple life. Such activities were taboo for a Christian. But to exclude oneself brought social isolation and threatened economic hardship.

One can imagine the discussions in the church at Thyatira. Some may have argued that to eat food offered to idols meant nothing. An idol is only an inanimate carving. Why worry? Paul stated as much. But others probably reasoned that the meat's presentation to a pagan god constituted an insult to Jesus.

When is compromise only harmless cooperation on an issue that is not moral and does not violate a principle? The church in Thyatira debated the issue at great length, and the letter addressed to them by Jesus seems to imply that some went too far, while others held their ground at an appropriate point.

Jesus' evaluation. Which brings us to the letter itself. Jesus is presented as the one with eyes like blazing fire and feet like burnished bronze (verse 18). The description recaptures the legends of some of the first people in the area, soldiers waiting through long nights, sitting around open fires, peering into the darkness and wondering if a stealthy attack might be in the offing, bronze shields, reflecting the flames, at the ready. But Commander Jesus is also interested in the readiness and appropriateness of His contingent, the church. As He looked closely at the members of the congregation in Thyatira, He liked some of the things He saw—but not all.

His praise focused on their well-doing. The responsible members performed many good works of service, and He praised their love, faith, service, and perseverance, adding: "You are now doing more than you did at first" (verse 19). At the end of the letter He added that "the rest" of them had avoided the false teaching of Jezebel and as a consequence had not experienced "Satan's so-called deep secrets" (verse 24). He had nothing but praise for this remnant. But for the majority, the story sounded quite different.

Jezebel is the fourth personal name mentioned thus far in the letters and is the last. Three letters name a person who either blessed or thwarted the church. In Ephesus we noted Nicolaus, in Pergamos both Antipas and Balaam, and in Thyatira, Jezebel. We observed earlier that nothing is known of Nicolaus and Antipas. But Jezebel recalls a whole catalog of crimes.

The marriage of Israel's king Ahab to Jezebel introduced such a degree of apostasy that it became a legend in Israel's whole history. When Ahab married his chosen bride, he probably had little idea of how far they would go together to destroy the kingdom.

Jezebel, the daughter of the Sidonian king Ethbaal, promoted Baal worship vigorously. With her husband she built a large center of Baal worship in Samaria. Following Elijah's prediction of a drought, the relationship of both king and queen to the Lord deteriorated even further. Jezebel attempted to kill the Lord's prophets, and only the action of Obadiah, hiding 100 of them in two caves and feeding them a prison diet of bread and water, saved the day. Then came the great contest on Mount Carmel.

When the altars had been built and the sacrifices placed on them, Elijah took a day to mock Baal and his prophets, who could not ignite the sacrifice. At the end of a day of frenzy and mockery, Elijah ordered the Lord's sacrifice, as well as an area on the cinder-dry hilltop, to be doused with water. Then he prayed that the God of Israel would answer and show His power.

As Elijah prayed, a bolt of fire hit the altar atop Mount Carmel, consumed water and wood, sacrifice and stones, and left nothing but a blackened hole in the dust of Carmel's crest. Immediately Elijah acted to eliminate from Israel the curse of Baal worship. He commanded the faithful to take *all* the prophets of Baal to the brook Kishon and let it flow with the blood of these apostates. In this way God cleansed Israel and turned back the tide from the kingdom of Satan, caused by the nefarious work of Jezebel.

The letter of Jesus to the members of the Thyatiran congregation mentions a situation reminiscent of Israel when it was led astray by Jezebel. About the activities of some of the trade guilds it could be said: "She misleads my servants into sexual immorality and the eating of food sacrificed to idols" (verse 20). The Jezebel mentioned here is not a person living in Thyatira; rather, she symbolizes all who deny a saving faith, like Ahab's wife.

Second and third levels of application. At a personal level this letter challenges us to examine our dreams and place them before God for His approval in order to avoid compromise.

Jesus' instruction to the little remnant in Thyatira reads: "Hold on to what you have until I come" (verse 25). (Each of the last four letters has a reference to the return of Jesus.) And the promise offered the overcomer authority over the nations, an authority that the small church in Thyatira completely lacked.

We have talked about the local and experiential aspects of this message, but we must also take a moment to see the historical setting. Thyatira represents the fourth major period of church history, the Middle Ages, from the sixth to the fifteenth century, the compromise period of church history during which the remnant of Jesus held steadfastly to the truth that all around them was being abandoned. As the age of Thyatira closed, so did a terror-filled age of "sacrifice."

SARDIS—A REMNANT CHURCH

"To the angel of the church in Sardis write:

"These are the words of him who holds the seven spirits of God and the seven stars. I know your deeds; you have a reputation of being alive, but you are dead. Wake up! Strengthen what remains and is about to die, for I have not found your deeds complete in the sight of my God. Remember, therefore, what you have received and heard; obey it, and repent. But if you do not wake up, I will come like a thief, and you will not know at what time I will come to you.

"Yet you have a few people in Sardis who have not soiled their clothes. They will walk with me, dressed in white, for they are worthy. He who overcomes will, like them, be dressed in white. I will never blot out his name from the book of life, but will acknowledge his name before my Father and his angels. He who has an ear, let him hear what the Spirit says to the churches" (Rev. 3:1-6).

As I stood with my movie camera trained on the heights of Mount Tmolus, adjusting the focus on full telephoto, movement caught my attention.* Looking up from the eyepiece, I realized that while I had been setting up the equipment, a contingent of Turkish soldiers had appeared. The sight of the soldiers in battle uniforms brought the history of Sardis rushing into memory, and standing at the foot of that hill vividly enhanced my imagination.

When Jesus wrote to Sardis, the city's history lay in the past, not

the present or future. *Sardis* may mean "remaining," and precious little remained then, or now, of the glory of the days of the ruler who
brought into being the proverb "As rich as Croesus." To the north of
the valley of the river Hermus is the long ridge called Mount Tmolus.
Extending out from the ridge are several elevated peninsulas with
steep sides and relatively flat surfaces. The king of Lydia recognized
this spot as a natural fortress and built his capital 1,500 feet above the
valley. So from about 600 B.C. the king of Lydia ruled in Oriental
splendor from the heights of Mount Tmolus.

King Croesus (560-547 B.C.) grew complacent living in such a
secure fortress. He decided to wage war against Cyrus, king of
Persia, but first sought the advice of the oracle of Delphi. The oracle told him that if he crossed the river Halys and attacked Cyrus,
he would "destroy a great empire." Croesus did not see through the
ambiguity of the response and assumed that he would be the de-
stroyer, not the destroyed. Croesus attacked and suffered humiliat-
ing defeat. He retreated to the heights of Sardis, and Cyrus followed
to lay siege to the city.

After two weeks of waiting, Cyrus offered a reward to anyone who
could devise a way into the elevated fortress. Shortly after this, a soldier named Hyeroeades noticed a helmet falling down the steep sides
of the mountain, and he assumed a break must have developed in the
walls. That night he took a small group of soldiers, crawled up the cliff
in the area in which the helmet had fallen, and found a gap where the
plateau had fallen away. Through that break the soldiers entered the
city, found it unguarded, and overthrew Croesus. No one had been
watching, and the city fell.

Two centuries later a soldier named Laoras repeated the drama of
Hyeroeades for Antiochus, one of Alexander's surviving generals.

Jesus' evaluation. Jesus presents Himself to the congregation of
Sardis as the one who has the seven Spirits and the seven stars. It
seemed as if Sardis had lived in the heavens in the company of the
stars. But the stars represented the churches, and Jesus assured
Sardis that He held them, He comforted them, and He guided them,
because *He alone could be their security*. Position cannot mandate it;

walls and fortresses cannot guarantee it; soldiers cannot produce it. But Jesus is our life and security.

He had no praise for this church that lived in the past rather than the present. Jesus said: "You have a reputation of being alive, but you are dead. Wake up! Strengthen what remains and is about to die, for I have not found your deeds complete in the sight of my God. . . . If you do not wake up, I will come like a thief, and you will not know at what time I will come to you" (verses 1-3).

Those cryptic words summarize the long history of Sardis. The greatest tragedies of their city had come through complacency. Thus the King James Version's translation is appropriate: "Be watchful."

Second and third levels of application. The personal meaning of this letter needs little comment. Modern life is filled with substitutes for eternal security. Insurance policies, education, and Social Security can make life seem secure. But the only security of ultimate consequence is our spiritual security based on a continuous relationship with Jesus Christ.

Then beyond the local and personal is the historical perspective. The letter from Jesus to Sardis represents the church coming out of the Middle Ages. Little remained of the vibrant kingdom established by Jesus. It seemed that the church faced extinction, not glorious new life. What remained needed to be strengthened. The remnant that survived needed to be alert to receive light from the Scriptures. This would be a time for the restoration of the truths long corrupted and forgotten by the church, a time to reestablish the mission to reach the globe in preparation for Jesus' return.

The promise to the members in Sardis was that their names would remain in the book of life. It must have appeared often to those who lived during the Sardis period of church history that their names had been written in a book of death. But the tide turned through the work of the Reformation during the sixteenth to eighteenth centuries. The Sardis period established a foundation for reaching out to the world with the good news of the returning Saviour.

PHILADELPHIA—A LOVING CHURCH

"To the angel of the church in Philadelphia write:

"These are the words of him who is holy and true, who holds the key of David. What he opens no one can shut, and what he shuts no one can open. I know your deeds. See, I have placed before you an open door that no one can shut. I know that you have little strength, yet you have kept my word and have not denied my name. I will make those who are of the synagogue of Satan, who claim to be Jews though they are not, but are liars—I will make them come and fall down at your feet and acknowledge that I have loved you. Since you have kept my command to endure patiently, I will also keep you from the hour of trial that is going to come upon the whole world to test those who live on the earth.

"I am coming soon. Hold on to what you have, so that no one will take your crown. Him who overcomes I will make a pillar in the temple of my God. Never again will he leave it. I will write on him the name of my God and the name of the city of my God, the new Jerusalem, which is coming down out of heaven from my God; and I will also write on him my new name. He who has an ear, let him hear what the Spirit says to the churches" (Rev. 3:7-13).

As we were driving the 30 miles between Sardis and Philadelphia, we were impressed by the perfect marriage that seemed to have taken place between the volcanic soil and grapevines. Philadelphia is grape country just as much as France, Greece, and the Napa Valley in California. And as the fruit had come to full sweetness, the farmers were busy bringing in the crop.

Nearing the city, I exclaimed to the driver of our car, "See those men and women carrying baskets of grapes on their heads? That's a perfect picture." He pulled to a stop, and we set up the camera. But we needed to get closer to the action, so we moved the equipment closer to the vines. Just about the time we finished the shot, I noticed a tractor headed at full speed in our direction. We quickly put away the equipment, suspecting we had unwittingly trespassed on private property. I mused silently that at least we had captured the scene before being turned away.

The owner, driving the tractor, could speak little English, but that did not seem to be much of a hindrance. He had come merely to offer his help, the use of the tractor or anything else, and he gave us some of the fruit just picked from his vines. We went away with about 10 pounds of the most delicious grapes. This was our first introduction to the city of *Philadelphia*—"brotherly love."

This city had the distinction of being the baby of the seven churches. Colonists from Pergamos came to the area in the middle of the second century B.C., during the reign of Attalus II, who had such a devotion to his brother, Eumenes II, that he acquired the nickname *Philadelphus*, and thus the origin of the name of the new settlement he formed.

Geographically, it is located in a volcanic area called the Burned Plain. Volcanos, now extinct, once covered the area with volcanic ash and lava, making a lavish bequest of fertility to the soil.

In the first century, earthquakes frequently assaulted the area, and one particularly serious earthquake, the same one that wrecked Sardis in A.D. 17, devastated Philadelphia. The aftershocks lasted for years, and some of the citizens were afraid to go back into their homes. After Emperor Tiberius helped finance rebuilding the city, they changed its name to Neocaesarea, and a little later, when Vespasian did the same, the people gave it the family name of the emperor Flavia. But in time the original name came back and remains even today.

Attalus established a new settlement on the borders of three territories—Mysia, Lydia, and Phrygia—in order to spread Greek culture into all these areas. Philadelphians had been commissioned to be missionaries for Greece. A testimony to the effectiveness of their witness can be seen in the fact that by the second decade A.D. Lydians had stopped using their native tongue and spoke Greek exclusively. The letter from Jesus suggested history should be repeated, but this time with a noble difference, God's people were to be missionaries of the gospel.

Jesus' evaluation. Jesus presented Himself as the one with a special key to open a door that could not be closed against His will, but which could be closed forever at His will. This is the door of the gospel. In an important sense He opened it at His first coming, and it can never be closed until the end.

The praise Jesus spoke to the church living on the plains centered on their works of service. These people faithfully proclaimed the Lord's name. Jesus had no criticism for those in this missionary church who accepted their commission so enthusiastically and followed through so consistently.

But He had strong criticism for those who claimed spirituality but did not live spiritual lives. In keeping with the earlier words of Paul in Romans and Galatians, Jesus advised that a national Jew is not counted as a spiritual Jew because of direct lineage from Abraham. Spiritual Jews are members of the family of God because of their faith link with Jesus Christ, and only that relationship assures participation in all the promises. A synagogue without faith becomes a "synagogue of Satan," according to this letter (verse 9).

Then Jesus added that the overcomer would be made a pillar in God's temple and receive His new name in the New Jerusalem, which will come down from God out of heaven. The Philadelphians would have enjoyed the reference to their past history. A city ruined by earthquake and wrecked by aftershocks had no pillars left standing. The pillars of which Jesus spoke suggest grand buildings and temples that cannot be shaken down. That vision will be fulfilled when the New Jerusalem becomes the home of the redeemed.

And what about the new name? The names Neocaesarea and Flavia signaled a new city, a safe city, but not an eternal city. Only the New Jerusalem offers eternal security.

Third level of application. We have spoken about the meaning of Jesus' letter to the local Philadelphians, but the prophetic message is also powerful. Philadelphia symbolized the church in the late eighteenth and nineteenth centuries, when the church-at-large awoke to the missionary responsibilities Jesus had laid at its door. This period opens with the exploits of such well-known heroes as William Carey, Adoniram Judson, Hudson Taylor, Henry Martyn, Robert Moffat, and Allan Gardner.

In 1792 Carey wrote a tract on missions and the next year set sail for India. On arrival Carey's wife's health failed and she died. He found himself the lonely parent of six children. He worked for six years in that hostile environment before finally seeing one Indian take a stand for Jesus.

Two societies were soon formed: in 1795 the London Missionary Society and in 1804 the British and Foreign Bible Society. In 1805 Henry Martyn set sail for India, Persia, and Arabia. Martyn has been called the most heroic figure in the English church. In 1812 Adoniram Judson left for Burma. In that land he lost his first wife, his second wife, and two children. But his Burmese translation of the New Testament laid a foundation for all future missionary work in Burma.

In 1816 came the founding of the American Bible Society. The following year Robert Moffat sailed for Africa. By the middle of the nineteenth century, China and Africa were opening to the preaching of the gospel. And during that same period came the rediscovery and preaching of the grand news of Jesus' imminent return, a theme long lost in the Christian church. Mission stations around the globe heard the good news.

But there is more to Philadelphia than local and prophetic applications. There is also the personal aspect. The call of Jesus to missionary work is not only to heroic figures like Carey and Moffat. With the certainty of the return of Jesus comes the call for me—and you—to play some active role in sharing that good word. We cannot all act in the *same* way, but we can all act in *some* way with the people with whom we come in contact. If we have a bright star shining on our own horizons, we should brighten someone else's dark sky. The church of today grew from the soil of the church of the nineteenth century, and those roots of a not-too-far-removed past should fill us with missionary zeal for the Writer of the letter to the members of the church in Philadelphia.

Laodicea—A Lukewarm Church

"To the angel of the church in Laodicea write:

"These are the words of the Amen, the faithful and true witness, the ruler of God's creation. I know your deeds, that you are neither cold nor hot. I wish you were either one or the other! So, because you are lukewarm—neither hot nor cold—I am about to spit you out of my mouth. You say, 'I am rich; I have acquired wealth and do not need a thing.' But you do not realize that you are wretched, pitiful, poor, blind and naked. I counsel you to buy from me gold refined in the fire, so you can become rich; and white clothes to wear, so you can cover your shameful nakedness; and salve to put on your eyes, so you can see.

"Those whom I love I rebuke and discipline. So be earnest, and repent. Here I am! I stand at the door and knock. If anyone hears my voice and opens the door, I will come in and eat with him, and he with me.

"To him who overcomes, I will give the right to sit with me on my throne, just as I overcame and sat down with my Father on his throne. He who has an ear, let him hear what the Spirit says to the churches" (Rev. 3:14-22).

The last letter is the best known of the seven. Times without number in sermons and articles we have been chastised with the imagery of being neither cold nor hot, and the castigation "You do not realize that you are wretched, pitiful, poor, blind and naked" (verse 17). Jesus had no praise for Laodicea, "a people adjudged," but we must assume from the later visions that many do respond to the appeals and become "hot" for Jesus.

It is inappropriate to characterize every Christian in these last days as being *Laodicean*. Any message couched in imagery without explanation and presented for an extended period of time ceases to communicate. An intimate look at Laodicea is long overdue.

I could never forget the view of the peak of Heliopolis some three or four miles away as our car circled around the scattered ruins of once wealthy Laodicea. Acres of white calcium deposits form a mammoth lace shawl over the steep sides of the hill. A half hour later we were registered in a motel on the top of that hill and were bathing in the hot waters of Heliopolis. A giant underground hot spring comes to the surface on the top of the hill, flows down the side, and then makes its way to the valley directly past the site of ancient Laodicea. The spring is the basis of the message to the members of the church in Laodicea. The water flows hot from the spring, but cools as it flows down the hillside—depositing minerals—flows warm past Laodicea, and finally cools completely as it joins another stream miles from the original source.

Jesus said, "If you were hot like the stream at its source, you would have the missionary zeal of Philadelphia. If you were cold like the streams in the valley, you might sense your great need and be appealed to and warmed. But in this lukewarm temperature, like the waters flowing past the city, you sense no need. I can do nothing with you."

Nineteen hundred years ago business thrived. A hospital had been established, not the equal of the Pergamos facility, but with its own areas of expertise. Its doctors received such local acclaim that two of them, Zeuxis and Alexander, were featured on the coins of the city. The most famous treatments were for ear and eye complaints. For those who could not visit the hospital, an export trade made Phrygian powder available in tablet form.

The sheep of the area were selectively bred and became famous for their black glossy wool, from which clothing was manufactured, especially a tunic called a *trimita*. Driving through the nearest town, I noticed children walking home from school and smiled when I noticed the school uniform was a black tunic.

Both the hospital and clothing manufacture made Laodicea rich, and the flow of money led to the establishment of banks. The city could rightly claim to be one of the world's most wealthy centers. So great were its financial resources that when the city suffered a crippling earthquake in A.D. 60, the town fathers declined the proffered help of Rome and rebuilt the city with its own finances.

Jesus' message. It is against this backdrop of the past that we can understand the message Jesus sent to His church. The members were all involved in some way or another with the local industries—hospital, clothing manufacture, banking. They all became caught up in affluence and progress. Although there is nothing inherently wrong with affluence, wrongly handled, it is devastating.

Looking at Laodicea, Jesus wrote: "Despite the banks, you are poor. Despite the eye treatment, you are blind. Despite the tunics, you are naked. You don't need money from the bank; you need My gold purified in the fire of affliction. You don't need a black tunic; you need a white robe of My purest righteousness. You don't need Phrygian powder; you need the insight of My Spirit to see yourself as

you really are, and Me as I really am. You need discipline, so repent"
(see verses 17-19).

Third level of application. There is no need to comment further
on the obvious personal application of the message that Jesus so com-
pellingly drew for the benefit of Laodicea. And little needs to be added
about the prophetic application. Laodicea represents the church of
today awaiting the return of Jesus. Just two signs must yet be fulfilled
before the promise becomes reality: the gospel must be preached in
the whole world, and Satan must fill to overflowing his cup of iniquity
so that never in eternity will anyone have cause to question the consequences of rebellion against God. ●

----

* A 30-minute video on the seven churches, titled *Orders to Angels*, produced by the author, is available in VHS. For information, phone (800) 253-3000.

OUTLINE

1. The first major section of the Apocalypse corresponding with the first major section of Jesus' Olivet discourse

2. Heaven's throne room described

3. The 24 elders

4. The 4 living creatures

5. The sealed scroll

CHAPTER SIX

HEAVEN'S THRONE ROOM

ohn introduced Jesus in the first chapter of his book through several verses of symbolic description. In the next two chapters John recorded Jesus' letters. Chapters 4 and 5 are given over almost entirely to extolling our Saviour, so we should have no doubts that this work reveals Jesus.

In the book of Daniel the stories of personal exploits (chapters 1-6) become illustrations of the prophetic visions (chapters 7-12), and the same is true in a slightly different way in Revelation. The letters to the seven congregations of Asia Minor illustrate the great conflict throughout history between Jesus and Satan, the Lord's followers and Satan's host. All the main themes of the book are introduced in a subtle form in the three chapters we have already studied.

Revelation 4 brings us to the first of the three main sections of the book, according to the outline we are following. It is in recognition of the transition that John remarks, "After this . . ." It is an expression that often marks major transitions in his visions (see Rev. 7:1; 15:5; 18:1; etc.).

"After this I looked, and there [behold, KJV] before me was a door standing open in heaven. And the voice I had first heard speaking to me like a trumpet said, 'Come up here, and I will show you what must take place after this.' At once I was in the Spirit, and there before me was a throne in heaven with someone sitting on it. And the one who sat there had the appearance of jasper and carnelian. A rainbow, resembling an emerald, encircled the throne" (Rev. 4:1-3).

VISION OF THE THRONE ROOM

The word "behold" in the KJV of verse 1 is a Greek imperative, which we probably best recall from the Nativity story: "Fear not: for, behold, I bring you good tidings of great joy, which shall be to all people" (Luke 2:10, KJV). It is a strong expression designed to arrest our attention. John seems to be saying, "I have something of the greatest importance to share. Come with me into heaven, through the door that is now open, into the presence of the risen Christ. The veil has been swept away, the invitation is freely extended, and we now have continuous access to our Lord, so come."

John lets us know at the start that this is a symbolic presentation, not a literal one. He did not hear an actual trumpet; rather, the voice was "like" a trumpet—in volume, clarity, and authority. This is a voice one dare not ignore. John's words at this point reinforce an important part of the hermeneutic we are utilizing throughout the Apocalypse— we expect the presentations to be symbolic.

First, John describes God seated on heaven's throne. Next, he describes the sevenfold Spirit before the throne. Then in chapter 5 the Son is depicted as the Lamb.

The Father is described in terms of precious stones: jasper, sardius, and emerald. Morris warned that the lack of scientific terminology among the ancients makes identification of precious and semi-precious stones somewhat hazardous (see Morris, *The Revelation of St. John*, p. 87). But there is significance in that sardius and jasper were the first and last of the 12 stones set in the breastplate of the high priest, each of those stones being inscribed with the name of one of the 12 tribes. The Father bears all of us on His heart. Revelation is not just about galactic conflicts, although it includes them. It is concerned about each of us as individuals.

John describes a rainbow circling the throne. Since Noah's flood, the rainbow has endlessly repeated the promise that destruction by water will never again encompass the earth. All God's promises are as sure. The promises of everlasting life, a new heaven, and a new earth are sure. The promises of God are foundational to all that will be revealed in this book. God is still on the throne, surrounded by the symbol that reminds us each promise will be fulfilled (cf. Ps. 29).

THE 24 ELDERS

"Surrounding the throne were twenty-four other thrones, and seated on them were twenty-four elders. They were dressed in white and had crowns of gold on their heads. From the throne came flashes of lightning, rumblings and peals of thunder. Before the throne, seven lamps were blazing. These are the seven spirits of God. Also before the throne there was what looked like a sea of glass, clear as crystal" (Rev. 4:4-6).

Two major elements in the description of the throne are the 24 elders and the 4 living creatures. The number 24 (12 x 2) makes an important statement about the *kingdom*, and the 4 living creatures reveal some aspect of the theme of *universality*.

Erdman identified the 24 elders succinctly: "These are the ideal representatives of the glorified people of God" (Charles R. Erdman, *The Revelation of John*, p. 66). The question to ask is not how many, but who? The use of the numeral 12 alerts us that this is a depiction of the kingdom. In fact, these elders are mentioned precisely 12 times in this book (Rev. 4:4, 10; 5:5, 6, 8, 11, 14; 7:11, 13; 11:16; 14:3; 19:4).

History has had some notable moments when God has given the human race reassurance about the certainty of life in the kingdom of glory. In the patriarchal era He took Enoch to glory before he died to reassure the antediluvians that death would not forever hold sway. During the prophetic period both Moses (through a special resurrection) and Elijah (without experiencing death) ascended to God's throne. In the Christian era, at the resurrection of Jesus, a host of individuals rose from their graves. Matthew records: "The tombs broke open and the bodies of many holy people who had died were raised to life. They came out of the tombs, and after Jesus' resurrection they went into the holy city and appeared to many people" (Matt. 27:52, 53).

Paul seems to suggest that these resurrected ones were taken with

Christ to heaven: "When he ascended on high, he led captives in his train and gave gifts to men" (Eph. 4:8). In another place he refers to the resurrection of Jesus as the "firstfruits of those who have fallen asleep" (1 Cor. 15:20). And in a sense, those He chose to raise from the grave and take to heaven with Him also constitute a kind of first-fruits. The general resurrection comes at the end of the world, but here is a pledge that the harvest will be reaped, that all who have died in faith will be raised from their graves and taken to heaven.

The group selected to sit on thrones around God's throne consti-tute the kingdom in miniature. The group represents both Old and New Testament believers (12 x 2) clothed in white garments (repre-senting the righteousness of Jesus). Each wears a *stephanos*, "a crown of victory" (as worn by the winners of the Greek and Roman races). They had fought a good fight of faith. They had finished their ap-pointed earthly course. Now God grants them the crown of victory, the crown of eternal life, taking them bodily to sit at His throne to assure us of the reality of eternal life in Paradise.

THE FOUR LIVING CREATURES

"In the center, around the throne, were four living creatures, and they were covered with eyes, in front and in back. The first living crea-ture was like a lion, the second was like an ox, the third had a face like a man, the fourth was like a flying eagle. Each of the four living crea-tures had six wings and was covered with eyes all around, even under his wings. Day and night they never stop saying: 'Holy, holy, holy is the Lord God Almighty, who was, and is, and is to come.'

"Whenever the living creatures give glory, honor and thanks to him who sits on the throne and who lives for ever and ever, the twenty-four elders fall down before him who sits on the throne, and worship him who lives for ever and ever. They lay their crowns before the throne and say: 'You are worthy, our Lord and God, to receive glory and honor and power, for you created all things, and by your will they were created and have their being'" (verses 6-11).

The "four living creatures . . . covered with eyes, in front and in back" (verse 6) are described in the language of Ezekiel. Ladd asserted: "It is quite clear that these four living creatures are analogous to the seraphim of Isaiah 6:1-3 and the cherubim of Ezekiel 10:14. Their form is closer to Ezekiel's cherubim, each of which had four faces—those of a man, a lion, an ox, and an eagle—and four wings, whereas John's living creatures each have a single head and six wings" (George E. Ladd, *A Commentary on the Revelation of John*, p. 77).

Swete added that "the four forms represent whatever is noblest, strongest, wisest, and swiftest in animate nature" (Henry B. Swete, *The Apocalypse of St. John*, p. 70).

Interestingly, in Dakota culture the sacred hoop encompasses the entire universe. It has four points, representing the four compass points, and celebrates four creatures: the bison stands for wisdom; the bear, introspection; the eagle, illumination; and the mouse, innocence.

The early Church Fathers found in John's four creatures symbols of the four Gospels. They did not agree on which creature matched a particular Gospel, but Augustine developed the most widely accepted position when he equated Matthew with the lion, Mark with the man, Luke with the ox, and John with the eagle. And when John wished to describe Jesus as seen in vision, he painted four symbols (borrowed from Ezekiel and Isaiah) by which to show us the character of the Redeemer and His universal (4) power.

The four creatures sparkle with imagery. The lion spells royalty; the calf, sacrifice; humanity, intelligence; and the eagle, heavenly flight and farsightedness. In these factors we see Jesus our king, our substitute sacrifice, the all-wise, and the one who ascended to heaven to minister for us and who, with His ever-watching gaze, cares for us.

Understood another way, each of the four living creatures is a king in its own right: the lion, king of the forest; the ox, king of the field; the eagle, king of the air; and humanity, king of all creation. And Jesus our king rules universally—as denoted by the number 4.

Each of the four is known for a particular characteristic: the lion for majesty, the ox for perseverance, the eagle for untiring flight, a human being for superlative intelligence. Thus Jesus is represented anthropomorphically in ways with which we can identify. Majestically, courageously, farsightedly, wisely, He lived among us for some 30 years to show us the Father and provide the way to heaven.

During the Middle Ages the science of heraldry grew as individuals sought to produce visual symbols of their family's distinctive characteristics or the characteristics for which they wished to be known. Even today in Europe state occasions include some of these heraldic signs. This is John's approach also. He shows us Jesus through symbols that we can instantly recognize and appreciate. They are not drawn by an artist on wood, metal, or cloth. These are living creatures, the throne room's *living* royal coat of arms. Each creature has a characteristic that points us to an important aspect of our Lord's character, and grouped together reveal the salvation Jesus offers universally (4) to all who live in the world.

One might ask, If Jesus is on the throne, why would John paint these four creatures to illustrate Jesus' preeminent characteristics? The answer is that this is apocalyptic, not logic. If you walk into an artist's workshop, you expect to see many exhibits that reveal the artist. And in the Creator's "workshop," His throne room, John paints symbolic pictures, not reality, to reveal Jesus in His exquisite glory.

The Godhead is depicted in the throne room—Father, Son, and Holy Spirit (see Rev. 4:3, 5; 5:6). Together, the firstfruits of the Resurrection (the 24 elders) fill heaven with praise. The 24 alone, then the 24 with the 4 living creatures, sing of the worthiness of the Lord: "You are worthy, our Lord and God, to receive glory and honor and power [note the three elements, signifying unity], for you created all things, and by your will they were created and have their being" (Rev. 4:11).

"You are worthy to take the scroll and to open its seals, because you were slain, and with your blood you purchased men for God from every tribe and language and people and nation [note the four elements, signifying universality]" (Rev. 5:9).

"Worthy is the Lamb, who was slain, to receive power and wealth and wisdom and strength and honor and glory and praise [note the seven elements, signifying promised rest in Jesus]!" (verse 12).

Barclay exclaims: "The worship of God is not the preserve of liturgy and technically religious activities and intellectual pursuits.

Work and worship literally become one. Man's chief end is to glorify God and to enjoy Him forever. . . . Work well done rises like a hymn of praise to eternal God" *(The Revelation of John,* vol. 1, pp. 201, 202).

THE SEALED SCROLL

"Then I saw in the right hand of him who sat on the throne a scroll with writing on both sides and sealed with seven seals. And I saw a mighty angel proclaiming in a loud voice, 'Who is worthy to break the seals and open the scroll?' But no one in heaven or on earth or under the earth could open the scroll or even look inside it.

"I wept and wept because no one was found who was worthy to open the scroll or even look inside it. Then one of the elders said to me, 'Do not weep! See, the Lion of the tribe of Judah, the Root of David, has triumphed. He is able to open the scroll and its seven seals.'

"Then I saw a Lamb, looking as if it had been slain, standing in the center of the throne, encircled by the four living creatures and the elders. He had seven horns and seven eyes, which are the seven spirits of God sent out into all the earth. He came and took the scroll from the right hand of him who sat on the throne. And when he had taken it, the four living creatures and the twenty-four elders fell down before the Lamb. Each one had a harp and they were holding golden bowls full of incense, which are the prayers of the saints. And they sang a new song:

"'You are worthy to take the scroll and to open its seals, because you were slain, and with your blood you purchased men for God from every tribe and language and people and nation. You have made them to be a kingdom and priests to serve our God, and they will reign on the earth.'

"Then I looked and heard the voice of many angels, numbering thousands upon thousands, and ten thousand times ten thousand. They encircled the throne and the living creatures and the elders. In a loud voice they sang:

"'Worthy is the Lamb, who was slain, to receive power and wealth and wisdom and strength and honor and glory and praise!'

"Then I heard every creature in heaven and on earth and under the earth and on the sea, and all that is in them, singing: 'To him who sits on the throne and to the Lamb be praise and honor and glory and power, for ever and ever!'

"The four living creatures said, 'Amen,' and the elders fell down and worshiped" (Rev. 5:1-14).

An integral part of the description of the throne room is the drama of a sealed scroll. As chapter 5 opens, we read that a scroll rests in God's right hand. After the description of the throne room in chapter 4, the spotlight now rests momentarily on this scroll. Like a drama being enacted before a one-person audience, an angel asks the question "Who is worthy to break the seals and open the scroll?" (verse 2). No one is found to answer the challenge.

Sensing the supreme importance of the message contained in the scroll, John begins to weep. Perhaps he feels sad that God can find no one in heaven or earth with whom to share His secrets of the future. At this moment one of the elders tells John not to cry because "the Lion of the tribe of Judah, . . . has triumphed. He is able to open the scroll and its seven seals" (verse 5). Not the lionlike creature of chapter 4, but Judah's divine-human Lion had, through death and resurrection, the right to open the seals and reveal the scroll's contents.

So Jesus takes the scroll, and in typical apocalyptic style, the symbol changes and John sees not a lion but a lamb. Jesus the lion, who so courageously fought the battle with Satan, also had to die (like the sacrificial lamb) in order to become our substitute in death. Both death and resurrection are seen in this verse as John beholds the "Lamb, looking as if it had been slain" (verse 6).

Some translations of the Apocalypse substitute *book* for scroll in verse 1, but this masks the first-century setting. From the papyrus plant, papyrus was manufactured in sheets eight to 10 inches square. Artisans produced papyrus by cutting thin strips of the pith of the papyrus plant and placing them side by side. Next they glued other strips side by side at right angles to the first layer and smoothed the writing surface with pumice stone. Scribes wrote on the smooth side, with the grain, in narrow columns an inch or so apart. For a long document, the sheets were glued together horizontally and wound around a stick.

For a long work, several feet of papyrus would be required. The Gospel of Matthew, for example, would occupy some 30 feet.

Only in circumstances in which a great quantity of material needed to be recorded would the reverse side of the papyrus be used as well. The scroll Jesus had taken from the Father's hand contained, as we shall shortly see, the history of the world. Consequently, much had to be shared, so John describes it as being written on both sides.

Ladd commented: "The whole story of human history rests in the hand of God. What simpler or more sublime way of picturing God's ultimate sovereignty over all history could be found than this picture of the scroll resting in the hand of God?" *(A Commentary on the Revelation of John,* pp. 82, 83).

The reference to seven seals on the scroll is typically Roman and suggests a will. When a person's final will and testament had been written, the witnesses attached their personal seals. The scroll could not be opened until all the witnesses or their duly appointed representatives were present and personally removed their seals. In one sense, the slain Lamb had His will and testament written on the scroll pictured in Revelation 5 and 6. It had been sealed until His death. But in His resurrection glory He opened His own will, which revealed the triumph of His cause against His enemies. Someone dies then rises to open His own will? What striking images this book of symbols presents!

And how do God's children participate in this great unsealing of the future? With the scroll in His hands and ready to remove the seals one by one, Jesus sees the elders and living creatures taking bowls full of incense, "which are the prayers of the saints" (verse 8). The communication of prayer is our link with Him as we seek to understand and do His will.

Perhaps there is no better way to close these two chapters than by meditating on the slain Lamb. The King James Version translates Revelation 5:6: "Lo, *in the midst* of the throne . . . a Lamb." For each of us, Jesus must be the central fact of life. He must be "in the midst" of all plans and activities.

The Jews understood this concept well when they taught their children that there should not be a division between the sacred and the secular. For a believer there could be only sacred events. And when Jesus is "in the midst" of our lives, there is no secular either, only sacred.

In the world's first garden stood the tree of the knowledge of good and evil. In relationship with Jesus, that tree should have been for our first parents and their children only a tree of the knowledge of good. But through rejection it also became a tree of the knowledge of evil.

As a result, another tree had to be planted in another garden called Golgotha. And there "in the midst" of two thieves, Jesus offered eternal life to the one who had tasted the fruit of a tree of evil and now thirsted for the fruit of the tree of life. The thief had only two or three days of agonizing life left to live, but he used his only free organ, his tongue, to witness to his newfound faith.

When the unrepentant brigand accosted Jesus with the words "Aren't you the Christ? Save yourself and us!" the repentant thief called back, "Don't you fear God . . . since you are under the same sentence? We are punished justly, for we are getting what our deeds deserve. But this man has done nothing wrong" (Luke 23:39-41).

What made the change in the one and not the other? The repentant had beheld "the Lamb of God," and with broken heart received full pardon and the assurance that he would enjoy the bliss of Paradise.

There is still life in a believing look at the Lamb. ●

Outline

1. Background to the seals
   Expansion of part 1 of the Olivet address
   The principle of repetition and expansion
   Indebtedness to Zechariah
   Structure of each major seven: four/three or three/four

2. The first seal—the gospel horse

3. The second seal—the persecution horse

4. The third seal—the famine horse

5. The fourth seal—the death horse

6. The fifth seal—the cry for vengeance

7. The sixth seal—the final signs and judgment on rejecters

CHAPTER SEVEN

REMOVING THE SEALS

No symbols of the Apocalypse are better known to people from so many different walks of life than those of Revelation 6. Films, plays, books, and even some past members of the Notre Dame football team have been associated with the four apocalyptic horses and their riders.

But past associations pale when compared with the Branch Davidians of Waco, Texas. In early 1993 a self-proclaimed messiah who named himself David Koresh told the world that he alone had the truth about the seals of Revelation to reveal to the world. After an extended police standoff, the attorney general of the United States, Janet Reno, gave the order to attack and try to save the lives of the people in the compound. The ensuing inferno killed some 80 people—most of whom had lived inside.

Tragically, after the ashes were sifted for scattered bones and charred bodies, the world still knew no more than before about the meaning of the seven seals.

BACKGROUNDS

As we have noted previously, the seven seals are John's apocalyptic version of *the first part of Jesus' Olivet sermon*, which dealt primarily with the indicators of His return at the end of the age. That section of the sermon climaxes with the words "And this gospel of the kingdom will be preached in the whole world as a testimony to all nations, and then the end will come" (Matt. 24:14).

The first seal portrays the vigorous first-century proclamation of the gospel. Seals 2 through 6 illuminate much of the other information in Matthew 24:3-14: war, tribulation, hatred, earthquakes, famines, pestilences, falsehood, and lawlessness.

Then too, as we open this chapter we remember the hermeneutic of *repetition and expansion*. Each of the major visions of the book (for example, seals, trumpets, bowls) builds on and expands earlier material. Thus the outline of history detailed in the seven churches we see again in the seals, but from a different perspective. In the seven churches, we saw the perspective of the divine Shepherd. In the seven seals we see history from the point of view of the flock—what it will do, what it will endure.

John is *indebted to Zechariah* for much of the wording of the seven seals. The Old Testament prophet described a vision from God involving similar symbols. In Zechariah's description chariots were drawn first by red horses, second by black horses, third by white horses, and fourth by dappled horses. These charioteers were instructed to "go throughout the earth" (Zech. 6:7) and bring vengeance on the nations that had oppressed His people, especially Babylon and Egypt.

Interestingly, *the sevens of the book of Revelation are usually divided* into a four and a three, or a three and a four. For instance, here in the seals, the first four go naturally together because each uses the symbol of a horse. The last three have quite different symbolism. In the next major vision of seven, the trumpets, the first four also go together, while the last three are called *woes*. In the seven churches we noted that the first three go together, while the last four all climax with references to the coming Advent. This becomes an interpretive clue throughout the chapters.

With this background, the meaning of the vision of the seals is not difficult to understand.

THE FIRST SEAL—THE WHITE HORSE

"I watched as the Lamb opened the first of the seven seals. Then I heard one of the four living creatures say in a voice like thunder,

'Come!' I looked, and there before me was a white horse! Its rider held a bow, and he was given a crown, and he rode out as a conqueror bent on conquest" (Rev. 6:1, 2).

When Jesus opens the first seal, a living creature speaks in a thunderous voice, "Come!" and a white horse gallops away. From the dawn of recorded history, horses have been associated with war and conquest. Foot soldiers are a poor match for cavalry. In the days of Rome victorious generals returned from battle riding in chariots drawn by white horses, and they paraded their captives behind them. In Revelation white is associated with purity, heaven, and righteousness. We read of Jesus' white hair, the saints' white stones and white clothes, the 24 elders' white clothing, the white cloud, the white horses of Jesus and His angels, and the white throne. In another reference we read that the fine white linen in which the saints are clothed represents righteousness (Rev. 19:8).

In light of this information, we assume that the white horse represents the triumphant preaching of the gospel of the righteousness of Jesus. After centuries of Pharisaic legalism and degrading heathenism, the conquests of the preaching of the gospel in the first century are without parallel.

With the bow of the Spirit to send the arrow of the gospel to the heart of each hearer, dramatic results were seen, and shortly the church numbered in the hundreds of thousands.

This seal, with its white horse, symbolizes the same historical period as the church of Ephesus, the first century, when the gospel spread quickly and enthusiastically in the Roman world.

In another sense, the gospel horse still rides and must continue to ride until everyone has the opportunity to respond to its invitation. And each of us is called to participate in that work through our spiritual gifts. For some that may mean actively preaching at home or in other lands. For others it may mean a more private work of sharing Jesus' love wherever we meet people and sense a need. For still others it may mean a heartwarming hospitality ministry or a teaching ministry, because all of us have been equipped in some way to have a part in sharing the good news of Jesus' love.

THE SECOND SEAL—THE RED HORSE

The colors describe in a single word the import of the message of the seals. The purity of the gospel is contrasted with the blood shed by the church as it fell into the hands of ruthless caesars.

"When the Lamb opened the second seal, I heard the second living creature say, 'Come!' Then another horse came out, a fiery red one. Its rider was given power to take peace from the earth and to make men slay each other. To him was given a large sword" (Rev. 6:3, 4).

The description is not about civil strife or Rome's territorial battles. Ladd has written about the state of Rome in the period covered by the second seal: "The time when John lived, the late first century, was not a time particularly characterized by warfare. In fact, the might of the Roman armies had crushed effective resistance so that peace reigned from Armenia to Spain. The great Pax Romana gave to the Mediterranean world several centuries of peace which the Western world has never since experienced" (A Commentary on the Revelation of John, p. 100).

The red horse is another representation of the war against the church. The preaching of the gospel, symbolized by the white horse, turned Rome against the church. It could neither understand nor tolerate the thought of any kingdom but Rome. As we noted in the church of Pergamos, emperor worship required an annual symbolic act of loyalty to the emperor as a deity. The failure of Christians to perform this act led to increasing persecution, until the caesars attempted the annihilation of the entire Christian movement. The church had good reason to fear the sharp sword of the state, but not a fear of death; rather, the fear that Rome would inhibit the preaching of the gospel.

This seal runs parallel to the second church, Smyrna, and covers the persecution during the second and third centuries down to the conversion of Emperor Constantine.

THE THIRD SEAL—THE BLACK HORSE

"When the Lamb opened the third seal, I heard the third living creature say, 'Come!' I looked, and there before me was a black horse! Its rider was holding a pair of scales in his hand. Then I heard what sounded like a voice among the four living creatures, saying, 'A quart of wheat for a day's wages, and three quarts of barley for a day's wages, and do not damage the oil and the wine!'" (Rev. 6:5, 6).

The rider of the black horse carried a pair of balances with which to weigh rations. Barclay has commented: "In the Old Testament the phrase *to eat bread by weight* indicates the greatest scarcity. In *Leviticus* it is the threat of God, that, if the people are rebellious and disobedient 'they shall deliver you your bread again by weight' (Leviticus 26:26)" *(The Revelation of John,* vol. 1, p. 8).

Barclay went on to explain that in the ancient world a laborer's daily allowance would be a quart of grain and a day's pay would be a denarius *(ibid.,* p. 9). According to this description, the worker's daily food allowance required a full day's pay. There would be no money for any other purchases, and if the worker was married, there would be no way to provide for a family. A worker could elect to purchase nutritionally inferior barley to keep the family alive, but that would be a hard decision.

In the New Testament world the three main food commodities were grain (chiefly wheat), grapes, and oil. The grapes provided a staple beverage, and the oil constituted a regular part of the diet in food preparation. John notes no restriction on oil and wine, indicating that this is a period of scarcity rather than starvation.

This third seal is parallel to the third church, Pergamos, and describes a period of compromise and spiritual scarcity during which Jesus' teachings were corrupted or lost. The church maintained purity under persecution, but lost it in times of political acceptance.

THE FOURTH SEAL—THE PALE HORSE

Spiritual decline continues in the fourth seal. The church began with victory, but quickly experienced bloodshed, famine, then death. Swete observed that the color of this horse, from the Greek *chloros*, is the color of vegetation, the color green; but he added that in his opinion an alternate meaning of the word fits better here: "the grey, ashen color of a face bleached by fear" *(The Apocalypse of St. John,* p. 87).

"When the Lamb opened the fourth seal, I heard the voice of the fourth living creature say, 'Come!' I looked, and there before me was a pale horse! Its rider was named Death, and Hades was following close behind him. They were given power over a fourth of the earth to kill by sword, famine and plague, and by the wild beasts of the earth" (Rev. 6:7, 8).

The sequence described seems to follow a natural progression: War brings death to the male population; when those who farm are removed, famine results. When there is poor diet, ill health follows, and a sick population cannot protect itself from attack. A similar sequence is found in Ezekiel 14:21.

The fourth seal runs parallel to the fourth church, Thyatira, and represents the fifth to the fifteenth centuries, the period we call the Middle Ages. They were dark decades not only because of the lack of the light of the Scriptures but also because of the persecution and death that overtook so many who chose to follow God according to their personal convictions.

Once released, each horse continues to ride until the Second Coming. Although each seal represents a particular period, it also symbolizes an experience that is seen again and again in history. The gospel horse will ever ride until all have heard and made a decision. The persecution horse galloped especially in early centuries, but still is found in some countries today. The experiences of the black and the pale horses also have continuous selective applications.

THE FIFTH SEAL—SOULS UNDER THE ALTAR

The imagery and message of this seal is drawn directly from John's apocalyptic twin, Daniel. In the third of his major visions, chapters 8 and 9, Daniel recorded the exploits of "the little horn," which took away the daily sacrifice, tore down the sanctuary of God, slaughtered a host of martyrs, and prospered in apostasy. This is a scenario one would expect in fiction, not reality. In the midst of this presentation Daniel heard someone ask how long the situation would continue, and heard the crushing reply that it would continue for 2300 days. At that announcement Daniel fell ill.

"How long?" has been a constant question throughout the centuries.

"How long?" the martyrs have always wanted to know. And as the church emerged bloodied and decimated from the Dark Ages, the cry constantly went up to God, "How long? How much more must we suffer?"

"When he opened the fifth seal, I saw under the altar the souls of those who had been slain because of the word of God and the testimony they had maintained. They called out in a loud voice, 'How long, Sovereign Lord, holy and true, until you judge the inhabitants of the earth and avenge our blood?' Then each of them was given a white robe, and they were told to wait a little longer, until the number of their fellow servants and brothers who were to be killed as they had been was completed" (Rev. 6:9-11).

Although there is no way to explain the indiscriminate intrusion of death and pain, we believe that although God's mills grind slowly, they grind up the opposition exceedingly fine. It does seem a long time, and it is. But compared with eternity, it is but a moment. A few minutes to a hungry child waiting for supper seem like hours, but for someone fully occupied with interesting work or a hobby, they seem only a few seconds. God can respond to the inquiry only by saying that it will not last forever and that although others also will lose their lives, in this way some will find theirs—eternally. True faith supports us when we cannot see the future. True faith does not demand that God withdraw pain. True faith trusts God to support us as we pass through the pain.

The imagery of the souls under the altar is drawn from the regular daily sacrificial service of Israel. The blood, because life is in the blood (Gen. 9:4), took a central part in these services. "The rest of the bull's blood he shall pour out at the base of the altar of burnt offering" (Lev. 4:7). The souls of the martyrs are *beneath the altar*. That is to say, the lifeblood of the martyrs has been poured out as an offering and sacrifice to God (Barclay, vol. 2, p. 13).

The theme of the fifth seal (based on the vision of Daniel 8, where the question "How long?" was posed) also highlights a major theme of both apocalyptic books. *Judgment* is the air that all last-day events breathe. In the fifth seal the saints call for judgment, calling for their God to honor them because they have honored Him. Jesus promised that in heaven He would stand for those who stood for Him on earth, and in the final judgment, pronounced in Revelation 22, Jesus shows how fully He keeps His word.

As Fredericks has noted: "It should be stressed that the events of the fifth seal introduce a crucial aspect of the judgment theme in the Apocalypse: that judgment is brought against those who opposed the Lamb by opposing His people on earth. The cry of the martyrs of the fifth seal evokes 'the wrath of the Lamb' which smites those who persecute and slay the saints" ("A Sequential Study of Revelation 1-14 Emphasizing the Judgment Motif," pp. 173, 174).

The fifth seal runs parallel to the fifth church, Sardis, "that which remains," and aptly portrays the church emerging from the Middle Ages as it rallied itself to strike back at the kingdom of darkness and fully proclaim the gospel.

THE SIXTH SEAL—JESUS RETURNS

"I watched as he opened the sixth seal. There was a great earthquake. The sun turned black like sackcloth made of goat hair, the whole moon turned blood red, and the stars in the sky fell to earth, as late figs drop from a fig tree when shaken by a strong wind. The sky receded like a scroll, rolling up, and every mountain and island was removed from its place" (Rev. 6:12-14).

The joy of all the major visions of Revelation is that they end in glory for the believer. The seventh part of each seven-part vision ushers in the Sabbath rest of Paradise.

In comparison with the brevity of the preceding seals, the sixth has several fact-filled verses that describe an earthquake, a darkened sun, a blood-red moon, a star shower, and a shaking of the entire planet in which mountains are toppled and islands disappear. And all this transpires at the hand of the victorious Christ.

The natural phenomena of the sixth seal remind us of the Old Testament's prophetic mosaic (cf. Amos 8:8; Isa. 13:13; Joel 2:31). But we especially find these words a reflection of a segment of Jesus' Olivet sermon, in which He predicted earthquakes and signs in the sun, moon, and stars (Matt. 24:7, 29).

The reference to an earthquake is intriguing. Earthquakes appear to be occurring more frequently in recent decades and continue to cause great devastation. For example, the western states of America are affected by the movement of the Pacific tectonic plate as it inches under California and dives under southern Alaska.

The most devastating of all quakes probably occurred in Shensi, China, in 1556, when more than 750,000 people perished. A mighty shake in Calcutta, India, in 1737 killed more than 250,000. Quakes in China and Japan, in 1920 and 1923, respectively, each caused the deaths of some 100,000 people. The Lisbon earthquake of 1775 is reported to have rocked a wider area than any quake recorded, but the loss of life did not compare with the above-mentioned killers.

Does John mean for us to identify one particular quake? It would not seem so, but rather a pattern of increasing numbers of quakes that shake the earth and climax in that ultimate seventh plague quake.

Celestial phenomena also merit careful examination. Every time the sun is eclipsed, the event attracts a great deal of attention. In earlier times, when the prediction of such occurrences was not widely known or advertised, eclipses caused panic. The obscuring of the sun on May 19, 1780 (probably caused by extensive brushfires on the northeast coast of America), brought consternation to New Englanders.

The library of Princeton University, in New Jersey, displays a poem (which the author neglected to sign) with a notation that it was "A Few Lines Composed on the DARK DAY of May 19, 1780." The poem has 22 four-line verses, of which three of them read (in modern spelling):

"Nineteenth of May, a gloomy day,
   When darkness veil'd the sky;
   The Sun's decline may be a sign,
   Some great event is nigh.

"Then safe shall he, forever be,
   That doth to Jesus come;
   He need not fear though death be near,
   Since heaven is his home.

"All nature stands, when He commands,
 Or changes in its course;
 His mighty Hand rules sea and land,
 He is the Lord of Host."

The obscuring of the sun on May 19 certainly caught the attention of this unknown New England citizen.

And meteorite showers are always an awe-inspiring sight. There is a celestial phenomenon of "falling stars" (known as the Leonids) that occurs every 33¼ years. It has often shattered the complacency of earthlings, especially those unaware of this regularly repeated celestial feature. The years 1766, 1799, 1833, 1866, and 1966 brought particularly brilliant spectacles. But like the infrequent visits of Halley's comet, not every occurrence is as startling as its predecessor.*

Did John have just one particular shower in mind? It would not seem so, but rather the recurring cycles that keep our spiritual sights focused on the heavens, because it is there that we will see Jesus return.

Throughout the opening of the seals we have seen a symbolic presentation of history, and mixed in with the symbols we have read language that we cannot but understand literally: for instance, *conquering, take peace from the earth, men should slay one another, to kill with the sword, How Long, O Lord*? So should we view the earthly and astronomical phenomena as literal, symbolic, or both?

John's later use of sun, moon, and stars in chapter 12 symbolizes a church that shares the message of God's love. In the vision of the trumpets the darkening of sun, moon, and stars indicates the obscuring of the light of truth. So it would seem appropriate to propose that we should also see in the predictions of the sixth seal a "shaking" of the church by opposition, a "darkening" of the presentation of the gospel through apostasy, the shedding of the "blood" of still more of the members of the church (as Jesus warned under the fifth seal), and the falling of some of the brightest "stars" from the sky of our admiration as all are tested to the ultimate before the close of probation.

The events of the sixth seal cover the periods of both the sixth and seventh churches, that is, from the nineteenth century to the end of time. Today we stand between the events of verses 13 and 14. Immediately after the passage dealing with the signs in the heavens in His Olivet address, Jesus warned: "Now learn this lesson from the fig tree: As soon as its twigs get tender and its leaves come out, you know that summer is near. Even so, when you see all these things, you know that it is near, right at the door" (Matt. 24:32, 33).

Picking up directly on Jesus' words, John describes the heavenly signs and adds: "The stars in the sky fell to earth, as late figs drop from a fig tree when shaken by a strong wind" (Rev. 6:13). In the imagery of Jesus, summer is the end of the world, because summer is harvest-time. When the figs, the wheat, and the weeds come to fruition, you can be sure that Jesus is about to return.

At His return Jesus will respond to the martyrs' pleas to "judge the inhabitants of the earth and avenge our blood" (verse 10). Accompanied by millions of angels and in the glory of the Father and the Spirit, Jesus will split open the heavens to bring judgment and vengeance on the rejecters. John writes: "Then the kings of the earth, the princes, the generals, the rich, the mighty, and every slave and every free man hid in caves and among the rocks of the mountains. They called to the mountains and the rocks, 'Fall on us and hide us from the face of him who sits on the throne and from the wrath of the Lamb! For the great day of their wrath has come, and who can stand?'" (verses 15-17).

This is John's first major description of the final chaos in the last moments of this age. The words sound devastating enough, but much worse is reserved for later chapters. At the sight of Jesus, kings, great men, commanders, rich, strong, slave, and free shrink in terror. This is a full cross section of society. Evil men are not restricted to any social class any more than are the righteous. The wicked beg to be shielded from the glory, but unlike Moses, who had God to shield him in the rock, these rejecters cannot be protected. Their sinfulness lies fully exposed, and they are tortured by the fact that they have neglected salvation so freely offered.

John ends the presentation with the words "Who can survive it?" (verse 17, TLB). We are left waiting breathlessly for the answer in the breaking of the seventh seal, but John breaks away. We have reached this emotional high point, and rather than take us up the last step to eternal Sabbath rest, he pauses to answer the questions: *Who* can survive this cataclysmic nightmare? and *How*? After resting momentarily in the peaceful pastures of Revelation 7, John returns to conclude the vision of the seven seals in Revelation 8.

EXCURSUS ON REVELATION 4 THROUGH 7

In recent years some have suggested that revival in the church is being thwarted by a lack of understanding of the seals. Furthermore, it is alleged that we should understand this section of the Apocalypse to depict events surrounding the pre-Advent judgment rather than the events of the entire Christian Era. It is true, of course, that all Christians should certainly be concerned about revival, but there is no compelling evidence to believe that a futuristic view of Revelation 4-6, versus an historicist view, is a key to that eventuality. But for those who have an interest in this issue, the following excursus is included.

Soteriology. The assertion that the study of the Apocalypse in general should bring about personal revival is well-founded. As indicated in the hermeneutic that introduces this work, the most important symbol of the book is the Lamb, Christ Jesus. Thus an intimate knowledge of the book should bring us into a growing intimacy with the Hero of the book, with the result that in heart, life, and daily choices we will "follow the Lamb."

The greatest challenge to the Christian is not cognitive, however (for example, a better interpretation of symbols), but relational—a daily commitment to the Saviour. Despite the difficulties, studying John's Revelation should first fulfill the author's stated purpose—to reveal Jesus. Personal salvation and loving ministry are not based on great intellect or great exegetical skills, but on great commitments. Some of the world's Christian saints, such as Mother Teresa, may have doctrinal beliefs divergent from yours or mine, but their Christian commitment could never be doubted.

Structure. As introduced in chapters 1 and 2 of this study, Revelation has a finely balanced structure. At its basic level there are two halves, the first primarily historical and the second primarily eschatological, with chapter 11 a bridge between. This being the case, Revelation 6 is in the wrong half of the book to have an exclusively eschatological emphasis, that is, an emphasis on the pre-Advent judgment.

At another level, the book consists of four major sections, each introduced by a sevenfold vision: churches, seals, trumpets, bowls. Each successive vision builds on its predecessor and expands it, giving increasing emphasis to eschatological events (compare Daniel 2, 7, 8-9, 10-12 for a similar structure). As the seven churches paint the sweep of history during the entire Christian Era, we would expect the seals, to some significant degree, to do the same. This too denies a pre-Advent judgment emphasis.

At the more complex chiastic structure level, the historical chapters are mirrored in the eschatological chapters. In this case, chapters 4-7 are reflected in Revelation 19. And the multiplied reflections are impressive as outlined below. However, the entire comparison would not make the same sense if both sections were eschatological. Note some of the comparisons and similarities:

Revelation 4	**Revelation 19**
Door standing open, verse 1	Heaven standing open, verse 11
Overcomer's crown (*stephanos*), verse 4	Kingly crown (*diadem*), verse 12
Songs of praise, verses 8, 11	Songs of praise, verses 2-8
Revelation 5	
Slain Lamb, verse 6	Conquering King, verse 16
Revelation 6	
Seal 1, Proclaiming the gospel, verse 2	Gospel proclaimed no more, verse 12
Seal 2, Red horse conquers, verse 4	Red eyes of the Conqueror, verse 12
Seal 3, Wicked slay righteous, verse 4	Righteous One slays wicked, verse 15
Seal 4, Death for righteous, verse 7	Death for the wicked, verse 11

Seal 5, Judgment still **future**, verse 10	Judgment **is executed**, verse 11

The Content of the Fifth Seal Is a Crucial Observation
Note the contrast in the wording (KJV):
"How long . . . dost thou *not* judge?" (Rev. 6:10).
"He *doth* judge" (Rev. 19:11).

Seal 6, Wrath of Lamb, verse 16	Wrath of Almighty, verse 15
Revelation 7	
Righteous in eternal life, verses 9-17	Wicked in eternal loss, verses 20, 21
Following the Lamb, Rev. 14:4	Fighting the King, verse 19
Revelation 8	
Seal 7, Silence, verse 1	Commotion, verses 15-21

The words of Jesus. As already discussed, it is widely recognized that Revelation is an apocalyptic version of the Olivet sermon. The seals are the obvious outworking of Matthew 24:6-14, with their references to wars, famines, pestilences, faithlessness, and the preaching of the gospel in all the world. Clearly Jesus spoke in this passage not of just the end, but of events through history that would bring the world ultimately to the end. The words of Matthew 24:6-14 first describe the events preceding the fall of Jerusalem in A.D. 70 (the subject of the first trumpet as we shall shortly see), and second, the signs through history that will climax in the Lord's return. Note Jesus' own words: "When you hear of wars and revolutions, do not be frightened. These things must happen first, *but the end will not come right away*" (Luke 21:9). Thus the symbols and statements of the seals find applications through time, not exclusively for the end of time.

Old Testament foundations. It is legitimate to ask why John would utilize the imagery of Daniel 7, a judgment chapter, if he did not mean us to see that usage to indicate a judgment emphasis. Revelation 4 is John's first major throne room depiction. In order to do it justice, he searched the pages of the Old Testament, his Bible, looking for descriptions by the Old Testament prophets. He found several preeminent passages, including Isaiah 6, 1 Kings 22, and Exodus 19, but especially Ezekiel 1-10 and Daniel 7.

As Jon Paulien has noted, one theme binds these texts together, and it is the throne room of God, *not* the theme of judgment. In fact, in Revelation 4 and 5 John studiously avoided utilizing the judgment motif that is so prominent in Daniel 7, choosing instead those images that highlight the glory of the throne room setting. Paulien has noted some of these important differences: "There are, however, significant differences between Daniel 7 and Revelation 5. Many intervening elements in Daniel are left out and many other elements are added in Revelation. . . . Although John is familiar with the Danielic term 'Son of man' for Christ (Rev. 1:13), he deliberately avoids using it here. Rather, he prefers using the titles Lamb, Lion of Judah, and Root of David instead. In actuality, in spite of some general similarities, less than a quarter of Revelation 5 is drawn from Daniel 7.

"Most striking of all, however, is the fact that John studiously avoids the language of judgment in his throne scene. In the Greek language judgment is usually expressed by the nouns *krisis* and *krima*, and the verb *krinō*. . . . John is quite familiar with the language of judgment but deliberately avoids using it in the first half of the book of Revelation. The seeming exception (6:10) is not a description of the judgment, but a call for that judgment to begin" (Jon Paulien, "The Seven Seals" in *Symposium on Revelation*, book 1, p. 210).

Internal evidence. Probably the most persuasive evidence regarding the period of time depicted in Revelation 4 through 7 is found within the flow of the chapters themselves. Paulien has suggested that in this section of the Apocalypse John paints four pictures. First, in Revelation 4 we see a general, timeless view of God's throne room. Second, in Revelation 5 there is a climactic event that occurred in the first century—Jesus' ascension and enthronement—that enabled Him to be the One who could unseal the seven seals. Third, in Revelation 6 we encounter a series of events that span the centuries of the entire Christian era. And fourth, in Revelation 7 we read about the end of the great controversy, when Jesus returns, receives His own, and they enjoy fellowship eternally.

Such a view seems to allow the text to speak for itself without imposing meaning on it. Such a view also seems to honor John's structural flow. But such a view precludes a pre-Advent judgment focus for this passage. ●

---

* The Leonid meteor phenomenon has been traced back to A.D. 902. The 1833 event is consequential because it seems to have triggered serious study into the nature of meteors.

OUTLINE

1. Introducing Revelation 7
    Necessity of a hermeneutic
    Symbolic use of numbers
    Two different time frames
    Relationship to the seven seals
    Old Testament precedents

2. The sealing angel

3. The sealed

4. The great multitude

5. The Shepherd-Lamb

6. The 144,000

7. The seventh seal of silence

CHAPTER EIGHT

ABSOLUTELY SECURE

t is not difficult to understand Revelation 7 if we approach it on the basis of the hermeneutic we have established. But because these verses are generally read without a hermeneutic, they have caused considerable confusion. In some cases this has led to overt parochialism, in which certain individuals claim to be one of the exclusive 144,000, the elect of God, one of the few who will be saved when Jesus returns. Such mistaken literalism overlooks that the prophet identifies all the individuals of this "number" as Jews, which is hardly encouraging to a Gentile Christian.

To this point in the Apocalypse, we have noted just an introductory use of the numbers 3, 4, 7, 10, and 12. But this entire passage is built on numbers, primarily 4 and 12 signifying universality and the kingdom. The tribes of Israel depicted here are spiritual Jews, the Israel of God.

As we open this chapter we should note that John paints two pictures. He ends chapter 6 with the appearance of the Son of man in glory. The interlude between the sixth and seventh seals first *goes back in real time* from the moment of Christ's appearance to the beginning of the time of great tribulation that precedes His return (Rev. 7:1-8). Here John presents the 144,000 and their sealing. The second picture, verses 9-17, *moves forward* from the time of the Second Advent and describes the saints in heaven. But the main point of what John is about to share is to answer the questions Who will survive the judgment of Jesus in the last seven plagues? and How?

The falling of the plagues will be a time of unparalleled destruction, but God promises that the members of His family of faith will be protected and preserved. God will "seal" them against both the destructiveness of the plagues and the destructive intent of their enemies. The close of probation brings an irreversible separation between accepters and rejecters (see Rev. 22:11). A parallel can be seen in the experience of Noah's family. The saved entered the ark and were completely separated from the lost, who elected to remain outside at the mercy of the waters of judgment, and the saved were perfectly secure.[1]

The imagery of sealing is found in two Old Testament experiences. The first is well known; the second, relatively unknown. Before the Exodus the Israelites found protection from the savage assault of the tenth plague by "sealing" their doors with the blood of the Passover lamb. The angel of death simply "passed over" the homes of those who prepared for that Passover night, thus preserving their firstborn males. Similarly, at the end of this age, when the plagues are about to fall, God will protect or preserve all those who symbolically have applied Jesus' blood to the "doors of their hearts."

But there is a passage in Ezekiel on which John draws heavily to describe his vision: "I saw six men coming from the direction of the upper gate, which faces north, each with a deadly weapon in his hand. With them was a man clothed in linen who had a writing kit at his side. . . . Then the Lord called to the man clothed in linen who had the writing kit at his side and said to him, 'Go throughout the city of Jerusalem and put a mark on the foreheads of those who grieve and lament over all the detestable things that are done in it'" (Eze. 9:2-4).

The citizens of Jerusalem were to be divided between accepters and rejecters, and those who maintained a faith relationship with God were to be identified by a symbolic mark placed on the forehead—as will be the case at the end of the age.

THE SEALING ANGEL

"After this I saw four angels standing at the four corners of the earth, holding back the four winds of the earth to prevent any wind from blowing on the land or on the sea or on any tree. Then I saw another angel coming up from the east, having the seal of the living God. He called out in a loud voice to the four angels who had been given power to harm the land and the sea: 'Do not harm the land or the sea or the trees until we put a seal on the foreheads of the servants of our God'" (Rev. 7:1-3).

In the first verses of Revelation 7, we read of three sets of 4 (four angels, four corners, four winds) and a set of 3 entities that are to be protected (earth, sea, and trees). According to this passage, the earth is flat and has four corners (the way the people of ancient times spoke of it), and an angel at each corner restrains a particular wind of calamity. (The ancients believed that angels administered the forces of nature. For example, later in Revelation John referred to the angel of fire [Rev. 14:18].)

"It was the belief of the ancient peoples that the winds which came from due north, south, east and west were all good and favorable winds; but that the winds which blew diagonally across the earth were evil and harmful winds. That is why the angels are at the corners of the earth. They are about to unleash the winds which blow diagonally across the earth" (Barclay, *The Revelation of John*, vol. 2, p. 23).

That John utilizes the number 4 indicates the universality of the effects of the angels' action. The sequence of 3 entities to be spared indicates the unity of the remnant in their devotion to God. Calamity often brings out the best from people and draws them together. And when the church takes its last steps in the journey and faces Satan's last onslaughts, it will be fully united.

Land and sea is a readily understood metaphor to designate the entire world. The Bible uses *trees* as a symbol of people: alive, growing, leafing trees are a symbol of the righteous (Ps. 1:3). In contrast, dry, dying, leafless trees are a symbol of those who have no life-giving relationship with God (Luke 23:31; see also Rom. 11:17-24). Taken together, the 3 symbols in this passage depict God's family united in the kingdom even though scattered across the world.

After detailing the angels, John describes another angel "ascending from the east" (Rev. 7:2, KJV), carrying God's seal. As this angel flies to earth, he warns the other four angels not to allow any judgments to fall until the sealing work has been completed.

The mention of east, or the sun rising, is a biblical metaphor for heaven and God's throne. Ezekiel described the Lord's glory coming through the east gate into the tabernacle (Eze. 43:4), and the Wise Men who came to find the Messiah followed a star in the east. Orientals stood facing the east to identify the compass points, and named them in the sequence of east, west, north, and south. According to John's imagery, a messenger from God's throne is commissioned to protect God's family from the harm of the coming tribulation.

What is the purpose of this seal? First, in the setting of judgment, it is a seal of *approval, protection, and preservation.* Daniel said: "There will be a time of distress such as has not happened from the beginning of nations" (Dan. 12:1). Second, in this setting there will be the need for *provisions.* And as the angels provided for Elijah during the drought in the days of Ahab and Jezebel, God will provide for the saints during the time of coming trouble.

Third, we have the notions of *authenticity and possession.* In New Testament times a seal had an important role in the daily affairs of the empire, as had been the case back to Egypt and Mesopotamia. Seals are commonly found by archaeologists in their excavations in the Middle East. For convenience, these seals were frequently attached to a metal circle and worn as a ring.

The king had the most elaborate and important of all seals. When he dispatched goods or correspondence he impressed his seal into clay (in earlier civilizations) or wax (in later civilizations) and thus provided proof of authenticity. And people commonly used seals to identify their personal property (see Swete, *The Apocalypse of St. John*, p. 94). Also, in times when mathematics had been mastered only by a few professionals and when illiteracy was widespread, a personal seal on a document indicated agreement with the transaction.

These historical usages of a seal, authenticity and possession, are given spiritual significance in chapter 7. In John's end-time setting, God's "seal" symbolizes the love relationship between the believer and God, in contrast with the "mark of the beast," which symbolizes the coercive and manipulative relationship between Satan and his followers. John's description is not of angels applying a literal seal to the foreheads of the saved. Rather, he uses the symbol of their approval, protection, provision, and possession by God. Ladd asserted: "Certainly this sealing is a spiritual fact and not a visible bodily phenomenon" *(A Commentary on the Revelation of John*, p. 12).

This understanding is in harmony with Paul's comment: "Nevertheless, God's solid foundation stands firm, sealed with this inscription: 'The Lord knows those who are his'" (2 Tim. 2:19). The seal described by John identifies those who belong to God. They are the purchased possession of Jesus: "You were bought at a price" (1 Cor. 6:20).

In commenting on these verses, Hans K. LaRondelle warned us to keep in mind that sealing is part of the imagery of two experiences: "There is a real danger of confusing the apocalyptic seal of God at the end of time with the gospel seal that all Christians receive when they come to faith in Christ and unite with Him in baptism" *(Chariots of Salvation*, p. 169). In reality, only those who have received the gospel seal of faith will receive the protecting apocalyptic seal for the end-time tribulation.

To this point we have discussed the purpose of the seal, but we have not yet identified it. A full discussion of both God's seal and the beast's mark is in the discussion on Revelation 14.

THE SEALED

"Then I heard the number of those who were sealed: 144,000 from all the tribes of Israel. From the tribe of Judah 12,000 were sealed, from the tribe of Reuben 12,000, from the tribe of Gad 12,000, from the tribe of Asher 12,000, from the tribe of Naphtali 12,000, from the tribe of Manasseh 12,000, from the tribe of Simeon 12,000, from the tribe of Levi 12,000, from the tribe of Issachar 12,000, from the tribe of Zebulun 12,000, from the tribe of Joseph 12,000, from the tribe of Benjamin, 12,000" (Rev. 7:4-8).

These verses reveal that the 144,000 are made up of 12,000 from each of 12 tribes. The strange fact about the listing of the tribes is that this *exact* selection of 12 family names is not found anywhere else in Scripture.[2] It does not begin with Jacob's first son, Reuben, the son of Leah, but rather Judah, probably because Jesus came from Judah and the primary focus of the book is to reveal Jesus. And Dan is omitted.

On his deathbed Jacob said of Dan that he would be a serpent by the way (Gen. 49:17), and in rabbinical teaching Dan stood for idolatry. These are probable reasons for his exclusion.

That the list is contrived supports the view that the number 144,000 is symbolic and that we should seek a meaning along the lines of our hermeneutic. Here John paints a picture of the kingdom by using numerical symbols. Reduced to a set of symbolic factors, 144,000 can be expressed as 12 x 12 x 10 x 10 x 10—the kingdom, the kingdom, complete, complete, complete when Jesus returns. The sleeping righteous are raised, and together with the living righteous meet Jesus in the air (1 Thess. 4:16, 17). The kingdom of grace then becomes the kingdom of glory.

THE 144,000

Later in his work John adds further information about the 144,000. We include it here so that we can summarize all John has to say about this special group.

"Then I looked, and there before me was the Lamb, standing on Mount Zion, and with him 144,000 who had his name and his Father's name written on their foreheads. And I heard a sound from heaven like the roar of rushing waters and like a loud peal of thunder. The sound I heard was like that of harpists playing their harps. And they sang a new song before the throne and before the four living creatures and the elders. No one could learn the song except the 144,000 who had been redeemed from the earth. These are those who did not defile themselves with women, for they kept themselves pure. They follow the Lamb wherever he goes. They were purchased from among men and offered as firstfruits to God and the Lamb. No lie was found in their mouths; they are blameless" (Rev. 14:1-5).

Much of what we know about this special group sets them apart as unique.

Unique past, purpose, and privileges. They alone of all earth's inhabitants live through the climax of history when the plagues fall on the earth. They personally endure the great trials of the climax of history sustained by the Shepherd on the throne (Rev. 7:14). They alone receive the apocalyptic seal of God, the particular seal given at the moment of the close of probation to those in a faith relationship with Jesus (verse 3).

These people are the *aparchē* of God. Most translators choose the expression firstfruits as an appropriate translation. The word "firstfruits" is applied to Jesus, and in a sense to the 24 elders. But how can it be applied to the 144,000? It is easier to understand such a word when it is applied to those who arrive in heaven and stand at the throne *before* the main harvest is reaped at the Second Coming. But how can it apply to those who are part of the general harvest reaped at the Second Coming?

R. H. Charles observed that the word has a sacrificial character and might be accurately translated as "gift" or "sacrifice." Thus Williams' translation reads: "They have been bought at a price from among men to be an offering to God and to the Lamb" (Rev. 14:4, Williams). The Greek *aparchē* comes from *apo*, "derived from a certain source" and *archē*, "first place" or "eminence" *(The Analytical Greek Lexicon*, s.v. "Aparchē"). Thus the unique purpose of these individuals is to stand forever before God as the eminent ones from earth who stood faithfully for the Lamb during the final events of history.

This group that stands spotless, without guile, as pure as virgins in their faith in the Lamb, have certain privileges. They serve God continually before His throne. On occasions when the Lamb wishes to move from the throne, they travel with Him as His personal entourage (verse 4), and whether they travel or wait, a song comes spontaneously to their lips, the song of their experience, which has created a bond of an exclusive character between them and the Lamb.

"And they sang a new song before the throne and before the four living creatures and the elders. No one could learn the song except the 144,000 who had been redeemed from the earth" (verse 3).

Now we return to Revelation chapter 7.

THE GREAT MULTITUDE

"After this I looked and there before me was a great multitude that no one could count, from every nation, tribe, people and language, standing before the throne and in front of the Lamb. They were wearing white robes and were holding palm branches in their hands. And they cried out in a loud voice: 'Salvation belongs to our God, who sits on the throne, and to the Lamb.' All the angels were standing around the throne and around the elders and the four living creatures. They fell down on their faces before the throne and worshiped God, saying: 'Amen! Praise and glory and wisdom and thanks and honor and power and strength be to our God for ever and ever. Amen!'" (Rev. 7:9-12).

"After these things" begins another section of the sealing vision. Some have suggested that the group now pictured is the 144,000, but in another setting. However, Robert Mounce has observed: "The innumerable multitude includes far more than the 144,000 of the previous vision. All the faithful of every age are there" *(The Book of Revelation, International Commentary on the New Testament,* p. 171).

Revelation 7 opens with a picture of the 144,000 living through the tribulation of the last plagues. This is earth's last believing generation, the kingdom group that will be alive at Jesus' return. Then John describes the uncountable multitude from every age of earth's history standing before God's throne. This is the loyal army of believers from every age back to Adam. Together they sing: "Salvation belongs to our God, who sits on the throne, and to the Lamb" (Rev. 7:10). Then those at the throne (angels, the 24 elders, and the four living creatures) join in with their own song: "Amen! Praise and glory and wisdom and thanks and honor and power and strength [7 elements in the setting of eternal Sabbath rest] be to our God for ever and ever. Amen!" (verse 12).

Two aspects of this great multitude are significant. First, they all wear "white robes." All the redeemed must be clothed in the perfection of the Son. It is only His righteousness that permits their presence there. The second aspect is that they wave palm branches. This introduces a subject to which we have not yet referred.

The Apocalypse is written against the backdrop of the annual Jewish festivals.[3] Revelation 5, for example, alludes to the Passover service through the sacrificial lamb. The same is true of chapter 7, where protection is offered by a seal, as was the case at the time of the inauguration of the Passover tradition. Revelation 4 suggests the Feast of Firstfruits by the ransoming of the 24 elders to God's throne before the general harvest. In later chapters we will note allusions to the

Feast of Trumpets and Yom Kippur. But here in Revelation 7 the palm-waving multitude reminds us of the fulfillment of the last of the seven annual festivals, the Feast of Tabernacles.

Each year when the harvest had been gathered and the people could rest knowing they had adequate grain, wine, and oil for the upcoming winter, they would celebrate for a week in an outdoor camping adventure. Families would build temporary huts from branches and palm fronds. Coming each year in the pleasant autumn season at the end of the spiritual and agricultural year, the Feast of Tabernacles became the most joyous of the annual cycle of celebrations. It typified the ultimate celebration at God's throne when the harvest of the earth has been reaped by the Messiah at His coming and all the members of God's family have been gathered into their homes for a peace-filled eternity.

THE SHEPHERD-LAMB

"Then one of the elders asked me, 'These in white robes—who are they, and where did they come from?' I answered, 'Sir, you know.' And he said, 'These are they who have come out of the great tribulation; they have washed their robes and made them white in the blood of the Lamb. Therefore, they are before the throne of God and serve him day and night in his temple; and he who sits on the throne will spread his tent over them. Never again will they hunger; never again will they thirst. The sun will not beat upon them, nor any scorching heat. For the Lamb at the center of the throne will be their shepherd; he will lead them to springs of living water. And God will wipe away every tear from their eyes'" (verses 13-17).

The elder who addresses John asks a rhetorical question: "Who are these people?" The elders are well aware of their identity, but it is a joy to hear the story of their redemption through the Lamb, Christ Jesus. John quickly tells the elder, "My Lord, you know."

But the elder continues: "These are they who have come out of the great tribulation; they have washed their robes and made them white in the blood of the Lamb" (verse 14). One can never be far from the Lamb in the Apocalypse or in heaven. Jesus is the reason there is a great multitude in heaven.

The imagery in these verses is astounding. Clothes that are hopelessly soiled need to be washed, but the washing agent is blood rather than soap and water. Yet as a result, these clothes are made spotlessly white. Only the sacrifice of Jesus can make sinful lives pure.

The final verse of the chapter has an amazing mixed metaphor that may not pass the scrutiny of an English master, but is perfectly appropriate in apocalyptic literature. At the center of the throne, a Lamb is pictured, then without a transition, the Lamb is the Shepherd.

Jesus became the Lamb by virtue of the Incarnation. He took Adam's human nature and united it with His own divine nature and lived a life of perfection despite the limitations of the body that bore the marks of degeneration caused by many ages of sin. For all the years of Jesus' life, Satan tried to destroy Him and foil the plan of salvation. But each time, protected by the Father and the angels, Jesus escaped these evil designs. Finally, He chose the moment of His death as our substitute precisely at the time of the offering of the evening sacrifice. Then He rose from the dead and ascended to the throne to minister the benefits of His once-for-all sacrifice. Because He triumphed as the Lamb, He can now guide the sheep of the earth as their shepherd. Because He knows every inch of the path, the intensity of every temptation, the degrees of Satan's cunning, He can offer safety, succor, and security. There is no shepherd to compare with Him.

THE SEVENTH SEAL

"When he opened the seventh seal, there was silence in heaven for about half an hour.

"And I saw the seven angels who stand before God, and to them were given seven trumpets.

"Another angel, who had a golden censer, came and stood at the altar. He was given much incense to offer, with the prayers of all the saints, on the golden altar before the throne. The smoke of the incense, together with the prayers of the saints, went up before God from the angel's hand. Then the angel took the censer, filled it with fire from the altar, and hurled it on the earth; and there came peals of thunder, rumblings, flashes of lightning and an earthquake" (Rev. 8:1-5).

As we complete our exploration of Revelation 7, we step into Revelation 8 for the unsealing of the seventh seal, a description delayed by John's lengthy parenthetical presentation. John begins: "When he opened the seventh seal, there was silence in heaven for about half an hour" (verse 1). The brevity of the seventh seal is almost anticlimactic after such a vivid description of the horrors of the lost and the bliss of the saved. What is the meaning?

The first five verses of chapter 8 are set in the sanctuary and form a bridge between the seals and the trumpets, concluding one and introducing the other. Interestingly, each of the three judgment sets—seals, trumpets, and bowls—all open and close with visions of the sanctuary (Rev. 5; 8:2-5; 15:1-8; 8:1; 11:19; 16:17), because this is the only place in the universe where such authoritative decrees of judgment can originate. These five bridging verses mention three primary elements: silence, the golden censer at the altar before the throne, and a quartet of heavenly power described as "peals of thunder, rumblings, flashes of lightning and an earthquake."

The silence of the first verse is a dramatic surprise. After the chaos of the sixth seal in Revelation 6 and the songs of bliss of the redeemed in Revelation 7, one might expect a final elaboration of one or the other. But no, the reader experiences humbling, expectant silence.

Silence is often noted in the Old Testament as a powerful prelude when God is about to judge the enemies of His people. We read in Zephaniah, for example: "Be silent before the Sovereign Lord, for the day of the Lord is near" (Zeph. 1:7). And in Isaiah: "See, it stands written before me: I will not *keep* silent but will pay back in full" (Isa. 65:6, emphasis supplied), and again: "Be silent before me, you islands! Let the nations renew their strength! Let them come forward and speak; let us meet together at the place of judgment" (Isa. 41:1).

In view of the judgments at the close of the sixth seal and the judgments about to be described in the trumpets, nothing could be more fitting than a moment of contemplative silence.

The sequence of symbols in this passage is probably drawn from the daily service ritual: the offering of the lamb was followed by the taking of fire from the altar of burnt offering to the altar of incense and the burning of the incense.

The significance of the half hour is enigmatic and probably indicates just the briefest space of time. Interestingly, Niles has suggested, without a confirming citation, that each day approximately a half hour elapsed between the offering of the sacrificial lamb at the altar of the burnt offering and the offering of the incense in the holy place (D. T. Niles, *As Seeing the Invisible*, p. 63). If that is true, it would add a meaningful explanation to John's comment.

Ezell noted the significance of the sequence of events: there was a time of silence as the people waited for the priest to leave the sanctuary after offering the incense, then came the offering of the sacrifice, followed by the blowing of the priestly trumpets (Douglas Ezell, *Revelations on Revelation*, pp. 48, 49). This is the sequence of Revelation 8.

Mounce wrote this comment in a footnote of his commentary: "In reporting the siege of Jerusalem Josephus tells of a great light which appeared as a sign in the sanctuary for half an hour (Bell 6. 5. 3)" (Mounce, p. 179). Without any definitive word regarding the roots of the length of time, we are probably wise to see the greatest significance of the brief silence as a prelude to judgment.

The fragrant incense symbolizes the prayers of the saints, something that had always been intimately associated with the daily Temple ritual. We cannot help linking the prayers noted here with the prayer of desperation under the fifth seal: "How long Sovereign Lord, holy and true, until you judge the inhabitants of the earth and avenge our blood?" (Rev. 6:10). The saints continue to ask this question of God, and the symbols of the trumpets about to be described graphically depict God's response.

One aspect of this symbol is very meaningful as we continue to note the importance of the lamb symbol throughout the book. A vital link exists between the altar of burnt offering, the altar of incense, the rising of the smoke from the burning incense, and the priest who burned the incense. In the words of Ramsey: "Prayers go not up by themselves. They can only be carried up by the incense upon the golden altar, and kindled by the fire from the altar of atonement. The prayers of the saints can ascend only as embodied in the intercessions of the great High Priest, and resting on the merits of His atoning sacrifice. This is the secret of their power" (J. B. Ramsey, *The Book of Revelation: An Exposition of the First Eleven Chapters*, p. 360).

Finally, the bridge between the seals and the trumpets concludes with the fourfold description of "peals of thunder, rumblings, flashes of lightning and an earthquake." First we note the number 4, the symbol of the coming universality of God's judgments in answer to the prayers of the saints. The judgments will increase in severity and extent both in the trumpets and the bowls, climaxing in the sixth and seventh bowls that shatter the entire planet.

Only two occasions recorded in Scripture are described in terms reminiscent of Revelation 8:5—Sinai and Calvary. At no place in John's book are we allowed to walk out of sight of the cross. At Sinai God gave His eternal standard, the code and rule of life. At Calvary, Jesus, who had kept that law without exception, was treated as if He had rebelled against it all. Judgment fell on Him there instead of on you and me. And God's awesome power was revealed in earthly and celestial manifestations to mark the moment of earth's redemption. In these two events we can see law and grace—the eternal standard and complete substitution.

We have completed our journey through the seven seals and have seen that they follow the same historical sequence and contain the same basic message as the seven churches. In churches and seals we have seen Christian history from the point of view of both the Shepherd and His sheep. Now as we turn to Revelation 8 and 9, we will read the same history, but from a third perspective, a terrifying one—the point of view of the wolf, the spoiler of the flock. It is not a pretty picture. But those who are in God's care need not fear. If we must walk the dark valley of the shadow of death, we need not worry, because we will be with Jesus the Lamb, who has walked the path before us.

---

[1] Jesus referenced the Noah illustration in His Olivet address (Matt. 24:37).

[2] The list of tribes in Ezekiel 48 includes Dan and Ephraim; neither of which appears in Revelation 7.

[3] These festivals are recorded in Leviticus 23. Three were celebrated in the spring, one in the summer, and three in the autumn. The sequence was as follows: Passover, Unleavened Bread, Firstfruits, Pentecost, Trumpets, Day of Atonement, and Feast of Tabernacles.

OUTLINE

CHAPTER NINE

TRUMPET FANFARES

Revelation 8 and 9 contain the most graphic example of apocalyptic writing in the Bible. The complexity of the imagery has led to more speculative nonsense than can be found written about any other chapters of John's final work. If we are to avoid pure speculation as to what these symbols mean, we need to pay close attention to our principles of interpretation. The last word certainly has not been written on the trumpets. Perhaps hardly the first word has yet been written. For these reasons we will seek to establish with more detail than in previous chapters the background material on which John probably drew to describe his vision.

THE TRUMPET SYMBOL

Based on the Olivet address. Using the obvious structure of Jesus' Olivet address in Matthew 24 and 25 (introduction, three major points, conclusion), the trumpets are based on the second part of that address. As discussed earlier, the substance of the second part of Jesus' address detailed (1) physical attacks on Jerusalem and on the people of God, and (2) attacks on the substance of the gospel. Thus we expect to find these basic themes in the trumpets.

Progressive parallelism. According to the principle of repetition and expansion (observed in the prophetic visions of Daniel), we would expect to find in the trumpets much of the same material we found in the churches and the seals, but from a different perspective. Hendriksen termed this "progressive parallelism" (William Hendriksen, *More Than Conquerors*, p. 48). We would therefore expect that the vision begins in the first century and covers history to the Second Coming.

Clue from the fifth segment. As Milligan ably demonstrated, we find in the fifth part of each major septet a clue to the thrust of all seven. In the fifth church we read Jesus' comment: "Yet you have a few people in Sardis who have not soiled their clothes. They will walk with me, dressed in white" (Rev. 3:4). This concept of "walking with the Lord" is the dominant theme of all seven churches.

The fifth seal describes the souls of the martyrs crying out for vengeance from under the altar of sacrifice. They begged God to bring down Satan's kingdom and show the rightness of their witness for Him. All the seals contain variations of this theme.

The fifth of the seven trumpets gives us a clue regarding the thrust of all the trumpets. Among these grim symbols, we have one interpretive clue of more than average significance, a reference to those who do *not* have "the seal of God on their foreheads" (Rev. 9:4). Thus throughout the trumpets we are being introduced to the kingdom of darkness and its attempts to destroy the kingdom of light.

Biblical precedents. We search the Old and New Testaments to discover ways in which trumpets have been used and apply this information as a clue to the meaning of these two chapters. We know that throughout his book John has taken biblical gems and placed them in new and dramatic settings. Tenney has counted 57 from the Pentateuch, 11 from the historical books, 197 from the major prophets (in which he included Daniel with 53 references), and 38 from the minor prophets (Tenney, *Interpreting Revelation*, p. 104). As John reaches back into Scripture for appropriate words, he gives us clues to the meaning of the visions. This is especially true with the trumpets. We note six important examples.

1. A call to war (for example, Judges 7:19). The basic symbols in each of the first three seven-part series in Revelation (churches, seals, and trumpets) constitute a major clue to each section's basic meaning. Lampstands indicate an ecclesiastical milieu; seals, a legal illustration (for example, a will); and trumpets have often been associated with war.

2. *The daily sacrifice.* As the priest lifted the body of the lamb onto the coals of the altar, the trumpet would sound, indicating, "It is done; it is finished. The sacrifice has been offered for all the people." And when Jesus had been on the cross for some six hours that awful Friday, the weight of the sins of the world blotted out His Father's presence, and alone, separate, completely identified with sin, He cried, "It is finished," and yielded up His life. His voice sounded like a trumpet call to the universe: "It is done; it is finished."

3. *The fall of Jericho.* The reaction of the people to the report of the spies led to 40 years of wilderness wandering, and then a new generation crossed the Jordan and approached the walled city of Jericho. Beside the Exodus itself and the crossing of the Red Sea on dry land, what could compare in triumph with Jericho's fall? As the trumpet blasts at Jericho paved the way for Israel's entrance into the Promised Land, so the fanfare of the seventh trumpet will announce the entrance of the church into Paradise.

4. *The Feast of Trumpets.* Ten days before the Day of Atonement, the people would hear the trumpet announcement of this solemn day. No one was to come to this day of reckoning without warning. All must know that if they chose not to repent and make sacrifice for sins, there could not be any place for them in the camp of Israel. It has always been this way throughout history. God does not bring judgment without fair warning. Before the Flood, came the preaching of Noah. Before Christ's first coming, the preaching of John the Baptist. Before the fall of Sodom, the entreaties of Lot. Before the fall of Jerusalem, the sign of the encircling armies of Titus. God gives ample warning, and the symbol of the trumpet series reminds us of the approaching end, warning us that God's judgments have been restrained but soon will fall without restraint, and detailing how to be protected.

5. *The Jubilee celebration.* Every seventh year Israel followed a plan of agriculture in which the land was to lie fallow in order to restore its productivity. At the end of seven cycles of seven came the Jubilee celebration. Most Israelites would participate only once (at least as an adult) in the fiftieth year of Jubilee. Jubilee provided for at least two important issues: the restoration of land to owners and the

setting free of any who had become slaves.

As noted in chapter 1, it often happened that because of adverse circumstances a family would find it necessary to sell some of its land. But when Jubilee came, the land reverted to the original owners. In this way God preserved the original land allocation from the time of occupation. Also, through misfortune a person could become another's slave. But when Jubilee came, slaves were freed automatically.

In these two aspects of Jubilee we see symbols of what the trumpets signify for us as Christians. In the words of Wordsworth: "The sounding of the seven trumpets of the apocalypse ends in a universal *jubilee* for the deliverance of the people of God" *(The New Testament of our Lord and Savior Jesus Christ in the Original Greek*, vol. 2, p. 201).

6. Eschatological significance. In Jesus' Olivet address He incorporated the sounding of the trumpet into the events surrounding the Advent: "He will send his angels with a loud trumpet call" (Matt. 24:31). And Paul built on this theme when he said: "For the trumpet will sound, the dead will be raised imperishable" (1 Cor. 15:52). The prophecies of Joel, clearly eschatological in intent, contain trumpet imagery: "Blow the trumpet in Zion; sound the alarm on my holy hill. Let all who live in the land tremble, for the day of the Lord is coming. It is close at hand" (Joel 2:1).

The six examples just noted are some of the more important biblical precedents that help illuminate the meaning of the seven trumpets of Revelation.

Trumpets and bowls. The symbols of the trumpets and the bowls show an uncanny similarity.

Trumpets	Bowls
1. Earth	1. The same
2. Sea	2. The same
3. Rivers and fountains	3. The same
4. Sun	4. The same
5. Darkness	5. The same
6. Euphrates River	6. The same
7. "It is finished"	7. "It is done"

Faced with this apparent repetition, one wonders whether they are a description of the same events. A look at the chiastic structure of the Apocalypse, however, reminds us that the bowls reflect the trumpets rather than describe the same events at the same time. The first six trumpets sound before probation closes, while all the bowls occur after probation closes. So one is a type, a symbol of the other, but in a different time frame and with different intensity. The trumpets show preliminary, partial calamities and judgments. The bowls show final, intense judgments without the restraint of God's mercy (see the excursus at the end of this chapter for a further discussion on this point).

Two sets of plagues. We notice in the subject material of the trumpets and bowls a similarity to the plagues that fell on Egypt. Again the comparison becomes more obvious by placing the two sets side by side.

Last Seven Plagues (which parallel the trumpets)	**First Ten Plagues**
1, 4 affliction of the body— by sores and sun	3, 4, 5, 6, 8 affliction of the body—by flies, lice, murrain, boils, locusts
2, 3 water turned to blood	1 river turned to blood
5 darkness	9 darkness
6 frogs	2 frogs
7 hail and death	7, 10 hail and death

The similarity of the two series can hardly be coincidental. The plagues that fell on Egypt brought the release of Israel so that they could go to the Promised Land. It will be similar with the seven last plagues. As soon as they are over, Satan will cry, as it were, "It is enough; let them go!" and the redeemed will be caught up to meet Jesus in the air and go to the heavenly Promised Land.

Creation undone. There is also an intriguingly close parallel between the focus of the trumpets and the successive acts of Creation in earth's first six days. The trumpets catalog the systematic destruction of the earth, a series that reverses Creation.

Creation Focus	**Trumpet Focus**
Day 1—light	Trumpet 5—darkness
Day 2—pure atmosphere	Trumpet 5—polluted atmosphere
Day 3—vegetation made	Trumpet 1—vegetation destroyed
Day 4—sun revealed	Trumpet 4—sun obscured
Day 5—sea creatures made	Trumpet 2—sea creatures destroyed
Day 6—humans live	Trumpet 3—humans die
Day 7—rest	Trumpets 5, 6—torment

Could there be a more graphic demonstration of Satan's objective in his conflict with Jesus? One builds and beautifies, whereas the other destroys and despoils.

With this backdrop of interpretive clues, we now study the seven trumpets sequentially.

FIRST TRUMPET

"And I saw the seven angels who stand before God, and to them were given seven trumpets. . . .

"Then the seven angels who had the seven trumpets prepared to sound them.

"The first angel sounded his trumpet, and there came hail and fire mixed with blood, and it was hurled down upon the earth. A third of the earth was burned up, a third of the trees were burned up, and all the green grass was burned up" (Rev. 8:2-7).

When the first trumpet sounded, devastation in the form of hail and fire mixed with blood fell on the earth, trees, and grass. To mix hail and fire sounds implausible and points up the symbolic nature of these plagues.

Hail and blood are vivid reminders of Egypt's plagues of hail and of water turned to blood. But now the once protected are afflicted. God spared Israel in Egypt, but after centuries of disobedience His protection was withdrawn. In the devastation of Jerusalem in A.D. 70, Israel found itself the victim of the Roman armies.

The double reference to ⅓ is an apocalyptic metaphor of disunity (in contrast with the 3 of unity) and aptly describes the dislocation and disunity of Jewish life occasioned by the titan assault.

Trees, we have already noted, symbolize people, and grass is an Old Testament symbol of Israel. "All men are like grass, and all their glory is like the flowers of the field. The grass withers and the flowers fall, because the breath of the Lord blows on them. Surely the people are grass. The grass withers and the flowers fall, but the word of our God stands forever" (Isa. 40:5-8).

The imagery of the first trumpet seems to be drawn in part from Deuteronomy 29. God announced to Israel the consequences of abandoning the covenant. "The whole land will be a burning waste . . . nothing planted, nothing sprouting, no vegetation growing on it" (Deut. 29:23).

The first church, the first seal, and the first trumpet cover the same period: the first century. Each has a different perspective, however, with the trumpet focusing on Rome's attack on Jerusalem in A.D. 70— *the specific event Jesus described in the second part of His Olivet address.* Just a few recognized the sign of the encircling soldiers, heeded Jesus' warning, and escaped the carnage. Many Jews, symbolized as trees and grass, were "burnt up." For Jews it was, and still remains, one of the bitterest chapters in their checkered history.

Satan's attack through the armies of Rome had one important but unintended, positive consequence—it scattered the New Testament church headquartered in Jerusalem, and as a result the gospel spread more rapidly. Thus the meaning of the symbols of the first trumpet is to describe *the fall of Jerusalem* and the scattering of the Christian church.

SECOND TRUMPET

"The second angel sounded his trumpet, and something like a huge mountain, all ablaze, was thrown into the sea. A third of the sea turned into blood, a third of the living creatures in the sea died, and a third of the ships were destroyed" (Rev. 8:8, 9).

John's description of a burning mountain being thrown into the ocean and causing the water to turn to blood reminds us of the plague of blood that fell on Egypt. But here we have the additional symbol of a flaming mountain. The Old Testament has more than one reference to such a catastrophic image. The first is comforting: "'Before your eyes I will repay Babylon and all who live in Babylonia for all the wrong they have done in Zion,' declares the Lord. 'I am against you, O destroying mountain, you who destroy the whole earth,' declares the Lord. 'I will stretch out my hand against you, roll you off the cliffs, and make you a burned-out mountain'" (Jer. 51:24, 25).

Literal, local Babylon, likened to a burned-out mountain rolling downhill, is taken by John in the second trumpet and applied symbolically and worldwide. During the second period of church history (the second and third centuries) a spiritual Babylon, the Roman Empire, formerly the attacker, became the subject of increasing attacks. Hordes came down from the north, and Rome was powerless to resist them. Unhappily, the church became enmeshed in this battle for political supremacy. The repeated reference to ⅓ emphasizes the breakup of the once united Roman empire.

In his commentary on the trumpets, Thiele writes: "The second trumpet calls for some terrible, fiery, destructive force to fall into the troubled seas of the ancient world and to turn their turbid waters into blood. After the fall of Jerusalem came the fall of Rome. As the Jews had outlived their days of national usefulness, so also had Rome. . . . Like flames of fire from heaven came Genseric the Vandal, Alaric the Goth, and Attila the Hun, leaving in their wake scenes of ruin, desolation, carnage, and blood. Irresistible and destructive as a flaming mountain, the hordes of barbarians fell upon the peoples of Rome" (Edwin R. Thiele, *Outline Studies in Revelation*, p. 168).

The reference to ships at the conclusion of the second trumpet is fascinating. Perhaps John is alluding to the passage in Isaiah where, a century before the captivity, he predicted future agony and added: "For your sake I will send to Babylon and bring down as fugitives all the Babylonians, in the ships in which they took pride" (Isa. 43:14). Here, in the mind of Isaiah, Babylon is associated with ships, just as for Jeremiah Babylon had been associated with a burned mountain.

The second church, second seal, and second trumpet are parallel, describing events of the second and third centuries. In the trumpets we see depicted *the decline and fall of the Roman Empire.*

THIRD TRUMPET

"The third angel sounded his trumpet, and a great star, blazing like a torch, fell from the sky on a third of the rivers and on the springs of water—the name of the star is Wormwood. A third of the waters turned bitter, and many people died from the waters that had become bitter" (Rev. 8:10, 11).

The third trumpet is longer than the first and second trumpets, just as the third seal is longer than the first and second seals. The imagery has clear precedents that we can recognize instantly.

We have no difficulty identifying the falling star of the Old Testament. Isaiah writes, "How art thou fallen from heaven, O Lucifer" (Isa. 14:12, KJV) or as Moffatt translated it: "What a fall from heaven on high, O shining star of the dawn!" And Jesus confirms the association when He comments: "I saw Satan fall like lightning from heaven" (Luke 10:18). Some of the effects of this fall are detailed in the third trumpet.

John says the name of this star is Wormwood, one of a family of plants with an exceptionally bitter taste. In Roman times wormwood was the popular name of a plant used to prevent pregnancy and as such symbolized decline and death. Wormwood was used in Old Testament times as a symbol of God's judgment.

A well-known story from the Exodus also illuminates the text. When the people arrived at Marah, thirsty after travel, they found a stream and rushed to drink, but were appalled when they discovered this pure-looking stream tasted bitter like wormwood. Moses then took a tree and threw it into the stream, and it became sweet for drinking. Israel's acquaintance with this imagery of a bitter stream made sweet is turned around in the vision of the third trumpet and shows a sweet stream made bitter when the star called Wormwood descends from heaven and enters it.

Another Old Testament source seems to be the Deuteronomic curses. The picture is of generations of believers turning their backs on the covenant relationship, boasting of their achievements only to receive the curses in all their severity (Deut. 29:19-22). What had been predicted for literal local Israel is now poured on apostate spiritual Israel worldwide.

The third trumpet vividly symbolizes the events of the third period of history, when the streams of truth, originating like the river in the wilderness from the Rock, Christ Jesus, were polluted and made bitter, and those who drank them died spiritually. The ⅓ symbolizes the disruption and disunity of the church during a period of difficulty and declension. We noted the same content in the third church and the third seal, covering the period of the fourth and fifth centuries. "Polluted streams" says it as well as anything can. The third trumpet details *the fall of the church at large.*

FOURTH TRUMPET

"The fourth angel sounded his trumpet, and a third of the sun was struck, a third of the moon, and a third of the stars, so that a third of them turned dark. A third of the day was without light, and also a third of the night"(Rev. 8:12).

The fourth trumpet is exceedingly brief—sun, moon, and stars are obscured, and darkness covers the earth both day and night. Speaking of the creation of the sun, moon, and stars, Genesis records: "God set them in the expanse of the sky to give light on the earth" (Gen. 1:17). The prophet Micah uses this imagery in a reverse, symbolic sense: "Therefore night will come over you, without visions, and darkness, without divination. The sun will set for the prophets, and the day will go dark for them" (Micah 3:6). This is the sense in which John uses these symbols.

During the Middle Ages the prophets were silent and God's truth lay perverted, waiting the dawn of a new age when once again the Bible would be read and understood, and the full light of the gospel of faith would be preached. John uses the ⅓ symbol 6 times; the 6 is the symbol of agitation and restlessness that falls short of the 7 of Sabbath rest, and the ⅓, the symbol of disunity and separation, reveals what the kingdom of darkness brought to the kingdom of light during the Middle Ages. It is this terrifying experience that awakens the impassioned cry "How long, Lord?" The fourth trumpet runs parallel with the fourth church and the fourth seal, and covers the sixth to the fifteenth centuries. It is a symbol of *the fall of spiritual night.*

In summary: the first trumpet describes *the fall of Jerusalem*, the second trumpet describes *the fall of Rome*, the third trumpet describes *the fall of the church at large*, and the fourth trumpet describes *the fall of spiritual night on the world.*

THE THREE WOES

"As I watched, I heard an eagle that was flying in midair call out in a loud voice: 'Woe! Woe! Woe to the inhabitants of the earth, because of the trumpet blasts about to be sounded by the other three angels!'" (Rev. 8:13).

Revelation 9, detailing the first two woes (that is, the fifth and sixth trumpets), is one of the most remarkable passages of Scripture and of all apocalyptic writing, both canonical and noncanonical. Unfortunately, the extraordinary detail and complexity of the imagery confuses most readers. However, if we maintain the hermeneutic with which we began, the last three trumpets can be as clear as the first four.

Apocalyptic literature, by nature, has a face of eschatology. As we come to the climax of history, viewed from the enemy's camp, we would expect to hear about war games, strategies, and infamies of an intent and extent not seen in any other period of history (with the exception of the attacks centered on Jesus during His earthly life). The fifth and sixth trumpets detail the worldwide conflict as it approaches its climax. Here the final movements of the kingdom of darkness are being plotted, the hordes of angels at his command are being dispatched, and the most effective plans ever devised, implemented.

FIFTH TRUMPET

"The fifth angel sounded his trumpet, and I saw a star that had fallen from the sky to the earth. The star was given the key to the shaft of the Abyss. When he opened the Abyss, smoke rose from it like the smoke from a gigantic furnace. The sun and sky were darkened by the smoke from the Abyss. And out of the smoke locusts came down upon the earth and were given power like that of scorpions of the earth. They were told not to harm the grass of the earth or any plant or tree, but only those people who did not have the seal of God on their foreheads. They were not given power to kill them, but only to torture them for five months. And the agony they suffered was like that of the sting of a scorpion when it strikes a man. During those days men will seek death, but will not find it; they will long to die, but death will elude them.

"The locusts looked like horses prepared for battle. On their heads they wore something like crowns of gold, and their faces resembled human faces. Their hair was like women's hair, and their teeth were like lions' teeth. They had breastplates like breastplates of iron, and the sound of their wings was like the thundering of many horses and chariots rushing into battle. They had tails and stings like scorpions, and in their tails they had power to torment people for five months. They had as king over them the angel of the Abyss, whose name in Hebrew is Abaddon, and in Greek, Apollyon.

"The first woe is past; two other woes are yet to come" (Rev. 9:1-12).

Trumpet five contains the following chief symbols: a star that had fallen from heaven, the bottomless pit, smoke, polluted atmosphere, a multitude of locusts with the stings of scorpions, people who do not have God's seal, a king named Apollyon, and the number 5. We should examine the symbols separately before we attempt to integrate them.

A *star* that fell from heaven is a reminder of Satan's original fall. In a later vision, one third of the stars of heaven are seen falling. This is in contrast with the imagery of Daniel 8, where the prophet saw the little horn power that "grew until it reached the host of the heavens, and it threw some of the starry host down to the earth and trampled on them" (verse 10). There are stars in the firmament of the kingdom of light and stars in the kingdom of darkness. The star pictured in the fifth trumpet represents Lucifer and all the clouded "stars" that have led multitudes of human beings to turn their backs on God.

The *bottomless pit* is later described as the place where Satan is forced to dwell (Rev. 20:1-3). The bottomless pit, or Abyss (for that is the word in Greek), symbolizes the seat of Satan's kingdom.

As soon as the fifth trumpet sounds, *smoke* billows out of the bottomless pit. This aspect of the vision seems to be built on a passage of the Old Testament in which wickedness is symbolized as smoke.[1]

"Wickedness burns like a fire" (Isa. 9:18).[2] The sun illuminates; smoke obscures. This smoke is a vivid metaphor of the obscuring clouds of deception by which Satan seeks to negate the gospel.

The prophet Joel opens his book by describing the results of a plague of *locusts*. The prophet says the locusts represent the invasion of a "nation." As a result, the storehouses are empty and the barns torn down. Thus, we understand the locusts to represent great destructiveness. The name of the king of the locust horde is called *Apollyon* from the Greek meaning "to destroy." *Abaddon* in Hebrew means "destruction."

The *scorpion* is a biblical symbol of judgment (see 1 Kings 12:11, 14). Its sting is very painful, but usually not fatal. In the same passage that Jesus describes the way He saw Satan fall from heaven, He uses scorpions as a symbol of demons (Luke 10:19).

The meaning of a *seal* was introduced in the discussion of Revelation 7, where it is an apocalyptic symbol of protection, provision, and possession. But the New Testament also describes the Holy Spirit as placing the gospel seal on all those who become members of God's family. All Christians receive this seal of acceptance and belonging at the moment of their commitment to Jesus (Eph. 1:12-14).

When we link together destroying locusts and stinging scorpions from the smoky domain of Satan claiming all those who do not have God's seal of ownership, we have summarized the basic meaning of the fifth trumpet.

One other point focuses on the qualitative use of the number 5. The fifth trumpet mentions a period of five months. In the sixth trumpet a number is doubled to indicate intensification. Thus the halving of a number probably indicates a partial fulfillment. It has been established that the numeral 10 symbolizes completeness, therefore half of 10 could be understood to signify the notion of *incompleteness*.[3] If this is the intended meaning, then it would indicate that the destruction caused during the fifth trumpet in the fifth period of history is incomplete, and that only Satan's final assault (seen in the equally vivid symbols of the sixth trumpet) will bring it to completeness.

What we have noted in explanation of the symbols of the fifth trumpet fits into the scheme of history as outlined in both the churches and seals. As the church came out of the Middle Ages, it watched the flowering of the Renaissance and participated in the incredible events of the Reformation, drawing strength from the rediscovered truths of justification by faith, the priesthood of all believers, and the Bible as our sole rule of faith. This placed the kingdom of darkness firmly on the defensive. Satan had to devise approaches by which those rejoicing in the light of the gospel could be turned aside to pursuits that would sap their interest and energy.

Huntingford probably had these thoughts in mind when he wrote: "The locusts of socialism, communism, nihilism, intellectual pride, atheism, the deep and manifold deceits of Satan, are preparing the way for the final apostasy of the Gentiles" (Edward Huntingford, *The Apocalypse With a Commentary*, p. 174).

In summary, the fifth trumpet pictures fallen angels, commanded by Satan, the king of destruction, going into the world at the very time the Reformation is revealing again the light of the gospel and spreading the smoke of his lies. The opposition forces against which the church must fight are as numerous as locusts, as powerful as kings, as callous as evil men, as wily as evil women, as strong as lions, as swift as horses, and as uncontainable and ephemeral as smoke. What an opposition! Those who are faithful to God and His gospel cannot be infected, however; whereas those who accept the lies of Satan's imps and become infected with their heresies find themselves faithless and without salvation.

The fifth trumpet covers the same period as the fifth seal and the fifth church, the fifteenth to the nineteenth centuries, the long march out of medieval darkness into modern times.

SIXTH TRUMPET

"The sixth angel sounded his trumpet, and I heard a voice coming from the horns of the golden altar that is before God. It said to the sixth angel who had the trumpet, 'Release the four angels who are bound at the great river Euphrates.' And the four angels who had been kept ready for this very hour and day and month and year were released to kill a third of mankind. The number of the mounted troops was two hundred million. I heard their number.

"The horses and riders I saw in my vision looked like this: Their breastplates were fiery red, dark blue, and yellow as sulfur. The heads of the horses resembled the heads of lions, and out of their mouths came fire, smoke and sulfur. A third of mankind was killed by the three plagues of fire, smoke and sulfur that came out of their mouths. The power of the horses was in their mouths and in their tails; for their tails were like snakes, having heads with which they inflict injury.

"The rest of mankind that were not killed by these plagues still did not repent of the work of their hands; they did not stop worshiping demons, and idols of gold, silver, bronze, stone and wood—idols that cannot see or hear or walk" (Rev. 9:13-20).

The sixth trumpet marks a crisis point common to the six in each major series of seven in Revelation. As just noted, the number 6 represents a falling short of the Sabbath rest, symbolized by 7. Thus 6 is continual conflict without the peace that comes to those who are in Christ. The sixth church received a warning about the "hour of testing" that it would have to endure, the clear inference being that it would suffer eternal loss if it should fail the test. The sixth seal depicted the agony of the lost watching Jesus return, knowing they are eternally lost. The sixth trumpet focuses on the supremely important moment God has established on His universal calendar, when He will declare all people to be either part of His family and thus privileged to enter eternal rest, or not part of His family of faith and thus excluded from His eternal rest. It is a moment of extreme drama and magnitude. Thus the high point of the sixth trumpet comes when John writes of this supremely important "hour and day and month and year" (verse 15).

Milligan commented: "When *the hour, and the day, and the month, and the year*—that is, when the moment fixed in the counsels of the Almighty come, the chains by which destruction has been kept back shall be broken, and the world shall be overwhelmed by the raging stream" (*The Revelation of St. John*, p. 151).

As in the fifth trumpet, we need first to look at the individual symbols and then take the trumpet as a whole. The chief symbols are the river Euphrates, cavalry, and serpents.

The river Euphrates is given an even more detailed treatment under the sixth bowl. In that setting the angel pours out his plague, and the river dries up in preparation for the coming of the kings of the east. The imagery is based on the fall of Babylon in 539 B.C. Cyrus and Darius brought their army to the capital, diverted the river into marsh-lands, struggled up the muddy riverbed, found the city unguarded, and overthrew it. The drying up of the river signaled the beginning of a new world empire. Thus under the sixth trumpet the instruction is given: "Release the four angels who are bound at the great river Euphrates" (verse 14). In other words, the restraining that has been taking place is to end, paving the way for the eventual "drying up of the river"—the fall of spiritual Babylon and the founding of the eternal kingdom of glory.

The symbolism of *cavalry* riding their steeds is best understood by a comparison. In Revelation 19 King Jesus rides a white charger fol-lowed by His angelic host on horses. In Revelation 9 King Lucifer also commands an army on horseback, and as a grim reminder of his many aliases, we are told that the strength of these horses is like a *serpent*, the devil himself.

If we combine the individual symbols already discussed, we can see the clear import of the sixth trumpet. In these last days Satan will make his last frantic attempt to ruin as many of earth's inhabitants as possible. (However, John reminds us that during this onslaught, the prayers of the saints are still being heard at heaven's golden altar of in-cense [verse 13].) Some restraints long imposed on Lucifer are grad-ually released so that he will fully show his true character. But this trumpet reminds us that God has set time limits on Satan. The sixth trumpet ends at the appointed hour, on a day, in a month, in a year (note the fourfold description indicating the "universal" significance of the moment). When that hour strikes, probation will close and there will be no further opportunity for any person to change allegiance. The words reflect Jesus' comments in the Olivet sermon: "No one knows about that day or hour, not even the angels in heaven, nor the Son, but only the Father" (Matt. 24:36). The Father will bring down the curtain on probation history at the very hour already determined.

The army of Satan's kingdom is shown to be extremely powerful and complete—10 x 10 x 10 x 10 x 10 x 10 x 10 x 10 *doubled* (Rev. 9:16). They could not be more united (3 plagues), and the church, so bitterly attacked and scattered (⅓ "killed"), reels from the battle. The description of Satan's army is awe-inspiring: "Their breastplates are fiery red like the glow of a blazing furnace, smoky blue like the smoke rising from a fire, and sulphurous yellow like the brimstone from the pit of hell. The horses have heads like lions, and tails like serpents; they breathe out destructive fire and smoke and brimstone, and their serpent-tails deal out hurt and harm" (Barclay, *The Revelation of John*, vol. 2, p. 65).

We would imagine that in the face of this demonstration of stupendous satanic power people would pause long enough to consider God's claims on their lives. But hell-bent, Satan-controlled, and ignoring the Christ of Calvary, they come to "that hour" unrepentant and lost. The "universality" of their wickedness is highlighted by the naming of four sins: murder, sorcery, immorality, and theft (verse 21).

The sixth trumpet covers the time of the end, when Satan does all in his power to counter the final proclamation of the gospel right up to the hour of the close of probation. It is parallel to the seventh church and the first half of the sixth seal.[4]

SEVENTH TRUMPET

It might appear from the words of the sixth trumpet that Satan triumphs. But that is far from the case. God still has His "thousands" oppressed and scattered who have not bowed the knee to Baal—to use the language of Elijah's day. To complete the sequence, we read ahead to Revelation 10 and 11 and find John's description of the seventh trumpet. Like the seventh seal, it is brief and follows a parenthetical section.

"The seventh angel sounded his trumpet, and there were loud voices in heaven, which said: 'The kingdom of the world has become the kingdom of our Lord and of his Christ, and he will reign for ever and ever'" (Rev. 11:15).

"But in the days when the seventh angel is about to sound his trumpet, the mystery of God will be accomplished, just as he announced to his servants the prophets" (Rev. 10:7).

The end of the sixth trumpet and the beginning of the seventh trumpet comes at a universally significant hour, on a day, in a month, of a year, and it marks the close of probation. Only then can the Angel of chapter 10 joyfully announce there will now be "no more delay" in ending the ages of sin.

EXCURSUS ON REVELATION 8, 9

Just as some recent discussion has focused on the timing of the seals, so has there been discussion about the time setting of the trumpets. Those who see a pre-Advent judgment setting for the seals are inclined to see a post-probation setting for the trumpets on the basis that there are some remarkable similarities between the trumpet imagery and the bowl imagery, as has already been observed.

First, the recent arguments about the trumpets are based in some measure on beliefs about the seals discussed in the excursus at the end of chapter 7 of this work. If there is no validity in a futuristic view of the seals, there is not likely to be any for the trumpets, either.

Second, the trumpets chapters plainly indicate that probationary time continues to the end of the sixth trumpet. The last verse of chapter 9 records: "Nor did they repent . . ." The exclamation is made because the wicked *choose* not to repent; it is not the lack of opportunity, because the previous verses, describing the sixth trumpet, emphasize that the great conflict continues to that most momentous hour, in a day, in a month, in a year, when the gospel is preached for the last time and probation closes. That moment is the one at which the sixth trumpet ends and the seventh is *about* to sound (Rev. 10:7). There appears to be little reason to support a post-probation setting for all the trumpets when clearly the gospel is being shared right to the end of the sixth.

Commenting on this issue, Jon Paulien has written: "A further argument for the end-time interpretation of the seven trumpets notes the similarity in language between Revelation 7:1-3 and Revelation 8:7-9. According to Revelation 7 the earth, sea, and trees are not to be hurt until the sealing work is completed. Since these are the very objects affected by the first and second trumpets, it is suggested that these trumpets must follow the sealing chronologically and thus, occur in postprobationary times.

"However, it should be noted that Revelation 8:2 introduces a new series; consequently, it is necessary to demonstrate that the trumpet series follows *chronologically* the literary section that precedes it. Chapters 4 and 12 certainly go back to an earlier stage of history. Why not chapter 8 as well?

"Although it is true that the objects for destruction in the first two trumpets are protected in Revelation 7:1-3, they are also protected in the fifth trumpet (Rev. 9:4). This raises serious questions whether the trumpet series is to be related as an immediate sequel to the vision of chapter 7.

"Even more decisive, however, is the fact that the strongest parallel between the first part of Revelation 7 and the seven trumpets is in Revelation 9:14, 16. In both sections binding and loosing are related to four angels. In both sections a people are being numbered; in Revelation 7 the people of God; in Revelation 9 their demonic counterparts. And these are the only two places in Revelation containing the cryptic words, 'I heard the number *[ēkousa ton arithmon]*.' If probation remains open through the sixth trumpet and then closes with the sounding of the seventh, the sixth trumpet is the exact historical counterpart of Revelation 7:1-8. It is the last opportunity for salvation just before the end.

"The seven trumpets, therefore, do not follow the events of Revelation 7 in chronological order. The trumpets take their cue and commencement instead from the introductory vision of Revelation 8:2-6. The main theme of that vision is intercession at the altar of incense. This is an appropriate follow-up to the inauguration of the heavenly sanctuary as described in Revelation 5.

"The book of Revelation flows naturally, as shown above, from a view of the cross (Rev. 1:5, 17, 18; cf. 5:6, 9, 12), to a view of the inauguration of Christ's ministry in the light of the cross (Rev. 5), to a picture of the intercessory ministry that results (Rev. 8:3, 4), and ultimately to the judgment that precedes the end (Rev. 11:18, 19). The order of events is characteristic of the entire NT" ("The Seven Seals," in *Symposium on Revelation*, book 1, pp. 196, 197). ●

---

[1] Smoke is not used exclusively as a metaphor of evil. For example, smoke also symbol-

izes prayer (as in the smoke of incense) and protection (as in the smoke on Mount Sinai).

[2] Notice that both good and evil are consumed.

[3] Just as 1/3 is understood to indicate disunity and separation in contrast with the 3 of unity.

[4] It is worthy of note that this moment reveals the "remnants" of the great contest between Jesus and Satan. The first have been saved by God and will be completely protected and preserved by Him until Jesus' return. The second are Satan's remnant, those who have refused to repent despite God's most persistent entreaties. This remnant will go down into everlasting death with their leader, Satan.

Outline

1. Introducing Revelation 10, 11
   Seals and sealing are an interpretive clue

2. Heaven's mightiest Messenger

3. John's private message

4. No more delay

5. Bittersweet

CHAPTER TEN

SWEET AS HONEY

The Apocalypse is full of the most compelling contrasts. After the terror of locusts and lions and smoke and scorpions in Revelation 9 comes the peaceful vision of the majestic angel of chapter 10.

As we begin we need to review briefly Revelation 6 and 7. At the end of the sixth seal John paused. First he looked back and pictured the sealing of believers prior to the close of probation and the Second Coming. Then he looked forward and described the bliss of the redeemed in heaven. After that interlude he concluded the original presentation with a brief account of the seventh seal.

If John follows the same pattern with the trumpets, we might expect to see in Revelation 10 and 11 both a *backward* look in history, to be reminded of the setting of the final conflict, and a *forward* look to the ultimate vindication of the redeemed and God's wrath poured on the condemned. After that interlude he might conclude the original presentation by giving a brief account of the seventh trumpet.

And this is exactly what we find. While the sixth trumpet covers the last period in which the gospel is preached to the world, Revelation 11 takes us back through the centuries of the church's history from the time of Jesus and climaxes with the moment when Jesus returns, "rewarding your servants the prophets and your saints and those who reverence your name, both small and great" (verse

18). In this setting John twice gives the briefest description of the seventh trumpet.

HEAVEN'S MIGHTIEST MESSENGER

"Then I saw another mighty angel coming down from heaven. He was robed in a cloud, with a rainbow above his head; his face was like the sun, and his legs were like fiery pillars. He was holding a little scroll, which lay open in his hand. He planted his right foot on the sea and his left foot on the land" (Rev. 10:1, 2).

Wordsworth commented on the chapter in these poetic words: "The rainbow is an attribute of the Divine Majesty as already represented in a former vision (iv.3) and it is here like a halo round the Angel, and marks Him to be no other than Christ. . . .

"The rainbow expresses His mercy to the good, tempering His justice and judgments to the rebellious. . . .

"'His face as the sun,' proclaims His divine glory.

"'His feet as pillars,' firmly set, and 'of fire,' indicate that His kingdom is immoveable. . . .

"His feet are firmly planted 'on the sea' . . . the fluid element denoting nations in a state of turbulence and agitation. . . . And His feet are set on the earth, the emblem of worldly power opposed to the kingdom of heaven. . . .

"He is described as 'crying with a loud voice, like the roaring of a lion,' the king of beasts . . . a sign of wrath; and Christ, as King of the world, and Lord of the church, 'the Lion of the tribe of Judah' . . . is angry with, and will punish, all who usurp His sovereignty" (Wordsworth, *The New Testament of Our Lord,* vol. 2, p. 212).

Who else but Jesus could be represented by this symbolic portrait?

The word "angel" comes from a Greek word that means "messenger." In this case Jesus has a message of great importance that will sustain the church through the final struggle with Satan. This opposition has just been described as millions of horses with the cunning and venom of serpents (Rev. 9:16-19). Who can withstand such opposition? All who maintain their faith in Jesus.

JOHN'S PRIVATE MESSAGE

"And he gave a loud shout like the roar of a lion. When he shouted, the voices of the seven thunders spoke. And when the seven thunders spoke, I was about to write; but I heard a voice from heaven say, 'Seal up what the seven thunders have said and do not write it down'" (Rev. 10:3, 4).

In the midst of this vision God communicated some information for John's ears only. (This seems to parallel God's personal message to Daniel, recorded in chapter 12 of that book.) John heard seven peals of thunder, understood the meaning, and took his pen to record it, but he received the instruction not to write down the message, but to seal it. It would be fruitless speculation to attempt to unseal what God intended to remain sealed.

NO MORE DELAY

"Then the angel I had seen standing on the sea and on the land raised his right hand to heaven. And he swore by him who lives for ever and ever, who created the heavens and all that is in them, the earth and all that is in it, and the sea and all that is in it, and said, 'There will be no more delay! But in the days when the seventh angel is about to sound his trumpet, the mystery of God will be accomplished, just as he announced to his servants the prophets'" (Rev. 10:5-7).

After speaking through the rolling thunders, Jesus raises His right hand and proclaims: "There will be no more delay!" (verse 6). To understand this cryptic phrase in the context of the entire interlude of Revelation 10 and 11, one needs to ask if there is any Old Testament passage that might illuminate it. And one immediately recalls some striking resemblances in the last chapter of Daniel.

"Then I, Daniel, looked, and there before me stood two others, one on this bank of the river and one on the opposite bank. One of them said to the man *clothed in linen*, who was *above the waters* of the river, '*How long* will it be before these astonishing things are fulfilled?' The man clothed in linen, who was above the waters of the river, lifted his right hand and his left hand toward heaven, and I heard him swear by him who lives forever, saying, 'It will be for *a time, times and half a time*. When the power of the holy people has been finally broken, *all these things will be completed.*' I heard, but I did not understand. So I asked, 'My lord, what will the outcome of all this be?' He replied, 'Go your way, Daniel, because *the words are closed up and sealed until the time of the end*'" (Dan. 12:5-10).

The similarities are too numerous to be coincidental, especially when we have seen that John used Daniel's symbols and phrases more than those of any other Old Testament writer. Consider some phrases in Revelation 6 and 10 when compared with the Old Testament prophet. Daniel's question in the face of the final conflict was "What will be the outcome?" John's question in the face of the last conflict was "Who can survive?" The cry to the man in linen was "How long will it be before this all ends?" The cry of the souls under the altar was "How long before you step in and vindicate us?" It is deeply significant that the last two passages are in contrast rather than in parallel. The decree of the man in linen was "It will continue for a 'time, times and half a time.'" The decree of Jesus in Revelation 10 was "There will be no more delay."

From Daniel's perspective time stretched forward for centuries before Jesus' first advent. But when the sixth trumpet ends (and the seventh "is about to sound"), probation closes, and there will be no more delay in answering the cry of the souls under the altar for God to bring judgment on Satan and his kingdom.

The moment Jesus declares "No more delay," the seventh trumpet sounds, announcing: "The mystery of God will be accomplished, just as he announced to his servants the prophets" (Rev. 10:7), and "The kingdom of the world has become the kingdom of our Lord" (Rev. 11:15).

The expression "the mystery of God" is a synonym for the gospel (Eph. 6:19). John says it is the message "preached" to God's servants the prophets. The word "preach" here in Greek is *euaggelizō* and is the root from which we get the English word "evangelism." Why is it described as a mystery? Because many of its aspects are impossible to understand. For example: How can God be just and the justifier of sinners? How did the eternal God become human? How could Jesus be the lamb slain from the foundation of the world—before sin? How does God love the unlovable? How does faith make sinners righteous? How can a God of love destroy sinners?

It is important to note that just as there is an intimate content relationship between the seven seals and the seven trumpets (they cover the same historical period from two different perspectives), there is also an intimate content relationship between the interlude that comes between the sixth and the seventh seals and the interlude that comes between the sixth and the seventh trumpets. "No more delay," "The mystery of God is finished," and "Until we have sealed the bond servants of our God on their foreheads" are all descriptions of the climax of probationary time, a time of universal wickedness among the lost and of a complete trust in God on the part of the believing community.

BITTERSWEET

"Then the voice that I had heard from heaven spoke to me once more: 'Go, take the scroll that lies open in the hand of the angel who is standing on the sea and on the land.'

"So I went to the angel and asked him to give me the little scroll. He said to me, 'Take it and eat it. It will turn your stomach sour, but in your mouth it will be as sweet as honey.' I took the little scroll from the angel's hand and ate it. It tasted as sweet as honey in my mouth, but when I had eaten it, my stomach turned sour. Then I was told, 'You must prophesy again about many peoples, nations, languages and kings'" (Rev. 10:8-11).

The last four verses of Revelation 10 focus on some unusual imagery. In vision John hears the command to take the little book, or scroll (depending on which translation you read), from the hands of Jesus. As he takes it, John receives the further command to eat it, with the warning that although at first it will taste as sweet as honey, later it will taste bitter. John does as instructed, and at first it does taste sweet, but afterward the taste turns bitter.

What meaning is intended by this part of the vision? John is not talking about eating papyrus or leather. This little book is the symbol of a great reality that brings both sweetness and bitterness, joy and pain.

God gave Ezekiel a vision quite similar to John's, and that experience illuminates Revelation 10. God told the prophet that he must speak to Israel because they had rebelled, but warned it would be like walking through thorns and sitting on scorpions. Then He told Ezekiel to open his mouth and eat what he received, and then handed the prophet a scroll. As the prophet records the story: "So I opened my mouth, and he gave me the scroll to eat. . . . So I ate it, and it tasted as sweet as honey in my mouth" (Eze. 3:2, 3). At this point all seemed to be well, but a few verses further on Ezekiel records: "The Spirit then lifted me up and took me away, and I went in bitterness and in the anger of my spirit" (verse 14).

Presenting God's message is the sweetest work of all. But when you experience rejection, it can feel like the pricks of thorns and the stings of scorpions, and you may experience fear and anger, the sweetness turned bitter.

Apparently the experience surrounding the little book is something that had to be repeated despite rejection, for John was told: "You must prophecy again." In fact, it had to be repeated until heard by the world's "many peoples, nations, languages and kings" (Rev. 10:11).

For two reasons we assume that this symbolism portrays the experience of preaching the gospel. First, presenting the gospel is the commission of the church and the heart of everything it has to say to the world. Second, the story of eating the little book (verse 8) comes immediately after John's reference to preaching the gospel (verse 7). Thus it seems probable that the eating of the little book is an elaboration of an aspect of the preaching of the gospel.

The commission to take the gospel to all the world (Rev. 10:11; 14:6; Matt. 24:14) cannot help drawing our attention to at least six similarities between Revelation 10, 11, and Revelation 14.

1. These three chapters picture either one or several angelic messengers.

2. These three chapters focus primarily on the presentation of the gospel.

3. These three chapters alert the church that its work will not be complete until the gospel has been shared with every nation, kindred, tongue, and people.

4. These three chapters are written in the setting of the time of the end. (Chapter 10 is sandwiched between the sixth and seventh trumpets; chapter 11 climaxes with the eternal reward of the redeemed; and chapter 14 pictures the harvest of the world after the gospel's final proclamation has been made.)

5. These three chapters are written in the context of judgment being poured out on the unrepentant (Rev. 10:6, 7; 11:18; 14:18-20).

6. Most important of all, these three chapters are concerned with Jesus' return to vindicate the saved and bring vengeance on those who have chosen not to accept His salvation.

On the basis of these numerous similarities, we assume that the basic emphasis of Revelation 10, the eating of the little book and the elaboration of this theme in chapter 11, is the same as the symbols of Revelation 14:6-12; that is, the preaching of the gospel in the time of the end, a work that is the heart of the message of the three angels. This work inevitably brings two results—joy and sadness. For the one who shares the good news (and it is an evangelist, John, who was told to eat the book) comes the joy of sharing the love of Jesus and seeing some enter the faith community. But there is also sadness because so few choose to respond to God's message through His servants—precisely Ezekiel's experience from which the imagery is drawn. Then too, for all who enter the kingdom of God there is both a crown to wear and a cross to bear. It is well to be warned that after we taste the sweet news of the gospel, Satan will see to it that trial and sadness will quickly cross our paths. To use John's metaphor, we soon taste the bitterness of life in a world of sin and sadness that can be the more acute because it stands in such contrast with the sweetness of our faith experience with Jesus.

Interestingly, a mid-nineteenth-century experience illustrates the symbolism. Daniel had been shown that the preaching of the gospel would be interrupted and cast down to nothingness (Dan. 8:10-12), but that at the end of 2300 days (years) the sanctuary would "be restored" (Dan. 8:14, Moffatt). That is, among other things, the full gospel would be preached again.

The extensive preaching of Daniel 8 and 9 in the mid-nineteenth century provoked a revival of immense proportions. It began in America with the preaching of a Baptist lay preacher, William Miller, and spread rapidly across denominational boundaries and across the Pacific and Atlantic oceans to the world. Bible students constructed the chronology of the prophecy of Daniel 8 and 9, recaptured the lost good news of the Second Coming, and announced a date for Jesus' return. For the entire interdenominational movement involving tens of thousands of Christians and many of their pastors, this became the sweetest expectation. The news was "sweeter than honey, than honey from the comb" (Ps. 19:10). But when the time passed and Jesus did not appear, the experience brought great sadness—the sweetness turned sour.

And here we pause, for Revelation 10 is but the introduction of the vision that continues on into Revelation 11. ●

Outline

1. Introducing Revelation 11
   Bridge to the second half of book
   A part of the interlude between the sixth and seventh trumpets
   Qualitative significance of 3½, 42, and 1260

2. The sacred *naos*

3. The mourning witnesses

4. The power-filled witnesses

5. The seventh trumpet

6. John's summary statement

CHAPTER ELEVEN

WITNESSING FOR JESUS

I f Revelation 9 presents the most graphic apocalyptic writing of John's book, Revelation 11 is the most enigmatic. However, one commentator echoed the thoughts of others when he observed: "It has been said that this chapter is at one and the same time the most difficult and the most important chapter in the *Revelation*" (Barclay, *The Revelation of John*, vol. 2, p. 79).

Based on their understanding of the book's structure, some commentators see Revelation 11 as building a bridge to unite the two halves of Revelation. This position has merit, because the material contained in chapter 11 *introduces all the major themes of the rest of the book*. But we must move cautiously as we enter this highly symbolic chapter, or we will miss the wonderful forest and see only individual trees. To begin, as we have done before, we will look at the main symbols and then attempt to integrate them in a series of graphic pictures.

As mentioned earlier, the chapter that describes the two witnesses is part of *the interlude between the sixth and seventh trumpets*. John makes this clear by telling us at one point that the second woe (the sixth trumpet) is over and that the third woe (the seventh trumpet) is about to sound. The sixth trumpet describes the final preaching of the gospel amid the most vicious opposition of Satan. The seventh trumpet announces that probation has closed and that God's wrath in the seven bowls is about to fall on the world. *This is a time when God's elect require special protection until they are taken to heaven.*

In other words, because Revelation 11 is part of the trumpets' vision (a commentary on the second part of Jesus' Olivet address, attacks from without, corruption within), and particularly the sixth and seventh trumpets, this chapter as a whole is probably some variation on the three themes just referenced, namely: (1) the proclamation of the gospel amid the most intense attacks, (2) the close of probation and the protection of God's people, and (3) Jesus' return to receive His people.

It is important to note, however, that the interlude between the sixth and seventh seals deals only with the sealing of the saved at the close of probation and their bliss in heaven. The interlude between the sixth and seventh trumpets has a much wider focus. It too speaks of the sealing, but it also walks us back through the entire Christian era and then, like Revelation 7, climaxes with the saved in heaven.

Next, Revelation 11 *introduces us to three numbers* mentioned a total of five times in Revelation 11 through 13: the numbers 42, 1260, and 3½. Three and a half years equals 42 months, and assuming a standard 30-day month, this is equivalent to 1260 days. Thus these three apocalyptic designations of Revelation 11-13 are assumed to be equivalent, but in contrasting nomenclature for symbolic reasons. According to our hermeneutic, we assume these numbers first have a *qualitative* significance in interpreting the vision, and only second a possible *quantitative* application. We will also find a quantitative meaning in the historical experiences out of which the numbers have been drawn.

In Revelation 11 John gives some important clues to the qualitative meaning of the numbers by hinting at three of the most significant epics in religious history: the Exodus from Egypt and Israel's journey to the Promised Land; the drought in Israel during the days of Jezebel, who attempted to destroy the prophets of God; and the short ministry of Jesus, ending in crucifixion, burial, resurrection, and ascension (Rev. 11:6-13).

The first of these three experiences is linked with the number 42. There were 42 stages in the journey from Egypt to the Promised Land,[1] and the journey took 42 years.[2] The second of these three is linked with the number 3½. For three and one half years (1260 days) Israel suffered drought and oppression (1 Kings 18:1; Luke 4:25;

James 5:17). This period climaxed on Mount Carmel, where God was exonerated and all opposition slain. Then, too, Jesus spent three and one half years (1260 days) in publicly witnessing to His Father's love.[3]

According to our hermeneutic, that which was literal and local in the Old Testament is to be understood as symbolic and worldwide in the New. Thus the 42 of the Exodus of the Old Testament church from Egypt amid the signs and wonders from God reminds us of the journey of the New Testament church from the Egypt of this world to its safe entrance into the heavenly Promised Land.

The 3½ and 1260 remind us of the mission of the true Israel of God to witness in a world of spiritual drought where the prophetic word of God is usually spurned. The opposition of a spiritual Jezebel will always be encountered. However, final vindication on God's spiritual Carmel has been assured.

The 3½ and 1260 also remind us of the ministry of our Lord. Every day of His three and one half years of witnessing He suffered. He preached, as it were, in sackcloth, because there appeared to be such a small positive response to His revelation of the loving Father in heaven. And as it was for the Head, so it would be for the body—the church. The church too would witness, in a sense, "in sackcloth" because the gains would appear to be so modest when compared with the world's population.

The 3½ also reminds us of the "broken seven" of Daniel 9. Daniel wrote that the Messiah would confirm the covenant for a week of years, a 7, and that in the midst of the "week," after three and one half years, He would die, thus terminating all the animal sacrifices that pointed to Him. Daniel had written that by His sacrifice Jesus would make atonement for iniquity and "bring in everlasting righteousness" (Dan. 9:24). Thus the primary meaning of the numeral 3½ in a book written to point us to Jesus will always be to remind us of His substitutionary life and efficacious death. *Thus 3½, the broken 7, is an apocalyptic symbol of the gospel.* This is best illustrated by the fact that as soon as John writes the book's two central verses, Revelation 12:10, 11, a description of His victory at Calvary, he immediately proceeds to discuss this victory in terms of a 3½ in verses 14 and onward.

THE SACRED NAOS

"I was given a reed like a measuring rod and was told, 'Go and measure the temple of God and the altar, and count the worshipers there. But exclude the outer court; do not measure it, because it has been given to the Gentiles. They will trample on the holy city for 42 months'" (Rev. 11:1, 2).

The Temple in Jerusalem and the altar of burnt offering no longer existed when John wrote these words, so it is safe to assume that these references to the sanctuary are to be understood symbolically.

Measurement can be the prelude to building, but it can also be the prelude to *preservation*.[4] If we accept the meaning of preservation here (as we will in Revelation 21), then it corresponds perfectly with the sealing described in Revelation 7.

But if measuring represents preservation, what is being preserved? In other words, what does the Temple represent? Fredericks pointed out that the word translated "temple" some 70 times in the New Testament is *hieron*. It is the most commonly used word to describe the Temple as a whole. A less frequently used word is *naos*, which often refers to the inner sanctuary or the Most Holy Place. For example, we read that at the time of Jesus' death, the curtain in front of the *naos* was torn by unseen hands. And it is *naos* that John uses in Revelation 11:1.

Interestingly, Paul used *naos* to describe the church as a whole and its individual members when he wrote: "Consequently, you are no longer foreigners and aliens, but fellow citizens with God's people and members of God's household, built on the foundation of the apostles and prophets, with Christ Jesus himself as the chief cornerstone. In him the whole building is joined together and rises to become a holy temple *[naos]* in the Lord" (Eph. 2:19-21).

"Do you not know that your body is a temple *[naos]* of the Holy Spirit, who is in you, whom you have received from God? You are not your own" (1 Cor. 6:19).

Thus the measuring of the Temple can be understood as a symbolic way of saying that God preserves or "seals" His church during the final judgments poured on the wicked prior to Jesus' return. This meaning is essentially the same as the events in the interlude between the sixth and seventh seals.

John then elaborates on the church to make it a trinity of unity. He names temple, altar, and worshipers (Rev. 11:1). According to Paul's description, the symbolic temple includes all believers, and Christ is its foundation.

The mention of the inner temple and the outer court, one measured and one not (that is, one preserved and one not) is rooted in Jewish history and practice. Four courtyards surrounded the Temple in Jerusalem. The innermost corresponded to the original courtyard in the wilderness and became known as the *Court of the Priests,* where they offered sacrifices on the altar of burnt offering and washed their hands and feet in the laver.

The *Court of the Israelites* surrounded the first court. Only male Israelites could enter this area. The third court was reserved for Israel's women, and the fourth bore the title *Court of the Gentiles,* and no Gentile could move closer under the threat of death. With this meticulously observed segregation so intimately understood by Jews and Gentiles of the first century up to A.D. 70, John wrote that the outer court would not be measured, that is, it would not be preserved. It represented Gentiles, or unbelievers, in contrast with the Temple, which represented spiritual Israel. Revelation 11:2 ends with the words that the church would be trampled for 42 months.

The idea of preservation in the inner shrine is also rooted in a well-known experience. When Titus finally breached the walls and entered the city, the Zealots, one of the most dedicated of Jewish sects, vowed they would die before admitting defeat. According to one tradition, they fondly believed that God would never allow a reviled Gentile to enter the sacred rooms of the Temple, so they retreated into those holy places, believing they would be safe. But if that was their belief, it was misplaced, because it is said that they were slaughtered where they hid. The notion of protection in the inner shrine may have been in John's mind as he wrote this vision.

The deadly work of Satan against the Israel of God is described in terms of a 42 (a reminder of Israel's pilgrimage to the Promised Land).

In the setting of the sixth trumpet, this may be understood first as John saying that the opposition will continue clear through to the end of the church's long pilgrimage from the Egypt of this world to heaven. In a secondary quantitative application, it may also be applied to the years A.D. 538 to 1798.

The Mourning Witnesses

"'And I will give power to my two witnesses, and they will prophesy for 1,260 days, clothed in sackcloth.' These are the two olive trees and the two lampstands that stand before the Lord of the earth. If anyone tries to harm them, fire comes from their mouths and devours their enemies. This is how anyone who wants to harm them must die. These men have power to shut up the sky so that it will not rain during the time they are prophesying; and they have power to turn the waters into blood and to strike the earth with every kind of plague as often as they want.

"Now when they have finished their testimony, the beast that comes up from the Abyss will attack them, and overpower and kill them. Their bodies will lie in the street of the great city, which is figuratively called Sodom and Egypt, where also their Lord was crucified. For three and a half days men from every people, tribe, language and nation will gaze on their bodies and refuse them burial. The inhabitants of the earth will gloat over them and will celebrate by sending each other gifts, because these two prophets had tormented those who live on the earth.

"But after the three and a half days a breath of life from God entered them, and they stood on their feet, and terror struck those who saw them. Then they heard a loud voice from heaven saying to them, 'Come up here.' And they went up to heaven in a cloud, while their enemies looked on.

"At that very hour there was a severe earthquake and a tenth of the city collapsed. Seven thousand people were killed in the earthquake, and the survivors were terrified and gave glory to the God of heaven.

"The second woe has passed; the third woe is coming soon" (Rev. 11:3-14).

These verses detail the drama of the two witnesses in imagery that is quite complex. In summary, the two proclaim their message in mourning for 1260 days. They have tremendous power, enough to devour their enemies. When they finish their work, the beast comes from the bottomless pit, kills them, and leaves them unburied for a period of "three and a half." This causes a great celebration on the part of those who despise the witnesses. Then miraculously the witnesses are resurrected and brought up from earth to heaven in a cloud, the earth shakes with a mighty earthquake, 7,000 are killed, and from the remnant of the opposition comes a terrified acknowledgment of God's glory.

We now must identify the witnesses. We begin by seeking Old Testament references on which John could have built this descriptive picture. He gives such obvious clues that it is not difficult to find the source. He says that the witnesses are two olive trees and two lampstands. John began his book by identifying the seven lampstands as the seven churches (Rev. 1:20), and to this we add the words of Zechariah.

In his vision Joshua, the high priest, and Zerubbabel, the governor of Judea, were portrayed as doing the work of the Lord. To the prophet, the angel asked: "What do you see?" He answered: "I see a solid gold lampstand with a bowl at the top and seven lights on it, with seven channels to the lights. Also there are two olive trees by it, one on the right of the bowl and the other on its left" (Zech. 4:2, 3).

John has a slightly different version from Zechariah: the same two olive trees, but two lampstands rather than one. However, the apocalyptic picture is basically the same. In the Old Testament setting the focus is Israel doing God's service, glowing with the light of God's love just as a lamp lightens a dark place, which can be accomplished only by the power of the Holy Spirit, never in the power of humanity. Then too, in Zechariah there is the priest-king image of the church symbolized by Joshua and Zerubbabel.

In Revelation 11 the two witnesses are graphic images of the church that John at the beginning told us Christ had "made . . . to be a kingdom and priests to serve his God" (Rev. 1:6). Bruce asserted that these symbols reveal both the royal and priestly functions of the body of Christ (F. F. Bruce, *The Revelation to John*, p. 649). John later wrote that we shall be *"priests* of God and of Christ and will *reign* with him" (20:6). Thus the two witnesses are first symbols of the church in its joint priest-king functions.

But as we have seen in other visions, there can be more than one level of meaning. The witnesses may also be seen as apt symbols of the two Testaments of Scripture, inspired by the Holy Spirit, and the primary "weapon" to be used by the church. All faith and doctrine must come from the pages of Scripture.

In summary of this introduction: the interlude of Revelation 10 and 11 between the sixth and seventh trumpets contains a backward look at the church's mission since its inception and a forward look to the church's preservation and vindication in the future "time of trouble." It runs parallel to the interlude of the sealing between the sixth and seventh seals, which also had a backward look and a forward look beyond the Second Coming to the saints redeemed in heaven. To this point in Revelation 11 John has used numerous symbols for the church: temple, worshipers, witnesses, lampstands, and olive trees. Such diverse symbolism is the substance of apocalyptic literature.

THE POWER-FILLED WITNESSES

In Revelation 11:5, 6, John reminds us of the tremendous power entrusted to the church in order that she might accomplish her mission. Jesus told the twelve: "I will give you the keys of the kingdom of heaven" (Matt. 16:19). Those who reject the Saviour and harm the church will certainly be sent to the fires of destruction that Jesus described at the end of the Olivet address. John then illustrates the totality of the victory of the church when its mission is complete by reminding us of the victories of the prophets Elijah and Moses. In the days of Elijah drought covered the land for a three-and-a-half-year period, and during the days of Moses in 42 stages God's people were led from Egypt to Canaan in 42 years.

So again the 1260, 42, and 3½ (Rev. 11:2, 3, 11) are *numerical symbols of the preaching of the gospel from Calvary to the Second Advent* despite constant oppression from Satan (as depicted in the trumpets). For this reason, the witnesses are described as doing their work

clothed in sackcloth. Throughout history people suffered Satan's attacks when they gave their testimony for Jesus. During the entire period of the church's mission, it seems that the earth has been littered
with such victims (compare the cry of the fifth seal). Symbolically, it is
as if they had been sentenced to death and not given the benefit of a
decent burial, but rather held up continually to ridicule.

Three stories illustrate this point: the rejection of Lot's entreaties
by the people of Sodom, the oppression of Israel by the Egyptians, and
the refusal of the people of Palestine to accept Jesus during His ministry (see Rev. 11:8, 9).

On the other side of the coin, there is anger among Satan's followers, his pawns (verse 10), because they have heard the gospel, have
been convicted by the Holy Spirit, but have rejected it. This has caused
them to suffer guilt, or "torment" (verse 10).

At the end of the church's long pilgrimage of witnessing in sackcloth (at the end of the seventh trumpet), the church will rise triumphantly to meet Jesus in the air. For many there will be a bodily
resurrection from death. For the sealed ones there will be a symbolic
rising from living under the sentence of death, the change from mor-
tality to immortality. Jesus will call a halt to the great conflict and shout
to His elect: "Come up here" (verse 12). And they will rise, vindicated,
in a cloud of angels, their enemies silenced at last, to gather at the
throne. The same information, although in a far briefer form, was depicted in the corresponding interlude in Revelation 7.

The earthquake described in Revelation 11:13 is probably the same
earthquake described under the seventh bowl. But John gives additional meaning through the qualitative use of different numerals. In
the same verse he states that a tenth of the city (that is, the city of
Babylon) fell. The numeral 10 being the symbol of completeness, a
tenth would indicate that the destruction from the earthquake is only
a mere introduction, and that ultimate (complete) destruction will
come at a future time at the end of the millennium.

In the discussion of the seven bowls, the earthquake is said to split
the city of Babylon into three parts (Rev. 16:19). The reference to a
split trinity would indicate the collapse of the unity Babylon had been

able to forge during the final onslaught of the church under the sixth trumpet. The disunity is further elaborated in Revelation 17:11-17.

The description of 7,000 killed at this time is to be understood qualitatively, but is something of a conundrum. Those who are killed must be the unrepentant, because the remnant of the believers are preserved and give glory to God (Rev. 11:17). If John had said 6,000 were killed, it would have been understood as the complete number of the lost. The introduction of the number 7 is evidently to accent the time factor—the event takes place at the moment when eternal Sabbath rest is about to begin. The 7,000 (7 x 10 x 10 x 10) is probably to remind us of the complete (10) victory of Jesus and the beginning of the eternal Sabbath rest (7).

THE SEVENTH TRUMPET

"The seventh angel sounded his trumpet, and there were loud voices in heaven, which said: 'The kingdom of the world has become the kingdom of our Lord and of his Christ, and he will reign for ever and ever.'

"And the twenty-four elders, who were seated on their thrones before God, fell on their faces and worshiped God, saying: 'We give thanks to you, Lord God Almighty, the One who is and who was, because you have taken your great power and have begun to reign'" (Rev. 11:15-17).

In these words we read a second version of the seventh trumpet. In Revelation 10 the reference to the seventh trumpet indicates the *earthly* perspective of this period, the time the preaching of the gospel is terminated and the return of Jesus hastens without further delay. In Revelation 11 we hear the seventh trumpet sounding from a *heavenly* perspective. At God's throne the announcement is made that the everlasting kingdom of glory is finally established, thus the rejoicing as the 24 elders sing: "We give thanks to you, Lord God Almighty, the One who is and who was, because you have taken your great power and have begun to reign" (verse 17).

JOHN'S CONCLUDING STATEMENT

"'The nations were angry; and your wrath has come. The time has come for judging the dead, and for rewarding your servants the prophets and your saints and those who reverence your name, both small and great—and for destroying those who destroy the earth.'

"Then God's temple in heaven was opened, and within his temple was seen the ark of his covenant. And there came flashes of lightning, rumblings, peals of thunder, an earthquake and a great hailstorm" (verses 18, 19).

Revelation 11 closes with a sequential summary of the key events at the climax of history.

1. The nations were enraged.
2. The time comes for God's wrath to be expressed.
3. The dead are to be judged.
4. And to give rewards to His servants the prophets.
5. And to the saints.
6. And to those who fear His name, small and great.
7. And to destroy those who destroy the earth.

This is not a list of events that transpire at one moment. Rather, it is the sequence of major events that occur during the seventh trumpet.

Verse 19 has two important climaxing thoughts. John refers us back to the temple of God in heaven, where each major vision begins and ends, and he reminds us that the temple is still open, because our Father still extends the invitation for us to come boldly to His throne. Then to ensure that we connect the seventh trumpet with the seventh bowl, John again names lightning, thunder, earthquake, and hail coming from God's throne (cf. Rev. 8:5). *Judgment on God's enemies and vindication for the church have both been guaranteed. This is the great message of Revelation 11.* ●

---

[1] *"Forty-two*, a number which had already been distinguished in Holy Writ as the number of Mansiones or Stationes by which the People of God came to the Land of Promise." "On the number *forty-two*, often signifying in Scripture a time of *trial* leading to *rest*" (Wordsworth, *The New Testament of Our Lord*, vol. 1, p. 5). Again: "The number *forty-two* connects the History of the Christian Church with that of the *Israelitish* Church in the Wilderness. Its stations are enumerated in the book of Numbers, and they are *forty-two* (Num. 33:1-50)" (*ibid.*, vol. 2, p. 221).

[2] Israel had been journeying for nearly two years when the spies returned with their unfavorable report, and the sentence of a further 40-year wandering was pronounced (Num. 14:34).

[3] A precise dating of Jesus' ministry is not possible from the record of the four Gospels. However, John mentions three Passovers (John 2:13; 6:4; 13:1), and he also refers to a "feast of the Jews" (John 5:1), which many commentators believe was a fourth Passover. With His

baptism preceding the first Passover by some months, it is generally believed that the length of Jesus' ministry spanned three and one half years. This belief can find support by the reference to half of a "week" of seven years in Daniel 9:27. At the conclusion of the first half (three and one half years), Gabriel noted that Jesus would "put an end to sin" and "atone for wickedness" (verse 24).

[4] "The action of measuring is one of appropriation and preservation" (Wordsworth, vol. 2, p. 215; cf. Num. 35:5; Jer. 31:39; Hab. 3:6; and Zech. 2:2, which he references). "All true children of God, who worship him in spirit and truth, are measured, that is, protected. They are safeguarded, while the judgments are being inflicted upon the wicked, persecuting world. To be sure, these saints are going to suffer severely, but they will never perish; they are protected against eternal doom" (Hendriksen, *More Than Conquerors*, pp. 153, 154).

OUTLINE

1. Introducing the chapter
   The beginning of the second half of the Apocalypse
   God's ideal plan for the incarnation and ministry of Jesus

2. Birth of the Christian church

3. Satan begins and loses the great conflict

4. The church witnessing to the end

CHAPTER TWELVE

THE WAR HAS BEEN WON

I n a sense everything in Revelation to this point has been an introduction, and all that follows is a conclusion. Revelation 12 is the heart of the book. It details the great controversy in which this world is involved and that has made it the theater of the universe, and in the heart of Revelation 12 is the theme of the entire book. Here we read that Jesus won the war at Calvary (the cross is central in this book) and that His victory is our victory; thus we have nothing to fear.

Revelation is divided into two halves. In *Revelation 12 the second half of the Apocalypse begins.* Hendriksen expressed this view cogently: "Chapter 12 is the beginning . . . of *the second major division of the book.* This major division covers chapters 12-22. It forms a unit. The main characters that arise in opposition to Christ and His church are introduced in chapters 12-14. They are: the dragon, the beast out of the sea, the beast out of the earth, Babylon, and the men that have the mark of the beast. The visions that follow show us what happened to each of these antichristian forces: to those having the mark of the beast, chapters 15, 16; to the harlot Babylon and to the two beasts, chapters 17-19; and, finally, to the dragon, chapters 20-22" (Hendriksen, *More Than Conquerors*, p. 162).

In his Gospel John begins the story of Jesus' life on earth with His baptism. So in the Revelation we read John's *only* account of the poignant story of Jesus' birth.[1]

BIRTH OF THE CHRISTIAN CHURCH

"A great and wondrous sign appeared in heaven: a woman clothed with the sun, with the moon under her feet and a crown of twelve stars on her head. She was pregnant and cried out in pain as she was about to give birth. Then another sign appeared in heaven: an enormous red dragon with seven heads and ten horns and seven crowns on his heads. His tail swept a third of the stars out of the sky and flung them to the earth. The dragon stood in front of the woman who was about to give birth, so that he might devour her child the moment it was born. She gave birth to a son, a male child, who will rule all the nations with an iron scepter. And her child was snatched up to God and to his throne. The woman fled into the desert to a place prepared for her by God, where she might be taken care of for 1,260 days" (Rev. 12:1-6).

Revelation 12 opens with another of John's symbols for the church. This time it is a celestial mother. Of all the book's symbols, this would have been one of the most familiar to John's original readers. The Old Testament often refers to the covenant people of Israel in terms of a bride or wife. Some see the entire Song of Solomon couched in this metaphor. When the nation wandered, the image changed from a faithful to a faithless wife (for example, Eze. 16).

John's picture of the church includes sun, moon, and stars. All three we noted in our discussion of the fourth trumpet, but there they were dimmed to indicate the restraining of the light of the gospel during a period in which little was heard of the Christian faith. But in the vision of Revelation 12, the church is brilliantly endowed with the shining sun, the lustrous moon, and a "coronet of celestial diamonds" (Swete, *The Apocalypse of St. John*, p. 144). In other words, it is about to witness in the full light of the gospel.

John probably means us to see other levels of meaning as well. The church was to witness in the full glory of the New Testament gospel (the sun) as well as the reflected glory of the Old Testament sacrificial system (the moon). In the number 12 we see a reference to the kingdom nature of the organized church, begun with 12 patriarchs in the Old Testament and renewed with 12 apostles in the New.

Then John tells us the exact time frame of the vision's application:

Jesus was about to be born. The event to which the entire Old Testament had pointed was about to become reality.

Momentarily our attention is then turned from earth to heaven, and the dragon is introduced for the first time. This character will occupy a great deal of our attention in future chapters, and John's description is lurid. It had "seven heads and ten horns and seven crowns on his heads" (verse 3). A dragonlike figure is an important part of the Old Testament record, and it symbolizes all that is evil. The psalmist spoke of a dragon and Leviathan (Ps. 74:12-14). Isaiah also included a reference to Leviathan (Isa. 27:1).

Canaanite mythology included a seven-headed serpent named Lotan that personified evil because it fought constantly against good. But it is in Babylonian mythology that we find a bright-red dragon that seems to be remarkably like the dragon John describes in the Apocalypse. Babylon's figure was the dragon of chaos that had been defeated. This seems to be an appropriate reminder of all John wishes to convey. There is no doubt that this dragon represents Satan, because John spells it out beyond doubt: "The great dragon . . . that ancient serpent called the devil, or Satan, who leads the whole world astray" (Rev. 12:9).

John's dragon has seven heads with seven diadems and 10 horns. The 7 indicates that the influence of this monster will last until the church experiences eternal Sabbath rest. In fact, it is his work that delays the beginning of the eternal rest. The 10 horns indicate the apparent completeness of the many battles he wins—so many, in fact, that he seems sovereign of all. In every age Satan has won major successes. There are far more who walk his broad way than the few who walk the narrow way of Jesus. The 10 horns are adopted from Daniel's vision of the monster with 10 horns. A horn is a symbol of power, and blood was smeared on the horns of Israel's altar of burnt offering.

John jumps across the short life span of Jesus (covered in his Gospel and alluded to in Revelation 11) and next depicts Him caught up to God to the throne, where He now rules with a "rod of iron." The iron is taken from the Middle Eastern shepherd's rod. We are familiar with the crook on one end, based on the many pictures we have seen with that feature. It fit around a sheep's or goat's neck. But the other end of the staff, the end that tapped the ground, usually had a brass or iron ferrule. With this the shepherd could fight off an attack.

In the setting of this chapter Jesus rose to heaven to be the champion of His church. He had fought the dragon throughout His life, and the church must now follow in His footsteps and suffer the same attacks He suffered, but He would be with them, guiding, protecting, and sustaining. His iron rod is the pledge of the ultimate strike reserved for those who strike His church.

At Jesus' ascension the church entered its period of witnessing in sackcloth, as we noted in Revelation 11, and God promised to sustain it during the 1260 "days" of persecution. Again, as in chapter 11, the 1260 is primarily qualitative, describing the persecution of the church throughout its entire pilgrimage from the Egypt of this world to the heavenly Promised Land.

SATAN BEGINS AND LOSES THE GREAT CONTROVERSY

"And there was war in heaven. Michael and his angels fought against the dragon, and the dragon and his angels fought back. But he was not strong enough, and they lost their place in heaven. The great dragon was hurled down—that ancient serpent called the devil, or Satan, who leads the whole world astray. He was hurled to the earth, and his angels with him.

"Then I heard a loud voice in heaven say: 'Now have come the salvation and the power and the kingdom of our God, and the authority of his Christ. For the accuser of our brothers, who accuses them before our God day and night, has been hurled down. They overcame him by the blood of the Lamb and by word of their testimony; they did not love their lives so much as to shrink from death. Therefore rejoice, you heavens and you who dwell in them! But woe to the earth and the sea, because the devil has gone down to you! He is filled with fury, because he knows that his time is short'" (Rev. 12:7-12).

Verses 4, 7-12 give us one of the most profound pictures in Scripture of the insidious rebellion that initiated the great controversy that has enveloped our planet for thousands of years. Lucifer challenged Jesus[2] about His position. Lucifer seemed unwilling to occupy a place *under* the Most High. Rather, he wished to be *like* the Most High (Isa. 14:14). The discontent ultimately became an open war that led to the expulsion of Satan and those who sided with him. "His tail swept a third of the stars out of the sky" (Rev. 12:4). The number 3 is a symbol of unity, the broken 3 is a symbol of the disunity Lucifer introduced among the angels, not a percentage of the angels that rebelled.

That was how the conflict began, and the next verses indicate how the conflict ended, how the war was won through "the blood of the Lamb" (verse 11). Fredericks wrote: "In the battle scene it is Michael who takes the offensive action. The dragon puts up a vigorous defense, but his resistance is futile. The earthly reality behind this scene is the incarnation of Christ, His holy life, and substitutionary death on the cross. That this equals Michael's glorious victory highlights the paradox that through apparent weakness and defeat, Christ (and His saints) defeated the dragon (Rev. 5:5, 6; 12:11). It portrays the power of self-sacrificing love conquering the selfish love of power. Christ appeared to 'destroy the devil's work,' but He accomplished this goal only by laying down His own life, and thereby He destroyed 'him who holds the power of death—that is, the devil' (1 John 3:8; Heb. 2:14, NIV).

"God declared His verdict at the cross. Judgment was executed there upon all the sins of the believers and their progenitors. All further activity of divine judgment in the Apocalypse falls only upon those who *refuse* or *lose* a faith relationship with the Lamb" (Fredericks, "A Sequential Study of Revelation 1-14," pp. 266, 267, 265).

It is only in the light of the finished work of the cross that the Revelation can proclaim: "The accuser of our brothers, who accuses them before our God day and night, has been hurled down" (verse 10). The war has been won, and as Christians we live by that victory.

Verses 10, 11 proclaim the victory of Jesus over Satan in their great conflict. These are the central words of Revelation. In John's chiasm, all that precedes builds toward this central certainty, and all that follows emphasizes its truthfulness and details how the last scenes in the drama will play out. The war has been won!

Next John details the believer's overcoming, which is based on the finished work of Jesus on the cross. Any overcoming rests exclusively on this fact of history. Overcoming is often thought of in terms of what the believer does, and approached from that context, there will always be a desperate striving that is never satisfied, a life divorced from peace.

To think of overcoming only in terms of eliminating wrongdoing is a very narrow view. The paradox of the Christian life is that we must ever strive for the ultimate, and we will not be accounted worthy unless we continue that quest, knowing all the time that Jesus' perfect life stands in place of our imperfect lives.

As we become more intimate with Jesus, we see old duties more clearly and discover new duties to accomplish in love for our Lord. Thus there is no point of arrival in this life, no point of full accomplishment, no moment when we can say we have attained, that we have overcome in the ultimate sense, and that we, in ourselves, now equal Jesus' perfect life. Rather, as long as we live we must grow, always trusting in Jesus' overcoming to be the substitute for our imperfect lives. "Therefore rejoice!" It is a great reality that the closer we come to Christ the greater we sense our sinfulness and shortcomings.

THE CHURCH WITNESSING TO THE END

"When the dragon saw that he had been hurled to the earth, he pursued the woman who had given birth to the male child. The woman was given the two wings of a great eagle, so that she might fly to the place prepared for her in the desert, where she would be taken care of for a time, times and half a time, out of the serpent's reach. Then from his mouth the serpent spewed water like a river, to overtake the woman and sweep her away with the torrent. But the earth helped the woman by opening its mouth and swallowing the river that the dragon had spewed out of his mouth. Then the dragon was enraged at the woman and went off to make war against the rest of her offspring—those who obey God's commandments and hold to the testimony of Jesus" (Rev. 12:13-17).

In the last five verses of chapter 12, John returns to the theme of the witness and persecution of the church, which he interrupted to tell the story of the origin and climax of the cosmic war. In this repeat treatment we see another perspective of the same history already covered in the churches, the seals, the trumpets, and the two witnesses: the story of the church in the setting of the conflict between Christ and Satan.

To summarize these final verses: John pictures the church as a woman with two wings of an eagle, who flew into the wilderness where God cared for her in this three-and-a-half period, this "time[one], times [two] and half a time." The serpent poured out a great flood to try to drown the church, but the earth drank up this flood, and the church survived. Enraged, the dragon/serpent plotted a final battle with those who still remained—"the remnant" as the King James Version puts it. They were readily identified because they "obey God's commandments and hold to the testimony of Jesus."

The reference to eagles' wings reminds us of an Old Testament passage in which God told Israel He had taken them out of Egypt on eagles' wings and brought them to Himself (Ex. 19:4; cf. Deut. 32:11). John is reminding the New Testament church that God will lead His people out of spiritual Egypt and safely to spiritual Canaan, a repetition of the triumphant theme we noted in Revelation 11.

It is natural for those of us in the West to think of the desert as a place of danger and death, but for Israel, emancipated from Egypt, the desert became a place of freedom and safety. It was unthinkable for the remnants of the Egyptian army to attack Israel deep in the Sinai desert. Likewise, the assault on believers who chose to live by their convictions during the Middle Ages made it necessary to find a secluded wilderness. There, away from the centers of secular life, they were safe from the serpent's reach (Rev. 12:14).

The reference to Satan's design to sweep the church away "with the torrent" (verse 15) is an obvious reference to the deluge in Noah's day. At that time the wicked were swept away. Jesus referred to this epic in the Olivet address (Matt. 24:38-41). Now Satan is shown attempting to turn the tables, so to speak, and sweep away the church and leave only the host of wicked alive. Through the ages Satan has attempted to sweep away the church with two strategies, attacks from without and attacks from within—physical assaults and moral or doctrinal assaults. We have noted this in the trumpets based upon the second part of the Olivet address. Now John introduces the same theme using the metaphor of a flood. But the strategy failed, for God's earth rallied to the church's aid. No matter where they were forced to flee, God sustained them, and in a literal sense the very remoteness of the believers' hiding places helped them survive and preserve the truths committed to their care.

As in Revelation 11, the persecution of the witnessing church is presented through the numerical symbol 3½. Qualitatively, the broken 7 is a symbol of the gospel that the church so zealously guarded and preached, based on the Calvary event to which John has just given the brightest spotlight in the book's two central verses. In a general sense, it is the entire period between the first and second advents of Jesus, when the church undertakes her long journey from the Egypt of this world to the heavenly Promised Land.

The final verse reminds us that a remnant will survive even to the end. Jesus had asked rhetorically if the Son of man would find faith on the earth when He returned. We are not to expect conversions on a mass scale. But a remnant will be faithful, giving its testimony because they love Jesus more than they love their own lives.

The word "remnant" in the Scriptures is a translation of more than a dozen different Hebrew and Greek words, but always with the sense of what remains, what is left over after war, calamity, or destruction. Time and again during the Old Testament era, it seemed as if Israel's witness might become extinct. Apostasy occurred repeatedly, and attacks were endured times without number, but always a faithful remnant remained. For example, Elijah felt that no one else served God, and he had to be reminded there were thousands who had never worshiped Baal.

Similarly, as the church emerged from the turmoil of the Middle Ages it might have appeared as if the battle had been lost. But a remnant remained, and a remnant will remain even in the last generation during the rigors of the sixth trumpet, at which time they will be sealed for the time of trouble and ascend to heaven without seeing death.

As we use the word today, "remnant" has three dimensions: time, size, and substance. In terms of *time*, we see a remnant come to light when a bolt of cloth is almost exhausted. Just so, the remnant of God's church is mentioned only in the second half of the book, and only twice (Rev. 11:13; 12:17), and on both occasions in descriptions where the "bolt of time" is finally unraveling, that is, in descriptions of the church at the end of time.[3]

Then too, a piece of cloth is called a remnant when only a *small* amount remains—similarly for the church. In the final conflict under the sixth trumpet, there will be victories: the little book of the gospel will be studied and received by some, but not by many. Only a small number will make the hard choice, the choice for Jesus, and experience the joy that comes in that commitment plus the trials that inevitably follow (see Dan. 11, 12; Rev. 10).

And there is the notion of *substance*. The piece of cloth that comes off the bolt and is sold as a remnant is, in point of fact, the first piece of cloth wound onto the bolt. Thus the remnant has a perfect identification with the bolt's origin. This is true also of the church. The remnant of the Lamb has been called to a work of restoration, to look back to Calvary, to look up to Jesus and the truths that He once committed to His disciples. In this way the believers of the last days are to have a faith like those who heard and accepted the words of Jesus and His disciples. John makes it clear that these believers would keep the commandments of God and hold firm to the testimony or teachings of Jesus.

The words of J. H. Sammis capture the essence of the climaxing verse of Revelation 12:

> "Trust and obey,
> For there's no other way
> To be happy in Jesus,
> But to trust and obey." ●

---

[1] John's Gospel begins with a preamble regarding Christ's preexistence (see John 1:1-18).

[2] John refers to Michael in this description. Michael is mentioned only five times in Scripture: Daniel 10:13, 21; 12:1; Jude 9; Revelation 12:7. Jude describes Michael as the "archangel." Souter's Greek lexicon translated this word as "ruler of angels." Paul describes the archangel raising the dead at the Second Advent (1 Thess. 4:16). Daniel describes Michael as the protector of the saints during the final period of earth's distress (Dan. 12:1). All of these references point exclusively to Jesus. Only our Lord rules the angelic host, raises the dead, and assumes the responsibility for the preservation of the saints during earth's last conflict.

[3] The use of the term "remnant" is not exclusively eschatological. At the end of *any* historical period the term could be used to describe the small group of the faithful in contrast with the larger group of the unfaithful (cf. Jer. 23:3; Eze. 11:13; Micah 2:12; Zeph. 3:13; Zech. 8:1-6).

Outline

1. The beast from the sea

2. The beast from the land and the statue

3. Satanic masquerade

CHAPTER THIRTEEN

THE GREAT MASQUERADE

On a visit to New Orleans, my wife and I visited some of the shops near the river, the kind patronized mostly by tourists. Items that seemed to be selling well were the masks used in the annual Mardi Gras celebration. You hold the mask over your face. It is a cover, a camouflage, not reality, the appearance of someone else; but inevitably the real person is still underneath.

This is the tenor of Revelation 13. It is the description of a great masquerade in which Satan attempts to fulfill the dream he once voiced in heaven, that he would be like the Most High. And the lengths to which Satan has gone in this strategy should fill us with a kind of sad awe.

For non-Christians the apocalyptic horses are the best-known symbols of Revelation. For Christians the beast, the antichrist, and his mark are probably the best known. Without hyperbole, millions of books have been sold based on the fears aroused by these symbols. And while admitting that the picture John draws is far from attractive, we can enjoy security now based on the event already completed at Calvary.

THE BEAST FROM THE SEA

"And the dragon stood on the shore of the sea. And I saw a beast coming out of the sea. He had ten horns and seven heads, with ten crowns on his horns, and on each head a blasphemous name. The beast I saw resembled a leopard, but had feet like those of a bear and a mouth like that of a lion. The dragon gave the beast his power and his throne and great authority. One of the heads of the beast seemed to have a fatal wound, but the fatal wound had been healed. The whole world was astonished and followed the beast. Men worshiped the dragon because he had given authority to the beast, and they also worshiped the beast and asked, 'Who is like the beast? Who can make war against him?'

"The beast was given a mouth to utter proud words and blasphemies and to exercise his authority for forty-two months. He opened his mouth to blaspheme God, and to slander his name and his dwelling place and those who live in heaven. He was given power to make war against the saints and to conquer them. And he was given authority over every tribe, people, language and nation. All inhabitants of the earth will worship the beast—all whose names have not been written in the book of life belonging to the Lamb that was slain from the creation of the world.

"He who has an ear, let him hear. If anyone is to go into captivity, into captivity he will go. If anyone is to be killed with the sword, with the sword he will be killed. This calls for patient endurance and faithfulness on the part of the saints" (Rev. 13:1-10).

We have often noted that John borrows imagery from Daniel with which to paint his own apocalyptic pictures. As Revelation 13 opens, we see some more borrowing. The first creature is a composite of the four creatures of Daniel 7. John's creature has a lion's mouth like Daniel's first creature, a bear's feet like Daniel's second creature, the appearance of a leopard like Daniel's third creature, and 10 horns and speaks blasphemies like Daniel's fourth creature. And as a final artistic touch, John's creature has seven crowned heads like the dragon of Revelation 12. But this is not the creature of the previous chapter, because John states that the dragon gave this composite creature its power, throne, and authority.

We should resist the temptation immediately to identify this beast as a symbol of a particularly evil power we know, some monstrous political and/or religious organization in which we see our personal conception of the antichrist. We should first study the parts of the symbolism and then see what they might mean when drawn together.

The first three creatures of Daniel's vision represented Babylon, Persia, and Greece—empires all named or identified in Daniel 8. The fourth creature represented the power of Rome, still some four centuries away from grasping supremacy when Daniel wrote.[1] So we assume that whatever the creature from the sea represents, it incorporates those political powers that ruled the world for a millennium.

Then too, Satan gave this beast his throne, authority, and power. That is, Satan gave his full support to these powers so that he could utilize them. For example, he used *Babylon* to take Judah captive and desolate Jerusalem. Satan used *Persia* in the days of Queen Esther to attempt the annihilation of Israel. He used *Greece* in the days of Antiochus Epiphanes to attempt to destroy the Jewish religion and to kill or sell into slavery 80,000 of Jerusalem's population. Satan used *Rome* to attempt to take Jesus' life at birth and to order His execution some 31 years later. Four decades later Rome was used as the vehicle for the destruction of Jerusalem and the Temple, and the scattering and persecution of the infant Christian church. During the Middle Ages Satan exploited the state church, the Papacy, to prevent the spread of the gospel of faith and the study of the Scriptures, and to persecute those who held biblical truths sacred in opposition to ecclesiastical tradition.

But before Babylon, *Assyria* reigned in the Middle East, and Satan used that political power to take captive the northern kingdom of Israel. Earlier still, *Egypt* ruled much of the world, and Satan used it to enslave the Jews and attempt the systematic demise of the population by ordering the deaths of all male babies.

Satan claims this world as his own. He willingly shares his throne, power, and authority with anyone he can use. While God holds in His hands the ultimate control of all that transpires in the world, Satan does have and does exercise a degree of power that has been all too obvious throughout the tortuous course of history. The power of Satan, how much he has and how he exercises it within the ultimate power of God, is a mystery that we do not fully understand.

That this first creature had precisely seven heads would symbolize the fact that it spans *the entire course of history from the organization of the church until it enters Sabbath rest at Jesus' return*. We have seen this qualitative use of 7 consistently in Revelation. That it had 10 horns (like the dragon of the previous vision) indicates *the apparent completeness of his success*. That the beast is *blasphemous* indicates that its heart is the heart of Lucifer, seeking to be God. This is not to say that every civil and religious power he has used is by nature satanic, but rather that Satan attempts to involve every power on earth to accomplish his purposes. The beast is blasphemous because it seeks to be God, with all the prerogatives and worship accorded God. *This seeking to be God is the most important interpretive clue to the meaning of Revelation 13.*[2]

In the setting of John's previous chapter revealing the great conflict, we would suggest that the beast from the sea represents all powers, civil and religious, that Satan has used to advance his purposes since the organization of the church at the Exodus and down to the Second Advent. It is a 7 power. That is, it stretches through the ages to the dawn of the eternal Sabbath. This is further emphasized by the fact that John uses the expression 42 in connection with its authority, and as we have seen in Revelation 11 and 12 the designations 1260, 42, and 3½ (the broken 7) are all numerical symbols of the church witnessing to the gospel until it reaches the symbolic Canaan and experiences eternal Sabbath rest.

But beyond the qualitative significance, there can be a quantitative application as well. The heads may also be seen to symbolize the most aggressive persecutors by which the church has been oppressed, as detailed above.[3] Most Protestant commentators since the Reformation have applied the biblical principle that a prophetic day represents a solar year. Thus the 3½ (years), 42 (months), and 1260 (days) in their *quantitative* application can be seen to represent a period of 1260 years in the heart of the Christian era, during which there was the most intense persecution and the most abject spiritual darkness (Rev. 13:5; cf. 11:2, 3, 9; 12:6, 14). More than one set of dates have been proposed, but A.D. 538-1798 are the most widely cited.

The power of this creature "to make war against the saints and to conquer them," and his "authority over every tribe, people, language and nation," with the result that it appeared as if "all inhabitants of the earth" were worshiping him (Rev. 13:7, 8), was fatally fulfilled during the Middle Ages. The record has been ably described times without number. The Spanish Inquisition alone would be sufficiently convicting testimony and needs no elaboration here.

Where were the faithful during these centuries? They were still alive, still testifying, small in number, driven into remote areas, but still holding fast to God's Word as they understood it, waiting for the light of the Renaissance and the Reformation to release them to proclaim the gospel worldwide. Apostasy became the mark only of those "whose names have not been written in the book of life belonging *to the Lamb* that was slain" (verse 8).

This brief glimpse of the Lamb is the only relief in an otherwise terrifying chapter. Even in the darkest of situations, we must hold on in faith. As the Holy Spirit says to us through John: "He who has an ear, let him hear" (verse 9) and "This calls for patient endurance and faithfulness on the part of the saints" (verse 10).

The Beast From the Land and the Statue

"Then I saw another beast, coming out of the earth. He had two horns like a lamb, but he spoke like a dragon. He exercised all the authority of the first beast on his behalf, and made the earth and its inhabitants worship the first beast, whose fatal wound had been healed. And he performed great and miraculous signs, even causing fire to come down from heaven to earth in full view of men. Because of the signs he was given power to do on behalf of the first beast, he deceived the inhabitants of the earth. He ordered them to set up an image in honor of the beast who was wounded by the sword and yet lived. He was given power to give breath to the image of the first beast, so that it could speak and cause all who refused to worship the image to be killed. He also forced everyone, small and great, rich and poor, free and slave, to receive a mark on his right hand or on his forehead, so that no one could buy or sell unless he had the mark, which is the name of the beast or the number of his name.

"This calls for wisdom. If anyone has insight, let him calculate the number of the beast, for it is man's number. His number is 666" (verses 11-18).

This second beast comes from the earth rather than from the sea. It looks something like a lamb in that it has lamb's horns, but it is not a lamb because from its mouth comes the evil devising of the dragon. This reminds us of Jesus' warning: "Watch out for false prophets. They come to you in sheep's clothing, but inwardly they are ferocious wolves" (Matt. 7:15). This lamb*like* creature has a miracle-working power reminiscent of Elijah, who called fire down from heaven. This second creature exercises all the authority of the first and tries to coerce the inhabitants of the earth to worship the first beast—the one that had died and been resurrected.

The second creature then promotes the erection of a statue of the first beast. The statue comes to life and commands the worship of the world with the threat of death for the disobedient. It devises a mark that can be placed on hand or forehead to identify those who perform this worship. Those with the mark are free to go about their regular business, but those without it suffer economic boycott. With a final apocalyptic flourish, John tells us the beast has a human number—666.

Most scholars agree that in the main, future events, not present or past events, are portrayed in the last part of the chapter. And whenever attempting to delineate the exact nature of future events, especially those portrayed in symbols, one should move with diffidence. However, the most important truth of this last section of chapter 13 is also the most obvious. From the early chapters John has kept our attention on:

- *the Lamb*, the Lord Jesus, who chose to die for our sins,
- who *ascended to heaven* to sit on the throne surrounded by the four creatures of life,
- and is spontaneously *worshiped by the host of heaven.*

But at the end of history Satan will attempt his most ambitious fraud. His plot is couched in the imagery of:

- a creature who *looks like a lamb,*
- who *rises from the earth*, but not to the throne, and is depicted in the setting of *four wild creatures of death,*

● and is so desperate for the worship he can never merit that he *compels the host of earth to worship him.*

The most important and obvious significance of this part of the vision is the masquerade of the angel who wants to be treated like God, worshiped like God, in fact, be God. He is not the Lamb of the Apocalypse, but a vicious, marauding wolf that tries to look like the Lamb and receive worship like the Lamb. And his work is to be the wily facilitator that generates the worship of the beast from the sea.

Seeking John's intended meaning, we attempt first to identify John's Old Testament precedents; next to understand the meaning of the numerical symbol 666; and finally to integrate the total picture.

The second half of Revelation 13 has two players: a second beast (from the earth rather than from the sea), and a statue of the first beast that comes back to life. If we can use a sports metaphor, the first beast passes the ball to the second beast, who in turn passes it to the statue, which then comes to life and acts like a despot. In other words, despite the changing symbols, Satan, like a coach, is the controlling force of all three. Satan is working through every possible religious, social, and political organization. Thus *it is more important to see the face of Satan peering through all these sinister symbols and developments than to identify the ever-changing cast of characters.*

It is also important to note that in Revelation 13, 14, and 15 John brings together the symbols of *beast, image, and mark or number,* indicating that they are intrinsically linked.

In the third angel's message we read: "If anyone worships the beast and his image and receives his mark . . ." (Rev. 14:9).

In chapter 15 we read about "those who had been victorious over the beast and his image and over the number of his name" (verse 2).

And of the second beast it is said: "He also forced everyone . . . to receive a mark on his right hand or on his forehead, . . . which is the name of the beast or the number of his name" (Rev. 13:16, 17).

To honor one is to honor all, including Satan, who empowers and uses them all.

The image or statue symbol is clearly drawn from the book of Daniel. After the prophet successfully recalled and interpreted the dream God had given the monarch of Babylon (Dan. 2), the king learned he had been symbolized as a head of gold. In Daniel 3 we read that the king ordered the construction of a statue—presumably of himself. This statue had dimensions based on the number 6, that is, 60 cubits high and six cubits wide. We surmise that Nebuchadnezzar disliked a statue with only a head of gold, because it lacked continuity for Babylon, so he made a statue that gleamed gold from head to toe.

The king ordered all people to bow before the statue. Shadrach, Meshach, and Abednego refused, were bound, and thrown into the furnace. The heat of the inferno killed the soldiers who hurled the three into the flames. But the flames did nothing but free the worthies. It burned their ropes, and in those flames they met their Lord.

And as it was, so in some intriguing way it will be. In ways we do not fully understand, there will be another command to worship a symbolic "statue," to worship the fallen angel who wants to be God. Those who refuse this idolatrous act will be threatened with death. But Jesus will be waiting to encourage and protect all who are sentenced. After the close of probation there would be no purpose in any people laying down their lives.

Another obvious Old Testament reference in the chapter is fire being called down from heaven. On Carmel God honored Elijah's worship, and the forces of Baal were destroyed (alluded to in Rev. 11). In Revelation 13 the counterfeit system is depicted as a lamblike creature calling down fire from heaven. But his purpose is deception, and the outcome is his destruction. Only the future will reveal exactly how this symbol is to be fully interpreted.

The number 6, used at the climax of the chapter, is an easily understood symbol. The sixth church, sixth seal, and sixth trumpet have all shown incredible conflict—a falling short of the 7 of rest. To be identified with 6 is to experience conflict without the rest of the Lamb. The beast and his image have the number that identifies ceaseless striving modeled by their leader Satan. Thus 6 is the numerical symbol of the restless lost. Without the Lamb, they can never find rest.

Without a hermeneutic, 666 can lead as far as fertile imagination can devise. Hitler, Nero, and a legion of others have had their names attached to 666. In *War and Peace* Tolstoy depicts Pierre in an interesting search for the meaning of the number 666, which illustrates how, throughout the centuries, the number has been endlessly and foolishly manipulated (see Leo Tolstoy, *War and Peace*, pp. 788, 789).

Historically, Protestants have given Roman equivalents to each letter of the Latin title *Vicarius Filii Dei*, making a total of 666.[4] But following the hermeneutic established at the beginning of this study, it seems more appropriate to see 666 as a symbol of unmitigated, ungodly *restlessness and rebellion*, and a falling short of the Sabbath rest of the Lamb.

In 1851 J. N. Andrews, an American scholar, wrote an article suggesting that the lamblike beast was a symbol of the United States and that its two horns symbolized civil and religious liberty. But this vision says that the second beast will have the voice of a dragon, and someday will be an instrument to do Satan's bidding in the creation of an organization that is the image of the powers Satan has used successfully through the centuries. This image organization will promote economic boycott and a death decree against the people of God. Such an idea is diametrically opposed to the Constitution of the United States and the relevant amendments, although there are precedents. For example, in 1942 during World War II 120,000 Americans of Japanese descent were denied their freedom and interned. But exactly who will be the human instruments to accomplish each of the assaults named in the last verses of Revelation 13, and how this will all transpire, is for the future to unfold. What is perfectly certain, however, is that the members of God's family will be preserved through it all.

SATANIC MASQUERADE

With this general overview of the parts of a remarkable chapter, we look again to see the dominant thrust of it all. Revelation 13 is a portrait of Satan's great masquerade, in which the *entire history of the Lamb is copied.* Satan would like us to see him as a savior with all the power and authority of the Lamb.

We see the first hint of this masquerade in the names of the two contending powers. In the Greek these two names are similar and rhyme. The Lamb is *arnion* and the beast is *thērion*. And from that beginning we see Satan offering himself as a substitute savior with his own plan of "salvation." The contrasts and similarities are found throughout the Apocalypse, but especially in chapter 13.

- John describes Jesus as wearing many diadems and the beast as wearing 10 of them (Rev. 19:12; 13:1).
- The Father gave the Lamb all power, a throne, and authority, as Satan happily gave to the beast his power, throne, and authority (Matt. 23:18; 25:31; Eph. 1:20; John 5:27; Mark 1:22; Matt. 21:23, 24; Rev. 13:2).
- Jesus is the personal representative and the living embodiment of the heavenly Father just as the beast is the personal representative and living embodiment of Satan (Rev. 12:3; 13:1, 2; John 14:8-10).
- Both the Lamb and the beast have horns of power (Rev. 5:6; 13:1).
- Both wield a sword (Rev. 19:15; 13:10; 6:4).
- Both lead their forces into battle (Rev. 9:2-4; 19:11-15).
- Both are called "king" (Rev. 9:11; 19:16).

But perhaps the most remarkable mimicry of all is the beast's attempt to follow the course of Jesus through death, resurrection, ascension, and glorious return.

- Jesus died, and likewise the beast received a "fatal wound" (Rev. 13:3, 12)—not a bad bruise, but death.
- Jesus rose from death, and the beast in a sense rose too, much to the amazement of the "whole earth" (Rev. 13:3).
- The fearless devotion of the apostles to their Master after His resurrection is copied by the beast's followers, who call out, "Who is like the beast? Who can make war against him?" (Rev. 13:4).
- The picture of the Saviour's return in power and great glory (Rev. 1:7) appears to have an attempted imitation in a kind of "fire-fall" (Rev. 13:13), but it could only be a pale imitation of the reality.
- The worshipers of the beast come from every "tribe, people, language and nation" (Rev. 13:7), just as the worshipers of the Lamb come from all nations (Rev. 15:4).

But there are also some stark contrasts.

- While the beast's followers are marked for eternal death, the followers of the Lamb are sealed for eternal life.
- The beast came up from the waters of our planet's sea (Rev. 13:1), while the Lamb came down from heaven's sea of glass (Rev. 15:2).
- For one army, filled with satanic fury, comes defeat. For the other, filled with the Lamb's love, comes victory and vindication.

Satan will go to any lengths to snatch a life and abduct it. And there are no lengths to which the Lamb will not also go in order to snatch a brand from the burning of Satan's fiery empire of insurrection.

And what is the dreaded *mark* that Satan would place on the hands or foreheads of all people? This we will pursue in our next chapter.

How easy it would be to come to the end of the thirteenth chapter of Revelation and be so wide-eyed over beasts, statue, mark, 666, and death decree that we momentarily forget that this is *not* the real subject of our meditation. This is only a mimicry, a masquerade, of the glorious self-sacrificing Lamb. Our eyes must go back to Him. Our hearts must be laid at His feet. And our security must ever be centered on Him.

To read of the beast and the lamblike creature is to read a caricature of the story of the Lamb. The certainty of our vindication is rooted in the past experience of the cross. And there is no better way to end this chapter than singing the praises of the Lamb, who has written our names in His book of life and who was slain from the foundation of the world. ●

---

[1] A sixth-century B.C. writing is assumed.

[2] It is also significant that "creatures of life" in Revelation 4 appear to be parodied by "creatures of death" in Revelation 13.

[3] There is not complete agreement on the identity of the seven heads among those who interpret them as literal powers. Some begin with Assyria; others begin with Babylon and identify the fifth power as the little horn of Daniel 7, the sixth with the best of Revelation 11, and the seventh with the two-horned beast of Revelation 13.

[4] Exegetically, it is problematical to impose Roman numerical equivalents on Latin words.

Outline

1. The last warning

2. The gospel

3. Babylon's fall

4. The worship of the beast

5. A beatitude

6. Grain harvest

7. Grape harvest

CHAPTER FOURTEEN

HARVESTTIME

From Revelation 14 on, the Apocalypse addresses only events of the end-time, and with each successive chapter the picture becomes more narrowly focused, until the Revelation climaxes with the redeemed in the New Jerusalem. The original readers must have received great encouragement from knowing that the end would come, but our generation has the additional benefit of knowing that most of the events pictured in the earlier chapters have been fulfilled and that we can anticipate the imminent fulfillment of these last details.

THE LAST WARNING

One of the greatest lessons of the seven annual feasts of Old Testament Judaism is that God does not bring judgment without warning. Each year the Feast of Trumpets preceded Yom Kippur by 10 days. Warning first, then judgment. Similarly, Lot went from house to house in Sodom before the fireball fell; and Noah proclaimed the unthinkable, the unbelievable, for 120 years before the first black cloud rolled across the sky—always warning before judgment. Jesus poured out His soul to the religious leaders about their ministry and His desire to lead them back to it, but because there was no general receptivity, four decades after their rejection judgment fell on Jerusalem. Each epic is a symbol of the final judgment prior to the creation of the new earth.

The three angels of Revelation 14:6-12 are three messengers—*aggelos* means "messenger." And these three messengers reveal three different aspects of judgment. The first warns of the *inception* of judgment, the second of the *reason* for judgment, and the third of the *execution* of judgment. The final verses of the chapter detail that execution in apocalyptic brush strokes. The description of Jesus reaping the harvest confirms the fact that the events of Revelation 14 are eschatological.*

THE GOSPEL

"Then I saw another angel flying in midair, and he had the eternal gospel to proclaim to those who live on the earth—to every nation, tribe, language and people. He said in a loud voice, 'Fear God and give him glory, because the hour of his judgment has come. Worship him who made the heavens, the earth, the sea and the springs of water'" (Rev. 14:6, 7).

The words of this messenger run parallel to Jesus' words in the Olivet address that the gospel must be preached in all the world before the end can come. The angelic message of Revelation 14:6, 7 consists of five parts, each with its own special significance.

First, we note that the primary thrust of the first angel is to *share the good news*, the eternal gospel made available through Jesus' life, death, and resurrection. It is declared to be eternal because it cannot be changed and still be the gospel. The good news is that Jesus has made the atonement, the once-for-all sacrifice, allowing both His sinless life and His efficacious death to stand in place of ours so that we can be complete in Him.

Second, this gospel must go to *the entire world*. The great missionary movements born in the nineteenth century must see their work completed. It is not enough to send the good news to *many* people—*all* must give their response before probation can close. This constitutes a challenge to each believer to become involved in ministry. The idea of reaching every "nation, tribe, tongue and people" is awesome. Probably the greatest fallacy that has crept into the church is that modern tools such as television and radio will accomplish the work while members sit back to watch and listen.

But each Christian must get involved. The preaching of the gospel is not the work of some abstract entity called *church*. It is the personal responsibility of each one who has become His disciple. Each individual has a responsibility to make a personal, active contribution toward the fulfillment of the gospel commission.

Third, to return to the words of the first angel, we are to *fear God and give Him glory*. "Fear" is an old English word that means "respect," and this meaning is expanded in the second phrase "give God glory," or put God first in everything because this is where an acceptance of the gospel leads. At any hour we can be tempted to put something or someone ahead of God. But if the Christian life means anything, it means putting God first in everything. It means maintaining the commitment despite the many times we fail to maintain the standard. It is easy for us to allow the peripheral to take the place of the central, the optional for the essential.

Fourth, the last clause of the first angel's message is concerned with the Creator. The angel commands us to worship the One who made all things. The language of this part of the first angel's message is taken from the fourth commandment.

"Remember the Sabbath day by keeping it holy. Six days you shall labor and do all your work, but the seventh day is a Sabbath to the Lord your God. . . . For in six days the Lord made the heavens and the earth, the sea, and all that is in them, but he rested on the seventh day" (Ex. 20:8-11).

From earth's first week there has been a memorial of Jesus' creative power. He was the active agent in the creation of the world (John 1:10; 1 Cor. 8:6; Eph. 3:7-9; Col. 1:14-16; Heb. 1:1-3), and His memorial is the weekly Sabbath. As mentioned earlier, after sin entered, the Sabbath also became a symbol of our redemption. By the subtle inference of the number 7, John assures each believer that God's gift is eternal Sabbath rest, in contrast with the fate of each rejecter, which he now proceeds to describe.

Fifth, the announcement is made that *the hour of judgment has struck* on God's clock of universal activities. The proclamation of this hour of judgment began in 1844, the year of the Great Disappointment, which was rooted in the 2300 days of Daniel 8:14. Clearly there must be a reckoning, an investigation, a decision-making process about individuals *prior* to the Second Coming. When Jesus returns He will bring His rewards with Him. Thus, it is self-evident that He knows what reward will be given to each individual prior to His return. For the living, this pre-Advent judgment will take place simultaneously as the solemn declaration is made against the wicked, but in vindication of each believer: "Let him who does wrong continue to do wrong; . . . let him who does right continue to do right" (Rev. 22:11, 12). With this phase of decision-making or declaration completed, Jesus will come and *execute* judgment, or to paraphrase John, He will come and reward each person according to how each has chosen to relate to the invitation of the gospel.

The Theme of Judgment in Revelation

One of the most important themes for John in his Revelation is the theme of judgment. Judgment is referenced in every chapter of the book—as Fredericks has ably established. However, the judgment theme is somewhat covert in the first half of the book; whereas it is *overt* in the second half. Thus the Greek words for judging/judgment *(krisis, krima, krinō)* are to be found only in the second half of the book, with the single exception of Revelation 6:10, where judgment is explicitly stated to be a future action, not a present one. Explicit judgment references occur in each chapter of the Apocalypse from chapters 14 through 20.

One fact is quickly established by reading these judgment passages. In the Apocalypse, judgment is a highly negative activity directed against the wicked, never against the righteous. This stands out starkly when we consider the passages in reverse order. First, in Revelation 20:4, 12 the saved are in heaven judging the lost: "I saw thrones on which were seated those who had been given authority to judge. And I saw the souls of those who had been beheaded because of their testimony for Jesus and because of the word of God. They had not worshiped the beast or his image and had not received his mark on their foreheads or their hands. They came to life and reigned with Christ a thousand years."

"The dead [obviously the wicked, since the righteous are doing the judging] were judged according to what they had done."

Second, in Revelation 19:11 the subjects of the judgment are identified as the beast and his followers. "I saw heaven standing open and there before me was a white horse. . . . With justice he judges and makes war."

Third, Revelation 18:8 states: "Therefore in one day her [Babylon's] plagues will overtake her: death, mourning and famine. She will be consumed by fire, for mighty is the Lord God who judges her."

Fourth, Revelation 17:1 indicates: "And there came one of the seven angels which had the seven vials, and talked with me, saying unto me, Come hither; I will shew unto thee the judgment of the great whore [Babylon] that sitteth upon many waters" (KJV).

Fifth, Revelation 16:5-7 describes one of the seven last plagues: "Then I heard the angel in charge of the waters say: 'You are just in these judgments, you who are and who were, the Holy One, because you have so judged; for they have shed the blood of your saints and prophets, and you have given them blood to drink as they deserve.' And I heard the altar respond: 'Yes, Lord God Almighty, true and just are your judgments [against the wicked].'"

Sixth, in Revelation 15:4 the redeemed stand on the sea of glass and praise God in these words: "Who shall not fear thee, O Lord, and glorify thy name? for thou only art holy: for all nations shall come and worship before thee; for thy judgments are made manifest" (KJV). And immediately John describes the seven last plagues poured on the lost.

Seventh, Revelation 14:6-8 says: "Then I saw another angel flying in midair, and he had the eternal gospel to proclaim to those who live on the earth—to every nation, tribe, language and people. He said in a loud voice, 'Fear God and give him glory, because the hour of his judgment has come. Worship him who made the heavens, the earth, the sea and the springs of water.' A second angel followed and said, 'Fallen! Fallen is Babylon the Great, which made all nations drink the maddening wine of her adulteries.'"

All seven references indicate judgment as an activity directed against *un*believers, never believers. We notice three important points regarding judgment in the chapter 14 reference noted above.

First, the mention of judgment here is in the setting of the preaching of the gospel. The gospel has two things to say about judgment. One is that those who are in Christ never come into judgment in the apocalyptic sense, for they have already passed from death to life. Note three statements of Jesus that John recorded in his Gospel:

"Whoever believes in him is not condemned, but whoever does not believe stands condemned already" (John 3:18).

"My sheep listen to my voice; I know them, and they follow me. I give them eternal life, and they shall never perish; no one can snatch them out of my hand. My Father, who has given them to me, is greater than all; no one can snatch them out of my Father's hand. I and my Father are one" (John 10:27-29).

"I tell you the truth, whoever hears my word and believes him who sent me has eternal life and will not be condemned [krisis, "judgment"]; he has crossed over from death to life" (John 5:24).

This, then, is John's frame of reference as he comes to discuss judgment in the Apocalypse. Believers are completely secure; they have nothing to fear about the judgment.

Second, John's mention of judgment in Revelation 14:6, 7 is followed by a reference to Babylon, "Fallen! Fallen," and a righteous tirade against the beast that works so tirelessly against the righteous. Thus there is the clear indication that the judgment of which John speaks in the first angel's message is addressed to the wicked, not the righteous. John takes great pains to make clear that for the righteous there is only vindication in answer to the prayer for vindication heard under the fifth seal.

Third, the great judgment chapter that seems to have been in John's mind as he wrote the three angels' messages is Daniel 7 (as was also the case in Revelation 4). The judgment of Daniel 7 is not against the righteous, but against the little horn power. It is absolutely in favor of the saints. They are not in any danger, but are exonerated and vindicated. When Daniel sought an explanation of the vision of the four beasts and the little horn, he was told: "This horn was waging war against the saints and defeating them, until the Ancient of Days came and *pronounced judgment in favor of the saints of the Most High*, and the time came when they possessed the kingdom" (Dan. 7:21, 22).

Judgment in both Old and New Testament apocalyptic visions is absolutely *for* the saints, absolutely for their *vindication*. They are never in jeopardy. Judgment is triumphantly against the wicked, consigning them to eternal death on the basis of their choice against God's love and salvation.

Significantly, the last words of Jesus in the Olivet address are about judgment. Jesus pictures a shepherd dividing sheep and goats, saved and lost. Just so, the rewards John highlights throughout his book are only two: life or death, an amplification of the Olivet story.

BABYLON'S FALL

"A second angel followed and said, 'Fallen! Fallen is Babylon the Great, which made all the nations drink the maddening wine of her adulteries'" (Rev. 14:8).

The message of the second angel is the announcement of the fall of Babylon. The language John employs here is clearly drawn from two Old Testament passages. Isaiah said: "Babylon has fallen, has fallen!" (Isa. 21:9). Jeremiah cried: "Babylon was a gold cup in the Lord's hand; she made the whole earth drunk. The nations drank her wine; therefore they have now gone mad" (Jer. 51:7).

This is the first of six uses of the name Babylon in the book, and the word "Babylon" and the number 6 have the same meaning in the Apocalypse: "restlessness," "falling short of Sabbath rest." Babylon is another name for the religious features of the beast of Revelation 11-13, which preaches a false gospel. As Criswell has so ably demonstrated, Revelation 14 is the positive side of the negative story of Revelation 13.

"In chapter 13 is the beast; in chapter 14 is the Lamb, gentle and precious, on Mount Zion. In chapter 13 are the spurious, the counterfeit, and the false. In chapter 14 are the true, the genuine, and the lovely. In chapter 13 is the mark of the beast, and in chapter 14 the mark of God. In chapter 13 is the work of idolatry and the corruption of the earth. In chapter 14 is the worship of the true Lamb of God and the saints' disassociation from the corruption of the world. In chapter 13 are those who go with the beast and the idolaters down into damnation and perdition. In chapter 14 are those who are redeemed from the earth and who are taken into heaven. In chapter 13 are those who follow the beast in all of his ways. In chapter 14 are those who follow the Lamb wherever He goes. In chapter 13 is the number of the beast, 666. . . . In chapter 14 are the one hundred and forty-four thousand" (W. A. Criswell, *Expository Sermons on Revelation*, vol. 4, pp. 137, 138).

Babylon, according to our hermeneutic, suggests a worldwide application of what once occurred literally and locally at the site of the ancient city. Probably, Babylon was built near the ruins of the Tower of Babel. *Babel* means "the gate of God," and the builders planned, in the event of another flood, to reach the gate of heaven through the stairs of that tower.

But they took heaven to be much too low, and their tower much too high, and their efforts much too grand. Their work began on the basis of a lack of faith in God and a misplaced faith in themselves.

Which is a parable about life. The moment we allow our faith in God to slip, we immediately begin to make plans that are self-directed and self-reliant. This is the seedbed for false religion, which always rests on personal effort for redemption. In this way the first two angels' messages are firmly linked together. The first proclaims the true gospel, and the second warns against the false.

The *collapse* of the effort to build Babel's tower is as well known as its *commencement*. God changed the speech of the builders so that they could not communicate with one another, and the ensuing confusion struck a deathblow to the project. Ever since *Babel* has been a synonym for "confusion."

Which also is a parable. To doubt God, to allow oneself to dwell on negative thoughts about God's love and purpose, always ends in spiritual confusion. It is inevitable, as Babel illustrates.

But the more significant factor is that this pattern of behavior, seen at Babel and on through the history of the later city of Babylon, originated with Lucifer. He doubted God's word, and the more he nurtured that doubt, the more he rebelled. According to what we read in

Revelation 12, he finally made a bid for the loyalty of heaven's angels. This caused confusion and split heaven's unity, and those who sided with him were cast out of heaven.

THE WORSHIP OF THE BEAST

"A third angel followed them and said in a loud voice: 'If anyone worships the beast and his image and receives his mark on the forehead or on the hand, he, too, will drink of the wine of God's fury, which has been poured full strength into the cup of his wrath. He will be tormented with burning sulfur in the presence of the holy angels and of the Lamb. And the smoke of their torment rises for ever and ever. There is no rest day or night for those who worship the beast and his image, or for anyone who receives the mark of his name.' This calls for patient endurance on the part of the saints who obey God's commandments and remain faithful to Jesus" (Rev. 14:9-12).

The third angel describes the fate of those who choose the path of disloyalty and disbelief. Those who receive the mark of the beast and worship the beast or his statue that came to life will drink God's undiluted wrath in the seven last bowls. Such people will meet their end in "fire and brimstone" in the presence of the Lamb. And for emphasis, the third angel repeats that this is *only* for those who worship the beast or his image and receive the mark of his name. In other words, every believer is secure.

In Bible times grape juice was the staple beverage. It was common for people to boil fresh grape juice into a syruplike texture and later to mix it with water to make a beverage. Alternatively, wine that had fermented (the Bible calls this "strong drink") was usually broken down substantially (up to 20 parts water to one of wine) virtually to eliminate the alcohol content. These everyday practices seem to be the background for the imagery here.

But the wording is quite strange. Morris explained: "The wine of God's wrath *is poured out without mixture*. The word rendered *poured* really means 'mix,' and it is used of preparing wine for consumption by mixing it with spices, water, or whatever was needed. It is paradoxical to say it is 'mixed without mixing,' but this is John's way of saying that it is not broken down in any way. The wrath of God will be visited on these sinners with no mitigation" (Morris, *The Revelation of St. John*, p. 181).

No verse of Scripture has a more severe warning of the consequences of willfulness and rejection. But the Lamb is in this chapter, even in the midst of the third message. John describes the wicked in the "presence of the Lamb." In chapter 11 we read that rejecters ultimately will give glory to God, so all the world, saved and lost, stand in His presence in this moment of destiny to reap the results of their choices, and all give glory to God.

The imagery of fire and brimstone is drawn from the experience of Sodom and Gomorrah, a compelling reminder of the thoroughness of extermination that comes from God's cleansing fires. Fire destroys; it does not preserve.

At this point we must answer the question raised in Revelation 7 and 13: What are *the seal of God* and *the mark of the beast*?

In this book of symbols, the seal and the mark are symbols of two opposing positions, the one for the saved, the other for the lost.

The apocalyptic seal identifies all who accept Jesus and will be caught up without death to meet Him at His return. The symbolic number of the saved is 12 x 12 x 10 x 10 x 10: the complete kingdom.

The mark identifies the lost, those who have chosen to reject Jesus' substitutionary death. The symbolic number of these restless people is 666. They refuse His works on their behalf, so they must stand in the merits of their own futile works. Such righteousness is as efficacious as filthy rags.

What is it, in the final analysis, that identifies, protects, and preserves a person who will be saved? What marks the one who will be lost? There are several answers to the questions, but most important is *character*. Those who stand secure in Jesus have chosen to place their wills in His hands and to say as He said in Gethsemane, "I choose to follow whatever You want for me." That *attitude* leads to a set of *actions* in harmony with God's will, which in turn develops *a character of submission to Him*. This is the seal of God. It is character that identifies those who belong to Him. *They model their leader, the Lamb.*

Those who follow Satan will model his attitude of rebellion. They disbelieve God's pronouncements and promises, reject His offer of salvation, and work to provide spirituality for themselves. It is this attitude of rebellion and self-sufficiency, first seen in heaven in the mind of Satan and later exemplified in the workers at Babel's tower, that mark individuals for eternal loss. *Such attitudes and actions form a character of rebellion like Satan's.* This character is the mark of the beast, and all marked this way must share his fate in the lake of fire.

And there is an inevitable extension of this issue of character. The decision regarding whom we serve will inevitably find expression in our worship. It is for this reason that both the seal of God and the mark of the beast have been associated with our weekly patterns of worship, referenced in the first angel's message. Character is seen through actions and worship patterns every day, and especially our worship of our Creator-Redeemer on the weekly Sabbath.

The words of Revelation 13:16 now come alive. John warns: "He also forced everyone, small and great, rich and poor, free and slave, to receive a mark on his right hand or on his forehead." These actions are a parody of Deuteronomy: "Hear, O Israel: The Lord our God, the Lord is one. Love the Lord your God with all your heart and with all your soul and with all your strength. These commandments that I give you today are to be upon your hearts. Impress them on your children. Talk about them when you sit at home and when you walk along the road, when you lie down and when you get up. Tie them as symbols on your hands and bind them on your foreheads" (Deut. 6:4-8).

God invites a heart relationship of choice; Satan coerces allegiance. God invites our worship; Satan forces it. God invites His people to take the symbols of their heart/love relationship and place them on their minds and hands; Satan would force allegiance, treating people like branded cattle.

After the announcement of the fate of rejecters, John returns to discuss the accepters, and he notes four characteristics of this group. John states that they *persevered.* They did not give up, no matter how heated the battle. They were *saints.* They always enjoyed a standing of holiness before God because they were clothed in His perfection despite any personal shortcoming. They were *commandmentkeepers.*

They firmly committed themselves to God's standard in all their plans and decisions. And they maintained *faith in Jesus*.

God's people will be known not only by their peace-filled hearts, but by their obedience-committed lives. They are dedicated to the Lamb. They follow the Lamb. They keep His commandments and the faith He lived and proclaimed in Palestine.

A BEATITUDE

"Then I heard a voice from heaven say, 'Write: Blessed are the dead who die in the Lord from now on.' 'Yes,' says the Spirit, 'they will rest from their labor, for their deeds will follow them'" (Rev. 14:13).

This beatitude after the third angel's message seems somewhat out of place at first reading. In the setting of the Second Coming and the rewards of accepters and rejecters, why did John talk about dying in the Lord? Throughout the centuries readers have been comforted with the knowledge that although some perish, some die in the Lord, some become victims in the battle between Christ and Satan, they are secure in the Lamb. The fruit of their sacrifice is an important contribution to the ongoing war. This verse is a commentary on the fifth seal. Some still ask why God does not do something to vindicate the casualties, and here God tells John again that all is under control, the fate of the persecutors will be exactly as defined in the third angel's message, so they have nothing to fear about the final vindication of the cause of the Lamb.

GRAIN HARVEST

"I looked, and there before me was a white cloud, and seated on the cloud was one 'like a son of man' with a crown of gold on his head and a sharp sickle in his hand. Then another angel came out of the temple and called in a loud voice to him who was sitting on the cloud, 'Take your sickle and reap, because the time to reap has come, for the harvest of the earth is ripe.' So he who was seated on the cloud swung his sickle over the earth, and the earth was harvested" (verses 14-16).

The last seven verses of Revelation 14 describe the coming of Jesus and the dividing of the world into the two categories established by the pre-Advent judgment, the saved and the lost. This passage is the direct counterpart of the conclusion of Jesus' Olivet address, in which He described His coming and the dividing of the world into sheep and goats. Although John changes the imagery from sheep and goats to wheat and grapes, references to the Son of man, the dividing, and the fire were all present in Jesus' original speech.

Three angels also figure in this final passage, just as three angels played a major role in the former section. And each of the latter is the counterpart of one of the former. As the first angel of the first trio cries: "The hour of His judgment has come," so the first in the second trio cries: "The hour to reap has come." As the second angel of the first trio announces: "Fallen! Fallen is Babylon the great," so the second of the second trio comes with a sickle to bring fallen Babylon's reward. The third angel of the first trio pours out God's wrath with fire, and the third of the second trio is called the angel with the power of fire.

GRAPE HARVEST

"Another angel came out of the temple in heaven, and he too had a sharp sickle. Still another angel, who had charge of the fire, came from the altar and called in a loud voice to him who had the sharp sickle, 'Take your sharp sickle and gather the clusters of grapes from the earth's vine, because its grapes are ripe.' The angel swung his sickle on the earth, gathered its grapes and threw them into the great winepress of God's wrath. They were trampled in the winepress outside the city, and blood flowed out of the press, rising as high as the horses' bridles for a distance of 1,600 stadia" (verses 17-20).

In this passage describing the execution of judgment, we read first about the vindication of those who have committed their lives to the Lamb. They are reaped with a sickle, like wheat or barley (the grain is not identified). At the Lamb's return the family of God is gathered from this earth.

Then John refers to the harvest of the grapes using Old Testament imagery. Grapes were a symbol of judgment. We read: "In his winepress the Lord has trampled the Virgin Daughter of Judah" (Lam. 1:15).

A Palestinian winepress consisted of two troughs, an upper and a lower, connected by a channel. As the grapes were trampled in the upper, the juice was squeezed out and flowed through the channel into the lower trough. In John's imagery this juice was blood, and it rose to the depth of the bridles of horses and extended a distance of 1,600 furlongs (Rev. 14:20, KJV).

Predictably, the number is qualitative in this symbolic portrayal. Virtually all commentators skip this particular numeral as of unknown significance. Barclay, for example, wrote about his "least unsatisfactory explanation" (The Revelation of John, vol. 2, p. 153). But according to the hermeneutic we are following, the number is simply 4 x 4 x 10 x 10. When God brings down His wrath, it spells "universal, universal, complete, complete." Nothing is spared, nothing left. Every sinner is destroyed by the brightness of Jesus' coming (2 Thess. 2:8). All opposition to the kingdom of God is brought to nothing as the saints are triumphantly taken home and eternal Sabbath rest begins. ●

---

* Revelation 14:1-5 is discussed in chapter 8 of this work.

Outline

1. Introducing Revelation 15, 16
   Jewish ritual is in the background
   An expansion of Revelation 14:9-11
   Repeated visions of the last days
   Differing views of different commentators
   Literal or symbolic?

2. Singing on the sea of glass

3. From the heavenly sanctuary

4. The first bowl—a sore

5. The second bowl—oceans turn to blood

6. The third bowl—rivers turn to blood

7. The fourth bowl—scorching heat

8. The fifth bowl—darkness

9. The sixth bowl—Babylon's fall and Armageddon

10. The seventh bowl—"It is done"

CHAPTER FIFTEEN

POURING OUT THE PLAGUES

The awesome verses of Revelation 16 have been a rich mine of speculation for commentators and an equally rich source of inspiration for novelists. For example, Dostoyevsky seems to have had these words in mind when he penned the last paragraphs of *Crime and Punishment*. Raskolnikov "dreamt that the whole world was ravaged by an unknown and terrible plague that had spread across Europe from the depths of Asia. All except a few chosen ones were doomed to perish. New kinds of germs—microscopic creatures which lodged in the bodies of men—made their appearance. But these creatures were spirits endowed with reason and will. People who became infected with them at once became mad and violent. But never had people considered themselves as wise and as strong in their pursuit of truth as these plague-ridden people. Never had they thought their decisions, their scientific conclusions, and their moral convictions so unshakable or so incontestably right. Whole villages, whole towns and peoples became infected and went mad. They were in a state of constant alarm. They did not understand each other. Each of them believed that the truth only resided in him, and was miserable looking at the others, and smote his breast, wept, and wrung his hands. They did not know whom to put on trial or how to pass judgment; they could not agree what was good or what was evil. They did not know whom to accuse or whom to acquit. Men killed each other in a kind of senseless fury. . . . Fires broke out; famine spread. Wholesale destruction stalked the earth. The pestilence grew and spread farther afield. Only a few people could save themselves in the whole world: those were the pure and chosen ones, destined to start a new race of men and a new life, to renew and purify the earth, but no one had ever seen those people, no one had heard their words or their voices" (Fyodor Dostoyevsky, *Crime and Punishment*, pp. 555, 556).

The Apocalypse begins with letters to seven *churches*, moves to unsealing the seven *seals*, continues with the fanfares of seven *trumpets*, in a long interlude details seven *mystical figures*—woman, dragon, Manchild, Michael, beast from the sea, beast from the land, Lamb (Tenney, *Interpreting Revelation*, p. 38)—and near the climax describes God's wrath being poured from seven *bowls*.

As observed earlier, the Apocalypse is written with *Jewish rituals recognizably in the background,* and to understand this section of the book we should note the basic sequence in Jewish liturgical practice surrounding the daily sacrifice. Following the sacrifice of the lamb came the offering of incense, next the trumpet blast, and then the drink offering. Farrar has reminded us: "The 'bowls,' *phialae,* are libation-bowls. Now the libation, or drink-offering, was poured at the daily sacrifice just after the trumpets had begun to sound, so that by placing bowls in sequence to trumpets St. John maintains the sequence of ritual action which began with the slaughtered Lamb, continued in the incense-offering and passed into the trumpet-blasts. Because the drink-offering had such a position, it was the last ritual act" (Austin Farrar, *The Revelation of St. John the Divine*, p. 174).

Revelation 14 through 17 are intimately connected. In chapter 14 in the third angel's message, we hear God's judgment *announced*. In the seven bowls of chapters 15 and 16 we read details of preliminary judgment *poured* on those who refuse to repent. In chapter 17 we find details of that judgment *executed* on the beast and its rider.

In Revelation 2 through 13 John passes through the *entire course of history* several times, but each time with a different perspective (churches, seals, trumpets, witnesses, woman, beasts). Similarly, beginning with chapter 14, he passes over the sequence of *events of the final days* several times, and on each occasion from a slightly different perspective (chapters 14, 16, 17, 18, 19, 20).

Following our hermeneutic, the majority of John's chapters have posed no major problem in understanding. Some of the more difficult chapters we have already discussed—Revelation 8 through 11. But close behind those visions in terms of the difficulty of understanding come the symbols of the bowls and the millennium, chapters 16 and 20.

Some *historicists* interpret the bowls as events of the French Revolution and the Reformation/Counter-Reformation. *Preterists* apply them to the days of Nero and the fall of the Roman empire. *Futurists* make every symbol literal and predict an ancient style battle on a small plain in Palestine.

In the face of the difficulty experienced by commentators in explaining the seven bowls, we ought to walk cautiously. To begin, there is a clear division, the predictable four/three (or three/four) division, that is evident in the other 7s. The first four bowls are said to fall on the natural world while the last three fall on the unspiritual world. This leads us to consider at least three possible interpretive approaches.

First, we might consider all the plagues to be literal, but that is unlikely in a book of symbols.

Second, we might consider some of the plagues to be literal and others symbolic. For example, some commentators consider the first four to be literal and the last three symbolic. But that constitutes a problem. If we consider the first four literal, then we would have to assume that they will not be universal, because no life could survive more than a few days without drinking water. But can you have God's final wrath on the lost being poured out selectively? It hardly seems likely.

Third, we can consider all seven bowls to be symbolic, which seems probable, based on it being part of an apocalyptic work.

However, in this book the Lamb is the central symbol, and in this vision John details the Lamb's victory over His opposition. Thus there is the strong indication of a gospel connection here that transcends all other meanings based on the fifth of the interpretive principles outlined at the end of chapter 2.

As is the case with all the chapters of the Apocalypse, readers must make their own prayerful decisions. There is no final, definitive answer to some of these questions.

SINGING ON THE SEA OF GLASS

"I saw in heaven another great and marvelous sign: seven angels with the seven last plagues—last, because with them God's wrath is completed. And I saw what looked like a sea of glass mixed with fire and, standing beside the sea, those who had been victorious over the beast and his image and over the number of his name. They held harps given them by God and sang the song of Moses the servant of God and the song of the Lamb: 'Great and marvelous are your deeds, Lord God Almighty. Just and true are your ways, King of the ages. Who will not fear you, O Lord, and bring glory to your name? For you alone are holy. All nations will come and worship before you, for your righteous acts have been revealed'" (Rev. 15:1-4).

Revelation 15 is the bridge between the three angels and the seven bowls. What setting does John choose to detail God's holy wrath? He chooses a familiar Old Testament setting, the liberation of Israel from Egypt, and once again makes it a symbol of the liberation of the new Israel from the Egypt of this world.

The vision begins on a sea of glass mixed with fire, and all those who have gained the victory over the beast, his statue, and the number of his name stand on that sea and sing the song of their deliverance. The mingled crystal and fire are reminiscent of the plague of hail and lightning that fell on Egypt (Ex. 9:23, 24).

The music sung is the Song of Moses, which Israel sang when they had safely traversed the Red Sea (Ex. 15:1-19). But the words John records are a rich mosaic from the psalms (Ps. 86, 92, 98, 111, 139, 145). It is called the Song of Moses because he liberated Israel, guided them safely through a sea of impassable water, and headed them directly to Canaan. However, John does not want us to think only of the Exodus because he adds that this song is the song of both Moses *and the Lamb,* and the experience of literal Israel with Moses is made a symbol of the experience of spiritual Israel and the Lamb. Moses brings a physical exodus; Jesus brings a spiritual exodus. Moses passed through the Red Sea of death; Jesus passed through the tomb of death. Moses struck a rock to provide a stream of life-sustaining water; Jesus is both the rock and the water of life. Moses recorded principles for life; Jesus perfectly lived those principles. Moses built a replica of the tabernacle; Jesus is the high priest in the heavenly tabernacle. Moses brought Israel safely to the borders of the Promised Land; Jesus will soon lead us securely into the heavenly Promised Land. Thus this is the song of Moses and the Lamb.

FROM THE HEAVENLY SANCTUARY

"After this I looked and in heaven the temple, that is, the tabernacle of the Testimony, was opened. Out of the temple came the seven angels with the seven plagues. They were dressed in clean, shining linen and wore golden sashes around their chests. Then one of the four living creatures gave to the seven angels seven golden bowls filled with the wrath of God, who lives for ever and ever. And the temple was filled with smoke from the glory of God and from his power, and no one could enter the temple until the seven plagues of the seven angels were completed" (Rev. 15:5-8).

Before the plagues are poured from their bowls, John pictures heaven's temple filled with the smoke of God's glory. The New Testament abounds with God's invitations to approach Him in His temple without fear. But for a brief time this invitation is suspended. When probation closes, no one can "enter the temple" in the sense of seeking forgiveness, seeking affiliation with the family of God. As Swete has reminded us, this is an allusion to the day of the sanctuary's original dedication in the wilderness when no one, not even Moses, could enter the tabernacle because the glory of the Lord reached such intensity (Ex. 40:35). As we have come to expect, each of the major visions begins and concludes in the temple in heaven, affirming God's sovereignty.

THE FIRST PLAGUE

"Then I heard a loud voice from the temple saying to the seven angels, 'Go, pour out the seven bowls of God's wrath on the earth.'

"The first angel went and poured out his bowl on the land, and ugly and painful sores broke out on the people who had the mark of the beast and worshiped his image" (Rev. 16:1, 2).

If the text is understood literally, the first judgment would be a corrupting sore to match corrupted hearts.

If it is understood symbolically, there is an intriguing clue in the fact that the Greek word for "sore" is used in the Septuagint version of Leviticus 13 to describe the dreaded Old Testament disease of leprosy. With no known cure and believed to be highly contagious, the afflicted were barred from society and lived and died outside their villages or cities.* Those afflicted by the last seven plagues will already have been excluded from the eternal Jerusalem because of their spiritual corruption. They will have been marked for eternal death because of their Satanlike character of rebellion.

THE SECOND PLAGUE

"The second angel poured out his bowl on the sea, and it turned into blood like that of a dead man, and every living thing in the sea died" (verse 3).

If the text is understood literally, then all sea life quickly dies. But if we draw on the Old Testament requirements regarding ritual uncleanness, this plague would instantly remind Jews of the symbolic defilement that came from contact with blood (Lev. 15:19-30).

Thus, if the text is understood symbolically, an ocean of blood is a cosmic figure of the uncleanness of the lost. First, they are declared unclean because of the corrupting sores as lepers, and second, as unclean because of their contact with blood. Therefore, they must die.

It must be injected here that God's holy wrath is an aspect of the gospel that is difficult to understand. This is God's strange act (Isa. 28:21), part of His moral justice. The unrepentant will have been given every opportunity to receive everlasting life, but not only will they reject it; they will cooperate in the most murderous assault on believers. Those who reject the blood of the Lamb will receive the wrath of the Lamb.

The Third Plague

"The third angel poured out his bowl on the rivers and springs of water, and they became blood. Then I heard the angel in charge of the waters say: 'You are just in these judgments, you who are and who were, the Holy One, because you have so judged; for they have shed the blood of your saints and prophets, and you have given them blood to drink as they deserve.'

"And I heard the altar respond: 'Yes, Lord God Almighty, true and just are your judgments'" (Rev. 16:4-7).

Heaven itself confirms the righteousness of this punishment. If the text is understood literally, those who have shed the blood of the saints will be forced to drink literal blood. If it is understood symbolically, those who shed the blood of others must prepare to be slaughtered. Jesus said: "All who draw the sword will die by the sword" (Matt. 26:52).

The Fourth Plague

"The fourth angel poured out his bowl on the sun, and the sun was given power to scorch people with fire. They were seared by the intense heat and they cursed the name of God, who had control over these plagues, but they refused to repent and glorify him" (Rev. 16:8, 9).

This plague brings blasphemy from the lips of the lost. If the passage is understood literally, this plague demonstrates the irrevocable rejection of God by the afflicted. Rather than acknowledge their wickedness, the unrepentant demonstrate their recalcitrance and suffer the most intense sunburn as they bake under the hottest sun. In Revelation 6:15, 16 John described the lost calling for the covering or protection of rocks and mountains.

If the verses are understood symbolically, the plague is highly meaningful. The issue is that every person needs protection, which God has always offered in the person of Jesus Christ and through His righteousness. But when the unrepentant reject the garment of righteousness, they are fully exposed in their unrighteousness and cannot but feel the "heat" of God's presence and punishment.

THE FIFTH PLAGUE

"The fifth angel poured out his bowl on the throne of the beast, and his kingdom was plunged into darkness. Men gnawed their tongues in agony and cursed the God of heaven because of their pains and their sores, but they refused to repent of what they had done" (Rev. 16:10, 11).

The last three plagues fall on the unspiritual world of the beast. God now strikes at the heart of Babylon, at the throne of the beast. In the fifth plague, if the text is understood literally, a dungeonlike darkness covers the earth.

If it is understood symbolically, a spiritual darkness envelops the lost. Helplessness and isolation (like a midnight without the relief of dawn) cause an intensity of pain never before known. Members of Satan's kingdom "gnaw their tongues," as it were, in their emotional pain. In this moment of mental agony, however, they do not acknowledge their sin or the justice of the consequences of which God clearly warned throughout Scripture. The justice of God's judgment could not be better illustrated than through the consistent attitude of the lost. They live in rebellion, and when confronted with the fruit of that rebellion they curse God.

THE SIXTH PLAGUE

"The sixth angel poured out his bowl on the great river Euphrates, and its water was dried up to prepare the way for the kings from the East. Then I saw three evil spirits that looked like frogs; they came out of the mouth of the dragon, out of the mouth of the beast and out of the mouth of the false prophet. They are spirits of demons performing miraculous signs, and they go out to the kings of the whole world, to gather them for the battle on the great day of God Almighty. 'Behold, I come like a thief! Blessed is he who stays awake and keeps his clothes with him, so that he may not go naked and be shamefully exposed.' Then they gathered the kings together to the place that in Hebrew is called Armageddon" (verses 12-16).

John passes through the first five bowls quite briefly and reserves his longest comment for the last two. Similarly, we noted that the first four seals and trumpets were brief compared with the fifth and sixth in each case.

It is in the sixth of the seven last plagues that we see the most intense conflict, and this is common to all the 6s of Revelation. The imagery of the sixth bowl is taken directly from Old Testament history, partially recorded in Daniel. Babylon had taken Judah captive and held them for 70 years. Near the end of that period, the fall of Babylon led to the establishment of the Medo-Persian Empire and decrees that allowed Israel to return home.

The strategy that overturned a world empire and introduced a new world power is the background of Belshazzar's feast, described in Daniel 5. That night while the Babylonian monarch toasted his friends, two kings from the east, Darius and Cyrus, had their armies stationed outside the city's walls. Chaldea assumed that its security could not be breached. But Persian forces dug a channel from the Euphrates River and diverted its water. When the level of the river dropped, under cover of night the soldiers waded up the shallow water and mud, entered the city unopposed, executed the king, and proclaimed a new world empire.

The Euphrates was Babylon's life. It flowed diagonally through the city, nurturing crops and providing water for the population. Without that river, Babylon would have died.

And what was literal and local we understand to be symbolic and worldwide. During the bowls of God's wrath, spiritual Babylon has a life source, the people who are its reality. As that support wanes, Jesus the king appears in the east, or heaven (see comment on Rev. 7:2, pp. 125, 126), to overthrow this Babylon and to announce the establishment of the kingdom of glory.

Next John elaborates the theme of the fall of spiritual Babylon in another way. Revelation 16:13-16 is the same story using different symbols. To begin, John introduces "the false prophet," a title that appears on only three occasions in the Apocalypse.

In His Olivet address Jesus warned: "False prophets will appear and perform great signs and miracles to deceive even the elect" (Matt. 24:24). True prophets tell the truth about God and nurture the elect.

False prophets tell lies about God and, if it is possible, mislead the elect. The false prophet of Revelation 16 is a member of the counterfeit trinity that leads the kingdom of darkness.

The *dragon*, John explained previously, is Satan. The *beast*, we have said, represents all powers through history that have done the work of Satan in oppressing God's people. And to this we add the *false prophet*, religiously oriented powers that have been exposed to the teachings of Jesus and the truths of Scripture and rejected them. They have turned truth into a lie. This is apostate religion at its worst.

The introduction of the imagery of frogs at this point adds a strange dimension that is almost tragic comedy. Barclay has suggested a play on words not apparent in the English rendering. "The word for *spirit* is *pneuma*, and *pneuma* in Greek is also the word for *breath*. To say, therefore, that an evil spirit came out of a man's mouth is the same as to say that an evil breath came out of man's mouth" *(The Revelation of John*, vol. 2, pp. 168, 169).

Wordsworth is exceptionally colorful in his nineteenth-century comment on the frogs, saying: "[They] shun the fresh streams of divine Truth, and dwell in the slime and quagmire of sordid cogitations, false Philosophy and skeptical Science, and Secularism, and speak swelling words, and come forth in the evening of the World's existence, and make it ring with their shrill discord" *(The New Testament of Our Lord*, vol. 2, p. 247).

Here Satan orchestrates the political and religious powers on earth in a last stand against God. With signs and miracles, the people of every nation on earth are solicited, and they are said to be gathered in a place called in Hebrew *Armageddon*.

Armageddon is another of the apocalyptic names that has found its way into secular parlance. And with this secularization have come abundant misunderstandings. Dispensationalists have made Armageddon a battleground in which the world gathers for a final showdown in the great conflict. Such literalism we would reject on the basis of both hermeneutic and common sense. Morris has stated: "No place of this name is known, and the term is surely symbolic. But its meaning is uncertain" *(The Revelation of St. John*, p. 199). Ladd has observed: "The problem is that Megiddo is not a mountain, but a plain" *(A Commentary on the Revelation of John,* p. 216).

Megiddo was also a city with an exceptionally long history. Established at the foot of the Carmel ridge to the northeast, it controlled the Plain of Esdraelon and the roads from Egypt to Syria and Chaldea. Excavations at the site date back to 1903 and the pioneering work of Schumacher, which revealed 20 levels in the tell. The ninth of those levels dates to the time of the Egyptian pharaoh Thutmose III, who took the city in the fifteenth century B.C. He recorded on the walls of the temple at Karnak the details of that battle, history's first detailed record of a battle.

It is in these historical precedents that we see the significance of John's reference to Armageddon. He recalled the literal, local area that saw some of the most decisive and important battles in Israel's history and imbued them with worldwide, symbolic applications. Hendriksen has observed: "Har-Magedon is the symbol of every battle in which, when the need is greatest and believers are oppressed, the Lord suddenly reveals His power in the interest of His distressed people and defeats the enemy. When Sennacharib's one hundred eighty-five thousand are slain by the angel of Jehovah, that is a shadow of the final Har-Magedon" *(More Than Conquerors,* p. 196).

John writes that we are to look to the Hebrew language for the meaning of the word he coined. As Wordsworth has explained: "Armageddon, or Har-magedon, is formed of two Hebrew words; the one . . . har, signifying a Mountain, the other, a cutting to pieces; from . . . gadad, exscidit; and thus it means the Mountain of excision, or of slaughter" *(The New Testament of Our Lord,* vol. 2, p. 248).

With that background, we can better understand what John had in mind by this cryptic verse.

First, it is part of the sixth bowl, and we must not separate it from the other parts of that bowl. What befell the city of Babylon will befall the world under the sixth bowl. Symbolic Babylon will fall when her support forsakes her, and the way will be paved for the establishment of King Jesus' new kingdom of glory.

Armageddon is another way of saying the same thing. The gathering of the "whole world" is involved here, a fact that immediately eliminates any suggestion of a battle on a small plain in Palestine. *They will not gather to fight a physical war. They are united in their resolve to destroy God's faithful followers and therefore will receive God's wrath.* The believers are all sealed, so they are absolutely secure.

THE SEVENTH PLAGUE

"The seventh angel poured out his bowl into the air, and out of the temple came a loud voice from the throne, saying, 'It is done!' Then there came flashes of lightning, rumblings, peals of thunder and a severe earthquake. No earthquake like it has ever occurred since man has been on earth, so tremendous was the quake. The great city split into three parts, and the cities of the nations collapsed. God remembered Babylon the Great and gave her the cup filled with the wine of the fury of his wrath. Every island fled away and the mountains could not be found. From the sky huge hailstones of about a hundred pounds each fell upon men. And they cursed God on account of the plague of hail, because the plague was so terrible" (Rev. 16:17-21).

In the sixth trumpet we read a vivid description of those opposed to God, who are unrepentant to the end and massed to attack God's faithful. But there is no battle. The moment the seventh trumpet sounds, we hear the announcement of victory. Similarly, in the sixth bowl the opposition is massed and unrepentant, but there is no battle.

Then under the seventh bowl there is a planet-enveloping declaration that the war has been won by the Lamb, and the news is stated in a variety of attention-demanding ways. First, there is a shout to the universe, "It is done! It is all over!" Then John names two sets of circumstances involving the number 3. As the angel shouts, "The end has come!" three shattering events are described to give dramatic flourish to the climax. It is reminiscent of the cymbal-clashing, trumpet-blaring, tympani-rolling finale of a Beethoven symphony. *Lightning* illuminates earth's darkened skies, rumbling *thunder* roars from hemisphere to hemisphere, and *an earthquake* shakes every inch of the earth's surface.

Lightning, thunder, and earthquake are all "acts of God" to begin with, and thus, perhaps, are to be understood as literal. These supernatural events bring about the destruction of earth's surface.

Then John adds another trio of events, which, combined with the first trio, make a total of 6—the number of chaos and restlessness for the lost. The final three will be the disappearance of islands, the toppling of mountains, and a hailstorm.

It is difficult to place a line of demarcation in the seven plagues between what John intends us to read symbolically and what he might intend for us to read literally in his description of this vision. But perhaps we do not need to be sure, for it all spells chaos, as "God remembered Babylon the Great and gave her the cup filled with the wine of the fury of his wrath" (verse 19), and at the end of this episode John observes, the "plague was so terrible" (verse 21).

At this point one might think that God would spare John further trials elaborating such chaos. But there is even more that must be said about God's wrath in the last days. In chapter 16 he describes the fate of the unrepentant world, and in chapter 17 he adds the fate of the beast and the great prostitute.

Before we leave this challenging chapter, there is a final, supremely important observation. At the beginning of this study we established the principles by which we would interpret the symbols of the book. One of those principles is the importance of the Lamb as the integrating principle; another is the central position of the cross. The singing of the song of the Lamb introduces the seven bowls. And it is in the experience of the Lamb of God at Calvary that we probably gain our keenest insight into Revelation 16. Clearly, the description of the vision of the plagues is written by John in words that recall his personal memories of the awesome Friday that the Christian world refers to as Good Friday in the Easter season. We must remember that this is a book of symbols, and we must seek constantly for the realities to which those symbols point us.

On that Friday Jesus was taken to Calvary outside the city. In this He was *treated as unclean, a spiritual leper*, as He became sin for us. And as earlier observed, the first plague is a sore, and the Greek word found in the Septuagint version of Leviticus 13 describes the dreaded disease of leprosy.

On that Friday Jesus *shed His blood* from 7 wounds—first on His back from the lacerating scourging at the hands of the Roman soldiers, next on His sacred brow from the sharp points of the thorns pressed onto His head, then from His hands and His feet as the soldiers pounded home the rugged nails, and finally from His side after being pierced by a Roman spear. And the second and third plagues each describe blood.

On that Friday Jesus hung in *the furnace of the wrath of His holy Father* and in submission reverently took upon His lips the name of His Father in the words "My God, why have You forsaken Me?" The fourth plague is the plague of intense heat in which the wicked take on their lips the sacred name of God—but in blasphemy.

On that Friday *darkness* mercifully enveloped the person of the Saviour so long exposed to and reviled by onlookers. The fifth plague is darkness at the seat of the beast.

That Friday all *the demons of Satan* were unleashed in a desperate attempt to deny the victorious death of the sinless Lamb. The sixth plague is the release of the spirits of devils to try to deny the victorious climax of salvation history.

On that Friday an awesome *earthquake* shook Calvary as the earth demonstrated in sympathy with the plight of its Maker. And the final plague includes a great earthquake.

On that Roman cross Jesus died in my place and yours so that we will never have to experience what He already has experienced as our substitute. But those who reject Him will experience the inevitable consequences of sin, and lacking a substitute, they will personally experience God's wrath in the seven last plagues. This is the primary significance of Revelation 16. ●

---

* It cannot be established with certainty that the leprosy of Leviticus 13 was Hansen's disease. It may have been. But it is also true that the same word is used in Exodus 9:10, Deuteronomy 28:35, and Job 2:7 for ulceration that may not have been leprous.

OUTLINE

CHAPTER SIXTEEN

FALL OF
THE HARLOT

The vision of Revelation 17 seems to be a sad reflection of the life and fate of Judas. This disciple had every opportunity to be an outstanding witness for Jesus, but instead he used his place of privilege for traitorous compromise, and his end was sudden death.

INTRODUCING REVELATION 17

Four Visions. In the context of the sixth and seventh trumpets, John shares four visions (a universal view) of the *conquering* people of God (see Rev. 10, 11, 12, and 14). In a similar way, in the context of the sixth and seventh bowls, he gives four visions (a universal view) of the *conquered* people who oppose God (see Rev. 17, 18, 19, and 20).

Throughout the Apocalypse John keeps directing our attention back to Christ, the Lamb. Predictably, the antichrist is the second most important power presented (after all, this is the story of the great conflict between Christ and Satan).

The opposition is portrayed in several guises, including dragon, beast, false prophet, and a woman and a city both of which are called Babylon. After the presentation of the seven bowls, John proceeds to detail the fall of each of these five: the woman Babylon in chapter 17, the city Babylon in chapter 18, the beast and false prophet in chapter 19, and the dragon in chapter 20.

Yom Kippur. John describes these judgments against the back-drop of the annual Jewish feast *Yom Kippur.* On that day anyone who had failed to heed the warning of the Feast of Trumpets would experience the Day of Atonement with sins unforgiven. Such a person would have been cut off from Israel, as will all who come to the final judgment day with sins unforgiven through the blood of the Lamb, Jesus Christ.

As we open Revelation 17 we understand that the vision is an extension of the seven bowls of Revelation 16, because John begins by saying that one of the seven angels with the bowls invited him to see "the punishment of the great prostitute, who sits on many waters" (verse 1).

The description is vivid. This lady offers sexual favors to the kings of the earth, and through them the entire earth gets drunk with the wine of such immorality. The woman lives in a wilderness and rides a scarlet beast that has seven heads, 10 horns, and is filled with blasphemy.

Matching the beast, the woman is dressed in purple and scarlet. Her jewelry includes gold, pearls, and gemstones, and she has a golden cup filled with abominations. On her forehead is the name "Mystery Babylon the Great, the Mother of Prostitutes and of the Abominations of the Earth" (verse 5).

At first reading, the angel's explanation seems as mysterious as the vision. John hears that the beast had an existence, lost its existence, but received it back through a resurrection, and came from the abyss to do its destructive work.

John then repeats almost verbatim the words of Revelation 13:8. (This and several parts of the description link the presentations of Rev. 13-17 together.) The earth was filled with wonder, or admiration, at the beast's resurrection, but those who wondered were individuals whose names had not been written in the Lamb's book of life.

Revelation's Two Women. The characteristics of the harlot in chapter 17 are more meaningful when compared with the characteristics of the pure mother of chapter 12.

The pure woman represents those who:	The harlot represents those who:
Maintain their faith in Jesus	Maintain their faith in self
Believe the gospel	Deny the gospel
Obey God's commandments	Disobey God's commandments

The Harlot Imitates Israel's Priests. The next set of comparisons is based on the ministry of the Old Testament priests in the sanctuary in both their daily and yearly functions. As the lamblike creature sought to mimic the story of the Lamb, so the harlot lives a life in contrasting counterpoint to the priests.

Israel's Priests:	The Harlot:
Dressed in pure white	Dressed in scarlet/purple
Bore the title "Holy"	Bears the title "Harlot"
Walked in gold of holy place	Wears gold/drinks from gold
Offers blood for repentance	Drinks blood/no repentance
Ate flesh of sacrifices	Flesh eaten by kings
Burned sacrifices with fire	Is burned with fire
Sent Azazel into the desert	Lives in the desert

Do the Women Represent Specific Churches? Because the pure mother of Revelation 12 represents the faithful from all communions through the centuries, we would expect the impure mother of Revelation 17 to represent the unfaithful from all communions through the Christian era rather than any particular group or church.

Awaiting the Advents. There is an interesting set of parallels between Jerusalem awaiting Jesus' first coming and Babylon awaiting Jesus' second coming. In Jerusalem lived a literal, local religious body that (1) became more concerned about institutionalism than godliness, (2) rejected the Lamb of God, and (3) finally condemned Him to death.

Likewise, in the last days Babylon, a worldwide body of seemingly religious people, will be more concerned about institutionalism than godliness and will legislate against the minority whose beliefs run counter to common opinion. They will persecute this remnant and pronounce the death sentence on it, doing to the church, the "body," what originally was done to Christ, the "head."

Though Jesus appeared to be fragile, helpless, and unable to protect Himself, through Him God's will was done; so also in the last days the church will appear fragile, helpless, and unable to protect itself, but will hold to the Father's will, be preserved by Him, and be caught up to meet Him at the throne. At the close of probation those who have rejected the Lamb as their substitute will experience in a personal way what Jesus experienced at Calvary in their place. This we noted is the chief message of the seven plagues.

With that introduction we now address the complex and often apparently contradictory aspects of this vision. The chapter is divided into three parts: first is a description of the woman and her mount, second is the explanation of the symbols, and third is the judgment on the harlot.

THE GAUDY HARLOT

"One of the seven angels who had the seven bowls came and said to me, 'Come, I will show you the punishment of the great prostitute, who sits on many waters. With her the kings of the earth committed adultery and the inhabitants of the earth were intoxicated with the wine of her adulteries.' Then the angel carried me away in the Spirit into a desert. There I saw a woman sitting on a scarlet beast that was covered with blasphemous names and had seven heads and ten horns. The woman was dressed in purple and scarlet, and was glittering with gold, precious stones and pearls. She held a golden cup in her hand, filled with abominable things and the filth of her adulteries. This title was written on her forehead:

MYSTERY
BABYLON THE GREAT
THE MOTHER OF PROSTITUTES
AND OF THE ABOMINATIONS OF THE EARTH.

"I saw that the woman was drunk with the blood of the saints, the blood of those who bore testimony to Jesus. When I saw her, I was greatly astonished" (Rev. 17:1-6).

The chapter opens by announcing judgment on the harlot, and the chapter concludes on the same theme. At the beginning John names the chief sin of this woman: she is guilty of immoral association. Some members of the worldwide community that falsely claims to be Christ's body become increasingly evil, until they are "drunk" with ungodliness.

This is a metaphor of the hypnotic attractions of worldly pursuits that are inconsistent with the Christian life. There can be uncanny subtlety about secular attractions. They can appear ever so innocent and offer great pleasure.

Christians should enjoy life, should find pleasure in life, and have a healthy self-esteem because of their acceptance by Jesus. But we do not seek our own will. Rather, we seek God's will and an intimate association with the Lamb. To seek first the kingdom of self and its pleasures stands in contrast with seeking first the kingdom of God and His righteousness. If we follow the wrong course, we ultimately will find ourselves in the wilderness (like Azazel on the Day of Atonement), cut off from spiritual Israel.

After describing the person of the harlot, John adds a brief comment about the beast and uses language that establishes a connection between the beasts of Revelation 12 and 13: the scarlet of the dragon, and the seven heads and 10 horns of the creature from the sea. In the earlier visions the creature speaks blasphemies, but when it is judged, the creature of chapter 17 is said to be "covered with blasphemous names" (verse 3).

There are only two sins that the New Testament specifically calls blasphemy: one is for a person to claim the power to forgive sins, and the other is to make oneself equal with God. It is the second that we note about Lucifer when he openly voiced his intention of being equal with his Maker. And that spirit of independence and self-exaltation has always marked his followers.

It is also important to note that it is the beast that blasphemes, not the woman. She is a professor of faith even though the profession does not find expression in a full commitment to do God's will. Thus both this woman and the false prophet of the sixth bowl are symbols of all who vainly claim to be God's people but without a corresponding commitment.

The description of the woman's gold, pearls, and gemstones, and the royal colors of scarlet and purple, have been mentioned in the comparisons above, but the source of the description of the contents of the gold cup comes from Daniel.

The phrase "abomination of desolation" or its equivalent Jesus used in His Olivet address, and we are never far from those words at any point in the Apocalypse. He identified that phrase as coming from Daniel, where it is used three times, once each in chapters 9, 11, and 12. Daniel's first reference is in the setting of the final judgment. John here uses the phrase in the identical setting—the final judgment. What else can God do to the self-righteous who become "drunk with the blood of the saints, the blood of those who bore testimony to Jesus" (verse 6)?

The woman has a mysterious name written on her forehead (one of the two places the mark of the beast is to be applied), indicating she is both the producer and reproducer of the abominations that have reduced the gospel to nothing in the lives of her followers. The gospel stands for life in the Lamb, acceptance of His righteousness, and a life of service in which He is glorified. The abominations of the harlot promote the growth of self-righteousness, the service of Satan, and the glorification of both.

THE PUZZLING EXPLANATION

"Then the angel said to me: 'Why are you astonished? I will explain to you the mystery of the woman and of the beast she rides, which has the seven heads and ten horns. The beast, which you saw, once was, now is not, and will come up out of the Abyss and go to his destruction. The inhabitants of the earth whose names have not been written in the book of life from the creation of the world will be astonished when they see the beast, because he once was, now is not, and yet will come.

"'This calls for a mind with wisdom. The seven heads are seven hills on which the woman sits. They are also seven kings. Five have fallen, one is, the other has not yet come; but when he does come, he must remain for a little while. The beast who once was, and now is not, is an eighth king. He belongs to the seven and is going to his destruction.

"'The ten horns you saw are ten kings who have not yet received a kingdom, but who for one hour will receive authority as kings along with the beast. They have one purpose and will give their power and authority to the beast'" (verses 7-13).

Because of the complexity of this passage, we will try to summarize it in the simplest language.

The woman sits on a beast with seven heads that are seven mountains that are seven kings: five have fallen, one exists, and one is yet to come to power who will rule for a short time.

The beast is intimately associated with 7, but is an 8, and is doomed to destruction.

The 10 horns are 10 kings who have no kingdom, but receive the authority of kings for "one hour." They are the devotees of the beast and together try unsuccessfully to wage war against the Lamb.

Ultimately, the 10 horns show their hatred of the harlot by stripping her, burning her, and eating her—the specific judgment God placed in their minds.

As stated above, the explanation seems more like a riddle than an explanation. But just as the beast of Revelation 13 mimics Jesus the Lamb, so this impure mother mimics the pure mother of Revelation 12. This observation is an important interpretive key. Now to the detail.

The primary meaning of 7 (heads), as we have observed in each application, qualitatively expresses eternal Sabbath rest, and in this case (like all the 7s) refers to the fact that the beast's power extends throughout the ages to the beginning of eternal Sabbath rest. The numeral 10 (horns) in this setting symbolizes the apparent completeness of the victories of antichrist.

Some expositors also see a quantitative and sequential meaning. The language reminds them of Daniel's four beasts and the prophet's words: "The four great beasts are four kingdoms that will rise" (Dan. 7:17). According to one view, the seven heads or mountains of Revelation 17 represent seven kings or kingdoms, five of which had already come to power and fallen before John's day, one was in power in John's day, and another that would come to power after his demise.

Because of the obvious similarity in the symbols of Revelation 13 and 17, some commentators consider the five powers prior to John's day to be Egypt, Assyria, Babylon, Persia, and Greece; the power of John's day, Imperial Rome; and a power yet future when John wrote— the religiopolitical power of the Papacy of the Middle Ages (see comment in the discussion of Revelation 13). Other commentators identify Babylon, Medo-Persia, Greece, Imperial Rome, and Papal Rome as the first five, as did Daniel. The sixth and seventh powers for these commentators may include France, the United States, or a revived Papacy.

According to a third view, the beast who is, is not, and will later rise is simply a parody on John's description of God, "who is, and who was, and who is to come" (Rev. 1:4). This approach has considerable merit on the basis of the numerous counterfeit approaches sprinkled throughout Revelation 13-17, which we have noted chapter by chapter.

The mention of 8 in the context of the 7 heads is not easy to interpret. Exegetically, 8 cannot refer to "heads," for while "8" is masculine in Greek, "head" is feminine. (In Greek, adjectives have to agree in gender with the words they modify.) Some commentators see 8 as symbolizing "resurrection" because Jesus rose on Sunday, the eighth day—a week (or octave) of 7 plus 1. This suggestion has some support because the beast had a resurrection after its death blow. Alternatively, 8 may also be understood as 2 x 4, that is, an intensified 4 (compare Revelation 9:16 for another number multiplied by 2, indicating intensification), alluding to the apparent universality of the power of Satan in the final days. But John adds that, despite appearances to the contrary, the power "is going to his destruction" (Rev. 17:11).

It is probable that the 10 horns, described as 10 kings, is a qualitative description of the complete support rendered briefly to the beast by the political powers of the earth in the final days of the conflict. Viewed together and interpreted according to the hermeneutic stated at the beginning, the numbers 4 (that is, 2 x 4) and 10 spell *universality* and *completeness*, and that no doubt aptly describes both the anger of the lost toward God and the bowls of God's retribution against the lost.

JUDGMENT

"They will make war against the Lamb, but the Lamb will overcome them because he is Lord of lords and King of kings—and with him will be his called, chosen and faithful followers.'

"Then the angel said to me, 'The waters you saw, where the prostitute sits, are peoples, multitudes, nations and languages. The beast and the ten horns you saw will hate the prostitute. They will bring her to ruin and leave her naked; they will eat her flesh and burn her with fire. For God has put it into their hearts to accomplish his purpose by agreeing to give the beast their power to rule, until God's words are fulfilled. The woman you saw is the great city that rules over the kings of the earth'" (verses 14-18).

The last verses of the chapter detail the judgment executed on the woman. Finally the showdown comes, and these verses expand the sixth and seventh bowls. Here we see another illustration of the principle of repetition and expansion: the last part of the three angels' messages (the fall of Babylon, recorded in chapter 14) is expanded in the pouring out of the bowls (chapter 16). And the last two bowls (Babylon's destruction and Armageddon, chapter 16) are further expanded in the judgment described in chapters 17 and 18.

The sixth bowl recalls the story of the fall of the city of Babylon through the drying up of the river Euphrates, along with the gathering of the world to the battle of God at Armageddon. This same war is depicted in Revelation 17:14. The forces marshaled by Satan will fight through the plagues to the Second Coming, but "the Lamb will overcome them because he is Lord of lords and King of kings—and with him will be his called, chosen and faithful followers" (verse 14).

John comments: "The waters you saw, where the prostitute sits, are peoples, multitudes, nations and languages" (verse 15). The words have two main points of significance. Despite the fact that the chapter began with the harlot sitting on a beast, she is now said to sit on water. John's mention of water reminds us of the sixth bowl, and we recall the water that dried up prior to the fall of the city of the same name—Babylon. A worldwide confederacy of religious and political forces will be gathered against the faithful remnant. The universal dimensions are indicated by a fourfold designation—people, multitudes, nations, and tongues. This chapter is about the battle of the ages that envelops the whole earth and has its effect on the whole universe.

Then John abruptly changes the apocalyptic symbol from water to horns (a biblical metaphor of power), but the focus remains the same—the worldwide liaison between the harlot (the world's apostate religious members and their leaders) and the world's political leaders. In the war between the saved and the lost (the forces loyal to Jesus the Lamb and those opposed to Him), the Lamb is the victor. When members of the religiopolitical federation against Jesus' followers see that their cause is lost, they will despise the harlot and "burn her with fire," a symbol of their anger and despair and continuing rebellion in the face of the Lamb's victory.

With such complex symbolism, we would do well to summarize before we conclude these thoughts on Revelation 17 in preparation for moving into Revelation 18.

The *beast* represents those major powers throughout history that have been used by Satan to accomplish his purposes. These have been mostly political powers. The *harlot* represents religious powers and followers who, believing they are doing God's work, are in fact persecuting His people. This symbol does not represent a single church or denomination. Babylon is seen wherever submission to God's will is rejected.

In the time of the end, particularly during the sixth and seventh bowls, there will be a worldwide federation of religious and political powers that will attempt to identify and destroy the faithful remnant, the people who keep the commandments and maintain their faith in Jesus. Such grandiose plans (which find their genesis in the heart of the angel who wanted to be God) come to nought at *Armageddon*, to use one symbol, or when the *"waters of the Euphrates"* dry up and Babylon falls, to use another. ●

Outline

1. Introduction to Revelation 18
   Rooted in the Old Testament, with references to four cities
   Summary of the chapter
   Seven interpretive clues
   Building an opposition temple
   Certainty of judgment

2. Sodom's fall

3. Babylon's fall

4. Tyre's fall

5. Nineveh's fall

CHAPTER SEVENTEEN

A TALE OF FOUR CITIES

Revelation 17:18 forms a bridge between the vision of the harlot called Babylon in Revelation 17 and the fall of the city called Babylon described in Revelation 18. John writes: "The woman you saw is the great city that rules over the kings of the earth" (Rev. 17:18). Then he immediately launches into a description of the city. Babylon's fall had been *announced* in the three angels' messages, had been introduced in the sixth bowl, and now is fully *detailed* in graphic language for an entire chapter.

INTRODUCING REVELATION 18

In Revelation thus far we have reviewed much of John's apocalyptic version of the Olivet sermon.

- In Jesus' introduction to that address He highlighted the sanctuary—and we find a similar emphasis in the seven churches.
- In the first part of His sermon Jesus detailed signs of His coming—and we read the same emphasis in the seven seals.
- In the second part of the sermon He detailed both physical and spiritual attacks on believers—and we find the same emphasis in the seven trumpets.
- And in the final part of His sermon Jesus judges rejecters and vindicates accepters—and we read the same emphasis in the

seven bowls during which rejecters suffer and accepters are sealed in protection and preservation.

● After Jesus concluded the basic content of His address, He shared several illustrations to bring His hearers to conviction. Following the identical structure, John now introduces several illustrations to bring us to conviction.

"After this I saw another angel coming down from heaven. He had great authority, and the earth was illuminated by his splendor. With a mighty voice he shouted: 'Fallen! Fallen is Babylon the Great! She has become a home for demons and a haunt for every evil spirit, a haunt for every unclean and detestable bird. For all the nations have drunk the maddening wine of her adulteries. The kings of the earth committed adultery with her, and the merchants of the earth grew rich from her excessive luxuries.'

"Then I heard another voice from heaven say: 'Come out of her, my people, so that you will not share in her sins, so that you will not receive any of her plagues; for her sins are piled up to heaven, and God has remembered her crimes. Give back to her as she has given; pay her back double for what she has done. Mix her a double portion from her own cup. Give her as much torture and grief as the glory and luxury she gave herself. In her heart she boasts, "I sit as queen; I am not a widow, and I will never mourn." Therefore in one day her plagues will overtake her: death, mourning and famine. She will be consumed by fire, for mighty is the Lord God who judges her.

"'When the kings of the earth who committed adultery with her and shared her luxury see the smoke of her burning, they will weep and mourn over her. Terrified at her torment, they will stand far off and cry: "Woe! Woe, O great city, O Babylon, city of power! In one hour your doom has come!" The merchants of the earth will weep and mourn over her because no one buys their cargoes any more—cargoes of gold, silver, precious stones and pearls; fine linen, purple, silk and scarlet cloth; every sort of citron wood, and articles of every kind made of ivory, costly wood, bronze, iron and marble; cargoes of cinnamon and spice, of incense, myrrh and frankincense, of wine and olive oil, of fine flour and wheat; cattle and sheep; horses and carriages; and bodies and souls of men.

"'They will say, "The fruit you longed for is gone from you. All your riches and splendor have vanished, never to be recovered." The merchants who sold these things and gained their wealth from her will stand far off, terrified at her torment. They will weep and mourn and cry out: "Woe! Woe, O great city, dressed in fine linen, purple and scarlet, and glittering with gold, precious stones and pearls! In one hour such great wealth has been brought to ruin!"

"'Every sea captain, and all who travel by ship, the sailors, and all who earn their living from the sea, will stand far off. When they see the smoke of her burning, they will exclaim, "Was there ever a city like this great city?" They will throw dust on their heads, and with weeping and mourning cry out: "Woe! Woe, O great city, where all who had ships on the sea became rich through her wealth! In one hour she has been brought to ruin! Rejoice over her, O heaven! Rejoice, saints and apostles and prophets! God has judged her for the way she treated you."'

"Then a mighty angel picked up a boulder the size of a large millstone and threw it into the sea, and said: 'With such violence the great city of Babylon will be thrown down, never to be found again. The music of harpists and musicians, flute players and trumpeters, will never be heard in you again. No workman of any trade will ever be found in you again. The sound of a millstone will never be heard in you again. The light of a lamp will never shine in you again. The voice of bridegroom and bride will never be heard in you again. Your merchants were the world's great men. By your magic spell all the nations were led astray. In her was found the blood of prophets and of the saints and of all who have been killed on the earth'" (Rev. 18:1-24).

Rooted in the Old Testament. As in every chapter, Revelation 18 is rooted in Old Testament material. The general tenor of the chapter is clear in the opening verses, where the second angel's message (Rev. 14:8) is repeated: "Fallen! Fallen is Babylon the Great!" (Rev. 18:2). Thus we would expect to find material drawn from the ancient Chaldean city's collapse. But we discover allusions to three other cities of antiquity as well: Tyre, Sodom, and Nineveh. To gain an insight into the chapter as a whole, we canvass its content in broad sections, then conclude with brief lessons from the four cities.

Summary of the chapter. A powerful angel descends from heaven, illuminates the entire earth, announces Babylon's downfall, and extends the invitation for the Lord's people to exit the city while there is still time.

Babylon's sins include self-gratification, idolatry, and immorality. Plagues are about to fall to give an appropriate reward for such sinful behavior. In the complex symbols of chapter 18, Babylon is still both a city and a woman. *Kings* lament her downfall as they recall the favors they enjoyed in her bedroom. *Merchants* mourn her passing as they recall the great business deals they had been able to arrange through her. And *transportation moguls* lament her passing as they recall the incredible business empires they created hauling merchandise arranged by her connections.

Finally an angel takes a giant rock and throws it into the sea as a symbol of the fall of the city/prostitute. Immediately all the commerce generated by Babylon ceases, all the immoral, idolatrous activities come to an abrupt halt, and Babylon is given the responsibility for all the deaths of all the martyrs in history. Thus finally is answered the cry of the fifth seal, "How long?"

Seven interpretive clues. First, Revelation 18 is an extension of the judgment theme of chapters 14-17. In particular, we note the point to which we have often referred in which *judgment in this book is judgment against the enemies of God and vindication for His people.* John says: "God has judged her for the way she treated you" (verse 20).

Second, as noted above, the opening announcement is identical to the second angel's message of Revelation 14:8, suggesting a common theme in both.

Third, what cheer to the believer to know that God's messenger will illuminate *all the earth* with his announcement! God wants all on earth to know the issues involved and to make a decision for Him. That decision will be revealed through a submissive character. If we choose Satan, a rebellious character will inevitably result.

Fourth, the birds and spirits that come to inhabit Babylon are based on the predictions of Isaiah and Jeremiah concerning the fate of the original city after it was overthrown. What once occurred literally now occurs spiritually. What was local is now worldwide. What once applied to a city now applies to an entire unspiritual worldwide kingdom.[1]

Fifth, the idea of being called out of a city before its fall is based on the Olivet address. Jesus warned of Jerusalem's fall. There would be a sign (the surrounding of the city by an army), and at that sign the people were to flee for their lives, not even stopping to go inside for clothes or supplies. This would introduce a time of severe oppression, so Jesus told His listeners to pray that it would not occur in winter or on the Sabbath.

The incident to which Jesus pointed came with devastating effectiveness. Titus moved his armies around Jerusalem, ready for a siege that he planned would end with Jerusalem's surrender. But before settling the troops into their positions, a message from Rome caused Titus to withdraw the soldiers for a brief time. Those who heeded that sign and its fleeting opportunity escaped with their lives. Those who did not leave immediately were trapped in the city and paid for their foolishness either with their lives or by being sold into slavery.

What happened to Jerusalem literally and locally will happen spiritually and worldwide when another city, Babylon, is about to fall. God would have His people separate themselves now from all that the city represents: a carelessness about God's will, idolatry (in its many and often subtle contemporary forms), and immorality (the sins of the flesh have never been more commonplace and so associated with devastating disease).

Sixth, in an interesting play on the Flood story, John describes the sins of the city as reaching up to heaven. At Babel a tower had been started, which the builders planned would reach heaven.[2] The tower never could reach heaven, but in the following generations the sins of the disbelievers did.

Seventh, the call to pay the city/woman "double for her trouble" causes concern to some Christians. It appears at first reading that God is being vindictive in His judgments, and that hardly seems to square with the Bible's call for justice. Morris commented: "It denotes not revenge but just requital. *Double unto her double* looks for punishment in full measure (cf. Isa. xl. 2). . . . In view of Babylon's fuller culture and enlightenment, a more severe punishment is required. She has mixed a cup for others (so rather than *filled;* the verb is that rendered "poured out" in xiv. 10, . . .). So the voice calls 'mix her a drink of double strength!'" *(The Revelation of St. John,* p. 217).

The lives of those who fall under the spell of this woman reflect the heart of the angel who wanted to be God. The woman is quoted as saying she is a queen and will never be a widow (that is, without male company), and will never be forced into mourning. For such spiritual arrogance that sees all life independent of God, plagues will come in a single day: pestilence, mourning, famine, and fire. This fourfold depiction symbolizes universal judgment and destruction. The reference to fire is drawn from Jesus' Olivet illustration of the sheep and goats. In that place Jesus said that all the goats would find themselves in the "fire prepared for the devil and his angels" (Matt. 25:41).

Opposition temple. In Revelation 18:9-20 we hear the laments of the kings, merchants, and shipowners who have thrived by their association with Babylon's queen. The long list of merchandise, which includes some 30 items, seems at first reading to be a meaningless mix of articles, but Carrington has observed that the list is a catalog of materials required for building a temple and the stores for maintaining it *(The Meaning of the Revelation,* p. 287). If this is right, then the symbol shows that while those in Christ are looking to the heavenly temple, where He sits on the throne, Babylon is bent on building and maintaining its opposition temple, where men and women will come to worship the dragon who wants to be God.

Certainty of judgment. Four times (universality) the chapter includes a reference to the fact that judgment falls at a certain "time" (verses 8, 10, 17, 19). It is reminiscent of the insistent tolling of a church bell announcing the demise of a person. All who have supported and been deceived by Babylon will be consigned to the flames in order that universal praise to God may sound again as it once did.

The last four verses describe this moment of judgment. The city is thrown down "with violence" under the seven bowls, and the city's burial is compared with throwing a boulder into the ocean.

The universality of this judgment is alluded to by two final sets of four: the cessation of music from Babylon's harpists, musicians, flute players, and trumpeters; and recognition that there will be no more tradesmen, sound of millstones, light of lamps, and happy voices of a bride and her groom.

So much for the graphic apocalyptic images in the chapter. But there is another level of meaning suggested by the Old Testament passages quoted, another 4, the ancient cities of Babylon, Tyre, Nineveh, and Sodom. Each city has its own message to apply to universal judgment at the end of time.

SODOM'S FALL

The references to fire and smoke (verses 8, 9, 18) and the insistent cry to get out (verse 4) rekindle the memory of the city that came to its end in fire and smoke. No city in history had such a spectacular end as Sodom. The degree of sinfulness among the inhabitants demanded a dramatic punishment.

And in this city's experience God underscores *the urgency of separating ourselves from un-Christlike practices.*

BABYLON'S FALL

On several occasions we have recalled the experience of Babylon. When Babylon fell, it meant the establishment of a new world empire and the issuing of the decrees that allowed the people to leave the land of their oppression and go home to Jerusalem.

And soon, at the fall of spiritual Babylon, we will hear the decree that we can leave *this land of oppression and go home to the New Jerusalem in God's heaven above.*[3]

TYRE'S FALL

The references to the city of Tyre John borrowed from Ezekiel 26 and 27, and with them he describes what he saw in vision (Rev. 18:3, 11, 15, 17-19, 22). Few cities have been the subject of such specific predictions as Tyre. God warned that Tyre would be attacked by many nations (Eze. 26:3), including Babylon, and that the city would be dumped into the ocean, left as flat as a rock-top, a place where fishing nets would be spread, and never rebuilt.

And just as predicted, it happened. First Babylon attacked, but the city was not destroyed. Later Alexander the Great brought about much of the fulfillment. Just before his attack, the Tyrians sensed imminent danger, and being a seafaring people, they boarded their boats and sailed from their walled city to a small island about a half mile from shore. No doubt they intended to return home as soon as the Greeks withdrew.

But Alexander refused to leave without overcoming these people. He ordered his army to level the mainland city and throw the ruins into the sea to make a causeway from the coast out to the island. In this way the city was destroyed, thrown into the ocean, and the original site left as flat as the top of a rock—as it remains even today.

And in the story of this city we hear the reminder that *when God destroys, it is total and permanent.*

NINEVEH'S FALL

The fourth city is Nineveh, and the words of Nahum 3, quoted in Revelation 18:23, remind us of Jonah's experience. When God entrusted to this man the duty of warning Nineveh of impending judgment, Jonah ran in the opposite direction. On the way west to Tarshish he was thrown overboard, taken by a giant sea creature God had prepared, and deposited safely on the coast—according to tradition, near Sidon, south of modern Beirut. After that miraculous intervention, Jonah decided to obey God, and he set off for the ill-fated city. There he announced with conviction that Nineveh had just 40 days to repent or the city's history would end. In response the city repented, and God granted a reprieve.

The story of this city reminds us that *God is not willing that any of us should perish and that He will do anything to bring us to repentance and eternal security.*

Revelation 18 is filled with stories of pathos and urgency. John utilizes many illustrations to woo us to the side of King Jesus and to help us voice a commitment that will make life meaningful now and the future secure. It is like reading the stories of Matthew 25 all over again, but an apocalyptic version. This is Jesus' appeal, His words, His wisdom. And as we hear His voice pleading for us to distance ourselves from all that the world offers, He waits for our response. ●

---

[1] It is interesting to note that the ancient city states were, in reality, religiopolitical kingdoms. Empires based in a city like Babylon illuminate the symbolism John utilizes here.

[2] The builders of Babylon also boasted buildings that reached heaven. The ziggurat upon which the temple to Marduk was built (the god who supposedly defeated YHWH) illustrated Babylon's religious pride and arrogance. The elevated palace rooftop from which Nebuchadnezzar boasted that he had built "this great city" symbolizes the personal pride and arrogance of Babylon.

[3] John draws heavily on Isaiah 47 for his description of the fall of spiritual Babylon he saw in vision.

Outline

1. Introduction to Revelation 19
   Judgment in the light of Calvary

2. Hallelujah chorus

3. Love feast

4. Alternate feast

CHAPTER EIGHTEEN

WEDDING BELLS AND DEATH KNELLS

All the judgments of Revelation 14-20 (and that includes the plagues of chapter 16) must be viewed through the prism of Calvary. We must never forget Jesus' agony, humiliation, unjust trials and brutal crucifixion, spilled blood, horrendous pain, and the weight of the sins of the world that He bore. And all the while He kept thinking of others and their needs. There was the thief who declared his faith and received the assurance of a place in Paradise, and His mother, distraught and lonely, whom He handed into the care of the one disciple who would not only have the will to care for her, but the length of life to do so.

The judgments at the end of the Apocalypse are the climax of the great conflict in which Satan has torn apart this once perfect creation, maligned God's name and character, and sought to snare every penitent. A universe once united has been shattered. A peace once enjoyed has evaporated. A joy once the rule has become the exception. What can God do to re-create a peaceful, joy-filled creation? Systematically, He must give every person an opportunity to see the issues for what they are, to make a response, and to accept the consequences of that choice, be it life or death.

The terror-filled chapters we have been studying are the inevitable consequence of an unhurried course of events. After God has given the invitations, extended the opportunities, and waited patiently for a response, He gives Paradise to the accepters and judgment to the rejecters.

HALLELUJAHS

"After this I heard what sounded like the roar of a great multitude in heaven shouting: 'Hallelujah! Salvation and glory and power belong to our God, for true and just are his judgments. He has condemned the great prostitute who corrupted the earth by her adulteries. He has avenged on her the blood of his servants.' And again they shouted: 'Hallelujah! The smoke from her goes up for ever and ever.'

"The twenty-four elders and the four living creatures fell down and worshiped God, who was seated on the throne. And they cried: 'Amen, Hallelujah!' Then a voice came from the throne, saying: 'Praise our God, all you his servants, you who fear him, both small and great!'

"Then I heard what sounded like a great multitude, like the roar of rushing waters and like loud peals of thunder, shouting: 'Hallelujah! For our Lord God Almighty reigns'" (Rev. 19:1-6).

We have become accustomed to John moving abruptly from earthly to heavenly scenes, and this is the case again between chapters 18 and 19. As this vision opens, John describes what he saw and heard in heaven. And the scenes at God's throne are stupendous. There is the sound of a universal hallelujah chorus, indicated by the fourfold use of hallelujah. Barclay observed that the word *hallelujah* literally means "Praise Yahweh" and comes from two Hebrew words, *halal*, which means "to praise," and *Yah*, which is the abbreviated name of God. Although hallelujah occurs only here in the whole Bible, it frequently occurs in a translated form. Psalm 113-118, called the *Hallel*, which means the "Praise of God," was learned by every Jewish boy. When *hallelujah* occurs in the Old Testament, it is translated "Praise the Lord," but in Revelation 19 the transliterated Greek form is retained (Barclay, *The Revelation of John*, vol. 2, p. 218).

One aspect of the hallelujahs is a little difficult to understand. At first reading it seems as if God is rejoicing over the destruction of the wicked, and this runs counter to all we know and believe about God.

"Hallelujah! The smoke from her goes up for ever and ever" (verse 3) is the message that fills heaven. Erdman pondered these thoughts and offered this explanation: "This is a moral universe. It would be impossible to believe that vice and virtue have the same reward, and that crime and cruelty and hate reach the same goal as innocence and sympathy and love. 'The wages of sin is death.' It cannot be otherwise. Heaven rejoices, not in the sufferings of men, but in the destruction of evil. Those who identify themselves with the life of Babylon must inevitably share her fate" *(The Revelation of John*, p. 137).

After the assurance that justice has been done, the second hallelujah repeats a phrase from the third angel's message. The smoke of Babylon's funeral pyre ascends for ever (Rev. 19:3; cf. 14:11). The phrase is repeated again in slightly different words in the description of the fate of the devil at the close of the millennium (Rev. 20:10).

Does this mean there will be a billowing smokestack for eternity, a reminder of the fate of those who rebel against God? Will the wicked be slowly burned, but not consumed, for ever and ever? The phrase "for ever and ever" (or "for ever") was sometimes employed by the Hebrews in ways quite divergent to Westerners. To us it means "time without end," but not necessarily so in the East. You can catch various meanings of this phrase in the Old Testament.

When Hannah brought her child Samuel to the tabernacle, she intended he should spend his life in the service of God in His holy sanctuary. She left him to serve God "for ever" (1 Sam. 1:22, KJV). The obvious meaning of the expression in that setting is "as long as life lasts." And Samuel served God all his life. To the Hebrew mind that meant "for ever."

Jonah described his experience in the sea creature as lasting "for ever" (Jonah 2:6, KJV). According to Jesus, it was three days and three nights. It must have seemed like eternity to the runaway prophet, but he remained confined in that cavernous stomach only as long as it took him to decide to cooperate with God's purpose. You see an incredible change after the sea creature dropped Jonah off on the beach: he quickly washed himself and headed for Nineveh, Tarshish now at his back. In this case the phrase simply means "until

God's purpose has been accomplished." And in Jonah's case that took a very short time, maybe 72 hours, but to the Hebrew mind that was "for ever."

The third meaning of the phrase is the one with which we associate the word "eternity," that is, time without end.

Whenever we read "for ever" in Scripture, we must seek to understand which of the three meanings applies. In the case of the words in Revelation describing the fate of the wicked, it would appear there are two ideas, both "as long as life lasts" and "until God's purpose has been accomplished." Fire does not preserve; it destroys. The smoke of the fires of that final hell will spiral toward heaven just as long as there is something to burn. Then the fires will go out, and as we read in Revelation 21, God will re-create the earth, restoring it to Edenic perfection.

The third of the hallelujahs celebrates the redeemed, all those who have developed characters of submission to God's will. The fourth celebrates the eternal reign of our loving God.

As we read the four hallelujahs, we note a progression. In the first there is a celebration of salvation that comes from God. This is followed by the assertion that all which has happened has been a fulfillment of the promise to avenge the blood of the martyrs recorded in the fifth seal (Rev. 19:2; cf. 6:10).

Love Feast

"'Let us rejoice and be glad and give him glory! For the wedding of the Lamb has come, and his bride has made herself ready. Fine linen, bright and clean, was given her to wear.' (Fine linen stands for the righteous acts of the saints.)

"Then the angel said to me, 'Write: "Blessed are those who are invited to the wedding supper of the Lamb!"' And he added, 'These are the true words of God.'

"At this I fell at his feet to worship him. But he said to me, 'Do not do it! I am a fellow servant with you and with your brothers who hold to the testimony of Jesus. Worship God! For the testimony of Jesus is the spirit of prophecy'" (Rev. 19:7-10).

The second part of Revelation 19 is devoted to the story of the great wedding feast in heaven, where the Lamb and the redeemed are united at the beginning of an eternal love feast. The passage is brief and remarkable because John does not describe the wedding feast, but merely announces it. The imagery is based on Middle Eastern custom and is incorporated in the Apocalypse on the basis of the wedding illustration Jesus used in His Olivet address, the parable of the virgins invited to the wedding (Matt. 25:1-13). In the words of John: "Blessed are those who are invited to the marriage supper of the Lamb" (Rev. 19:9). This is the fourth of the seven apocalyptic beatitudes.

Few exegetes have expressed the basis and application of Middle Eastern marriage custom in this passage as well as Hendriksen. He observed that the *betrothal* was taken more seriously than a Western "engagement." In betrothal, the terms of the marriage were spelled out in the presence of witnesses, and from that day groom and bride were legally husband and wife. But there was an *interval* between betrothal and the wedding feast, during which the bride's father paid the dowry. When those financial arrangements were completed, the way was paved for the *procession,* in which the groom came and received his bride from her home and in a procession took her to his home (or the home of his parents) for the wedding supper.

Similarly, the church was betrothed to Christ, and He paid the dowry with His blood. Then began an important interval of separation during which the bride prepares herself for the wedding supper. In the language of Revelation, she dresses in fine linen, her righteous acts. Soon the interval will be over, and the bridegroom will come and receive the bride, the church, and conduct her in a great procession of angels to the Father's house for the wedding supper celebration (see Hendriksen, *More Than Conquerors*, pp. 215, 216).

Three expressions in the wedding passage merit additional comment: "fine linen," "bride," and "the spirit of prophecy." In each case the meaning may not be immediately clear and probably should be viewed from more than one perspective.

Jesus' parable of the wedding garment (Matt. 22:1-14) illustrates the necessity of our accepting what is frequently referred to as "the robe of Christ's righteousness." We can offer Jesus nothing to merit His righteousness. Our salvation is entirely at His instigation and by His substitution.

The place of works in the Christian life and their part in God's evaluation of His saints are often misunderstood. Paul addresses this issue, in part, in Galatians. He points out that if a person looks to works or deeds of the law for salvation, all will be lost: "All who rely on observing the law are under a curse, for it is written: 'Cursed is everyone who does not continue to do everything written in the Book of the Law.' Clearly no one is justified before God by the law, because, 'The righteous will live by faith'" (Gal. 3:10, 11).

We assume that John is not contradicting Paul on this issue, so we must discover why the white linen the bride is wearing at the heavenly wedding banquet is called "the righteous acts of the saints" (Rev. 19:8). Ladd has captured an important aspect of the significance of the expression: "The fine linen of the saints consists of the decree of justification of God for believers" (*A Commentary on the Revelation of St. John*, p. 249). Christ's death stands in place of our death. Christ's righteous life stands in place of our unrighteous lives. The decree of justification makes His acts our acts just as if we had done them and demonstrated a life of perfection. We can never add *anything* to the gift of our salvation.

In addition, our ministry to others, utilizing our spiritual gifts, also constitutes "the righteous acts of the saints," but never to merit salvation, only as evidence of its accomplished fact. The Olivet sermon climaxes with Jesus dividing the sheep and the goats *on the evidence of a ministry of service to others or the lack of it.*

There also seems to be some confusion between who is the bride and who are the guests in the beatitude of Revelation 19:9. If the church is the bride, who are the guests? And if the saints are the guests, who is the bride? Ladd explained with a reminder of the apocalyptic license in such figures: "Jesus used the wedding motif to represent His relationship to His disciples in both its present and future aspects. He asserted that He was the bridegroom come to His people. 'Can the wedding guests fast while the bridegroom is with them?'

(Mark 2:19, RSV). The fact that His disciples are here viewed as wedding guests rather than the bride is because of the flexible character of parabolic language. If this language is to be literally pressed, there is no bride—only the groom and the guests" *(ibid.,* p. 247).

The third issue in the wedding passage concerns "the testimony of Jesus," which John explains is "the spirit of prophecy." John refers to the testimony of Jesus on several occasions in his book (1:2, 9; 12:17; 19:10 [twice]; 20:4). And because the first use of an expression in a biblical work is often normative, the first use of the expression "the testimony of Jesus" in Revelation is worthy of special note.

The verse speaks of both "the word of God" and "the testimony of Jesus." Kenneth Strand has suggested that the "word of God" is a synonym for the Old Testament and the "testimony of Jesus" for the New. According to this view, an angel came to John who gives his witness to the angelic communication based on both the Old Testament Scriptures (in which he was thoroughly versed as we can judge by the vast scope of the Old Testament references to which he alludes) and the New Testament (which had been written by the time the Revelation was concluded).

Thus, based on John's first use of this expression, we could think of the testimony of Jesus as the collation of manuscripts that would later be called the New Testament and which was a vital and influential reality in John's day.

Viewed from this perspective, the second use of the phrase, in Revelation 1:9, reveals that John's plight in being sent to the salt mines of Patmos was rooted in his devotion to the Old and New Testament Scriptures, which all witness to Jesus. The saints had an unswerving devotion to the Christ of these Scriptures and the truths of these Scriptures even if it meant giving up their lives. That is the significance of the cry under the fifth seal. Often those who faithfully witnessed found themselves martyrs in the cause. The same idea is to be found in the last reference to the testimony (or witness, it is the same word in Greek) in Revelation 20:4, where the saints judge the lost. There they are described as those who became martyrs because of "the testimony of Jesus."

It is important to canvass John's use of this term throughout his book before coming to a conclusion about its meaning in Revelation 19. Believers throughout history have been committed to the Word and the Testimony, or the Torah and the Testimony, or the Commandments and the Testimony. As LaRondelle has pointed out, the testimony of Jesus is not a body of literature exclusive to the modern era; it was extant at the birth of the New Testament church among the disciples who faithfully followed the Old Testament and the truths or testimony they had received from the lips of Jesus, truths recorded and expanded in the New Testament books.

John's equating of "the testimony of Jesus" with "the spirit of prophecy" highlights the Testimony's divine origin and authorship. The Holy Spirit breathed the thoughts of all Scripture to the prophets, who were His penmen. Thus He is the originator of this testimony to Christ just as He was the originator of the Word of God. "Prophecy" in this setting is not the prediction of future events, although it may include that. Its use is much broader and has the same meaning as in 2 Peter 1:21: "For prophecy never had its origin in the will of man, but men spoke from God as they were carried along by the Holy Spirit." In Revelation 19:10 John asserts that the testimony of Jesus is divine prophecy that shines it reassuring light equally on the past, the present, and the future.

Barclay has an additional point to make on this important phrase, which expands it even further: "(i) It can mean *the witness which the Christian bears to Jesus Christ.* That is the way in which Henry B. Swete takes it. He says: 'The possession of the prophetic spirit, which makes a true prophet, shows itself in a life of witness to Jesus, which perpetuates His witness to the Father and to Himself.' That is to say, the true prophet is the man who witnesses to Jesus by his words and by his life. . . . The true prophet, the man who really possesses the spirit of prophecy, is the man whose words and whose life witness to Jesus, and who thereby carries on and continues the witness to God of Jesus Himself.

"(ii) But this phrase can equally mean *the witness which Jesus Christ gives to men.* If we take that meaning, then the phrase will mean that no man can speak to men until he has listened to Jesus Christ; that the message which a true prophet brings to men is a message which he himself has first received from Jesus Christ; that no man can witness to men until he has received the witness of Jesus Christ.

"This is the kind of double meaning of which the Greek language is capable. And it may well be that John *intended* the double meaning; and that we are not meant to choose between the meanings, but to accept both of them. If we do that, then we can define the true prophets as the people who have received from Christ the message they bring to men, and the man whose words and whose works are at one and the same time acts of witness to Jesus Christ" *(The Revelation of John,* vol. 2, pp. 227, 228). (See the excursus at the end of the chapter for further comments.)

THAT OTHER FEAST

"I saw heaven standing open and there before me was a white horse, whose rider is called Faithful and True. With justice he judges and makes war. His eyes are like blazing fire, and on his head are many crowns. He has a name written on him that no one knows but he himself. He is dressed in a robe dipped in blood, and his name is the Word of God. The armies of heaven were following him, riding on white horses and dressed in fine linen, white and clean. Out of his mouth comes a sharp sword with which to strike down the nations. 'He will rule them with an iron scepter.' He treads the winepress of the fury of the wrath of God Almighty. On his robe and on his thigh he has this name written: King of kings and Lord of lords" (Rev. 19:11-16).

Revelation 19:11-21 is the longest of this chapter's three sections and presents the most graphic picture of the Second Coming given in the New Testament. John writes it in apocalyptic symbols, and we cannot help marveling at his choice of colorful imagery. The portrait is not all new; John uses earlier phrases and incorporates them into this climactic picture of the conquering Lamb.

The passage constitutes another description of the so-called grand battle of Armageddon. And just as there was no battle in Revelation 16, so there is no battle in Revelation 19, either. The lost are simply assembled to receive their judgment. Jesus rides a white horse, reminding us of the white horse of the gospel that came into view with the opening of the first seal. The faithful and true One has come to perform a work of righteous judgment.[1] His eyes are still on fire, as we saw in earlier descriptions (Rev. 1:14; 2:18), and He wears crowns—not a few like the beast, but many. And these are not crowns of victory celebrating the battle won at Calvary, but royal crowns, because He comes to reign as King of kings, a right He won at Calvary (Rev. 19:16).

It was not uncommon in centuries prior to John's writing for a king to wear more than one crown to illustrate dominion over more than one country. Ptolemy entered Antioch wearing two crowns, showing himself to be king of both Asia and Egypt. And the Lamb is now the monarch of all nations and peoples, heaven, and the planets of the universe, thus He wears many crowns.

That Jesus has a name which is not known except to Himself is a part of the mystery of our Lord. All eternity will not fully explore the wonders of His name or character. Two Old Testament stories remind us that it is not appropriate or possible for humans to know the names of God.

When wrestling with one of heaven's messengers, Jacob pressed his desire to know the name of the Visitor, but was refused. Gideon also wanted to know the name of his Visitor, but his curiosity remained unsatisfied. An old notion that had persisted from antiquity is that to know the name of a deity would mean power over that deity, so the name has to remain veiled. But this is not the case with our Saviour. Rather, it is simply the issue that He is infinite and beyond our full knowledge. But all that we know and have learned has reinforced the truth that He is absolutely trustworthy.

The robe of the Lamb is dipped in blood, but not His own. He is no longer the suffering Substitute of His people. He is the crowned Conqueror, and the imagery denotes His final battle. Apocalyptically, He bears the stains of those He slays, even before their demise! He is the divine judge Samson, the all-powerful. He is the divine judge Gideon, the mighty general. He is the divine King David, King of kings. He rides to conquer, clothed as if He had already conquered and slain, because with the promises of God, what is yet to happen can be described as if it has already occurred. On this basis John spoke earlier of Jesus as the Lamb slain from the foundation of the world.

That we should read here the ascription "the Word of God" is fitting, because this is reminiscent of the opening words of John's Gospel. Jesus has been a vital word in every generation of this planet's history. He originally spoke, and the world came into existence. He spoke on Sinai and gave an unchangeable statement of His will for each of us. He spoke in Palestine, and lepers lost their plague and corpses rose to life. He spoke at the cross, and a dying man found life. He speaks to our hearts today and changes the end of hope into endless hope. What a fitting title for the conquering Christ!

Then in keeping with the Olivet address description of the Second Coming (Matt. 24:31), Jesus is said to be accompanied by "the armies of heaven," the angelic host. As Jesus is pictured on a white horse, so they also ride white horses like a battalion of eminent soldiers.

The Head of this numberless battalion has a sword with which to smite the nations. This is part of earlier descriptions (Rev. 1:16; 2:12). And He holds a rod or scepter of iron to rule or judge those who have rejected Him as their leader. This repeats the words of the vision of Revelation 12. The reference to the wine press is taken from the vision of Revelation 14. The title "King of kings and Lord of lords" is borrowed from the vision of Revelation 17. So John draws together various aspects of the book's many visions and shows the Lamb supreme, fulfilling all He promised.

"And I saw an angel standing in the sun, who cried in a loud voice to all the birds flying in midair, 'Come, gather together for the great supper of God, so that you may eat the flesh of kings, generals, and mighty men, of horses and their riders, and the flesh of all people, free and slave, small and great.'

"Then I saw the beast and the kings of the earth and their armies gathered together to make war against the rider on the horse and his army. But the beast was captured, and with him the false prophet who had performed the miraculous signs on his behalf. With these signs he had deluded those who had received the mark of the beast and worshiped his image. The two of them were thrown alive into the fiery lake of burning sulfur. The rest of them were killed with the sword that came out of the mouth of the rider on the horse, and all the birds gorged themselves on their flesh" (Rev. 19:17-21).

The graphic language of these verses is another of John's apocalyptic marvels. It is not as lengthy as the description of the sixth trumpet, but it is still vivid. John borrows his description from Ezekiel (39:17-20), where the overthrow of Gog and Magog are depicted. John does not mention those names here, but he does in the following chapter, because literal/local Gog and Magog become spiritual and worldwide in John's application.[2]

In the last verses of Revelation 19 John pictures an angel calling the birds to God's alternate supper. This is a description based on Jesus' words on Olivet concerning the vultures gathered around carcasses (Matt. 24:28). The birds of prey gather to eat the flesh of the lost and their horses. These forces are assembled (Rev. 19:19) to make war, but no war eventuates, because the Lamb overcomes and overwhelms them. In climaxing this second last description of the lost, John names in particular the beast and the false prophet, who deceived earth's inhabitants and caused the lost to receive the mark of the beast and worship his statue. They all suffer the same fate together in the lake of fire.

We have now read the fate of Babylon the harlot and Babylon the city. We have noted the fate of the beast and the false prophet. All that remains is to read the end of the devil himself, the originator of universal misery and chaos, the planetary trauma that came in the train of this angel who plotted to be God and refused to be submissive to his loving Maker. This comes in Revelation 20 . . . and then eternal paradise!

EXCURSUS ON REVELATION 19:10

Since the birth of the Seventh-day Adventist Church in the mid-nineteenth century, its members have proudly affirmed that the gift of prophecy was manifested in the church's prophetic founder, Ellen G. White. As a Seventh-day Adventist, that is my belief too. Further, the writings of Ellen White have been traditionally called by Adventists "the Spirit of Prophecy," a phrase borrowed from Revelation 19:10 and used somewhat synonymously with the phrase "the gift of prophecy." I believe that the Holy Spirit inspired her in her worldwide ministry. However, I believe that if one is to be exegetically precise, the biblical prediction for her spiritual gift of prophecy is to be found in the eschatological words of Joel 2:28-32 and is to be affirmed in the gift lists of Romans 12, 1 Corinthians 12, and Ephesians 4.

Historically, and appropriately, in its statement of fundamental beliefs, Seventh-day Adventists have introduced Ellen White's prophetic gift by asserting that "the church is to come behind in no spiritual gift." However, the development of a full theology of spiritual gifts that includes Ellen White's prophetic gift is long overdue. Of course, such a study is not the focus of this present work. But the following paragraphs attempt to introduce a new paradigm of understanding that affirms the normative function of the "sure word of prophecy," the Scriptures, the gift-of-prophecy ministry of Ellen White, as well as the ministry of thousands of Christians worldwide in every local Christian congregation through the same spiritual gift of prophecy.

THE GIFT OF PROPHECY

God has a method to share the gospel with the unsaved of the world, to bring those who respond into the fellowship of the church, to nurture believers in this fellowship, and to encourage all members to identify the specific ministry for which He has already gifted them (to nurture the saved and/or to reach out to the unsaved) in preparation for Jesus' return. This comprehensive approach, rooted in Calvary, the Bible calls "spiritual gifts."

Through the spiritual gifts entrusted to each believer, God will accomplish *all that the church has been commissioned to do*. The health of each congregation of the body of Christ and its sharing of the gospel worldwide are all *gift based* and *Spirit empowered*.

The gift of prophecy is by its nature one of the most widespread of the Spirit's numerous gifts. It has to be, because it is the nurture gift, the gift that builds a church and maintains it in spiritual health. If this gift is not exercised by some members in each local congregation, those deprived churches would be denied the nurture intended by

God to deter spiritual ill health. On what basis can one make such an assertion? By the words of the apostle Paul to the *local congregation* in Corinth: "Follow the way of love and eagerly desire spiritual gifts, especially the gift of prophecy" (1 Cor. 14:1); "Prophecy, however, is for believers [i.e., in the congregational setting]" (verse 22); "For you can all prophesy in turn so that everyone [i.e., the entire local congregation] may be instructed and encouraged" (verse 31); "Therefore, my brothers, be eager to prophesy" (verse 39). This is the way God has planned to nurture the members of Christ's body.

Romans 12 names several ministries that one can expect in a local congregation. They include helping, teaching, exhortation, giving, leadership, mercy, hospitality, and prophecy (Rom. 12:6-13). There is no possibility of separating prophecy from the other gifts that operate at the *local* congregational level.

Ephesians names several spiritual gifts: apostleship, evangelism, pastor-teachers, and prophecy (Eph. 4:11). As in Romans, there is no suggestion that all but one will be found in local congregations. The nurture gift is essential if the fruit of evangelism is to remain in the ark of the church.

First Corinthians provides two gifts lists. The first list names nine gifts—including prophecy (1 Cor. 12:8-10). The second gift list, at the end of the chapter, names eight gifts—including prophecy (verse 28). The meaning is clear when you read all four New Testament lists of gifts: every local congregation must have someone ministering with the gift of prophecy.

It is worthy of note that Paul uses the same metaphor for an understanding of spiritual gifts in all three New Testament passages where the subject is discussed at any length. He always likens giftedness in the church to the human body. Exploring the body metaphor, we note that while some parts are optional (you can live a full life without a hand, a foot, an eye, an ear), other parts are imperative—without a heart or at least one kidney, the body dies. Similarly, the gifts of prophecy/nurture and evangelism are essential, or the congregation dies.

Every gift from the Holy Spirit to a human being is *perfect for its purpose*. Although the gifts are given to finite human beings, the Spirit's gifts still function perfectly for their divinely appointed purpose.

I have come to believe that the gift of prophecy operates in three spheres of influence. First are the "holy men of God" who penned the words of Scripture. No Christian questions that these individuals exercised the gift of prophecy. Second, as an Adventist, I believe that Ellen White had the gift of prophecy to lead the denomination she helped found. And third, I equally believe that today, as in every time of church history, both men and women are gifted by the Holy Spirit to exercise the gift of prophecy/nurture at the local congregational level. In all three spheres, while the prophecy gift differs in purpose and scope, it is still the same gift, and when used for its designated purpose it accomplishes God's purpose.

To summarize: according to this understanding, the *writers of Scripture* ministered through the gift of prophecy to the entire world for all time, *Ellen White* ministered and continues to minister through the gift of prophecy in the years of the "end-time" to the worldwide Adventist Church, and *someone in every local congregation* has the gift of prophecy and through this gift nurtures a small group of people in that local congregational setting. It is the same gift, but with a different purpose intended by God in each of these three spheres.

---

[1] The expression is based on the words of Isaiah 11:4.

[2] No historical person/place named Gog fits this passage. Whether or not Ezekiel used the name to represent the heathen hosts that would come against Israel is not known. In the same way, no person/place called Magog is known, but again Ezekiel may have used the name as a symbol of those lands from which Israel's enemies would come. For further comment on the possibility that the prophet used a cipher in this passage, see comment on Revelation 20:8.

OUTLINE

1. Introduction to Revelation 20
   Three views of the millennium
   Overview of the chapter
   Significance of the numeral 1,000
   Louis Were's view of a third application
   Summary

2. Satan bound

3. Judgment of the lost

4. Fifth beatitude

5. Close of the millennium

6. Gog and Magog

CHAPTER NINETEEN

ENDING THE CONTROVERSY

As we enter the verses of Revelation 20, we begin an examination of the most controverted chapter of the Apocalypse. Even those who read virtually none of this book want to stake their claims in this territory. Some interpret the millennium without giving any significant attention to the book as a whole. Predictably, such an uncontextualized approach runs a high risk of ending in delusion. Among the most vocal advocates are dispensationalists, who interpret the passage on the basis of a few words in Daniel 9 and predict the rapture of the church seven years before the Second Coming.

The word "millennium" does not occur in the Bible, but comes from two Latin words. It means 1,000 years. The word "chiliasm" is also sometimes used in connection with Revelation 20 and comes from the Greek *chilioi*, which means "thousand."

We should note briefly the three commonly held positions on the millennium, then move into an interpretation that honors the hermeneutic which we have attempted to follow consistently.

Amillennialism views the entire chapter as spiritual, dealing with the Christian in this present life who already, in a spiritual sense, is seated in heavenly places with the Lord. This view considers Satan as having been "bound" since the cross.

Premillennialism views the coming of Jesus as occurring *prior* to the commencement of the 1,000 years. An early Christian view stated that the history of the world from Creation to re-creation would be 7,000 years, the first 6,000 in history, and the 7,000th, the Sabbath age, the millennium of Revelation 20. At the close of this seventh 1,000-year period Satan will rise and with the lost attack the New Jerusalem, but be destroyed in the second death. That destruction will mark the beginning of an Edenic eternity.

Premillennialism comes in many variations. Today the most popular form is the dispensationalist view, which sees the church raptured to heaven before the Second Advent so that it will be spared the horrors of the great tribulation. According to this view, the redeemed will then spend the 1,000 years on this earth, after which Satan will be loosed to deceive the nations, only to be cast into the lake of fire. This paves the way for the beginning of the eternity of peace.

Postmillennialism views the Second Coming as beginning after the 1,000 years. But the nature of these years varies from proponent to proponent. Some see the 1,000 years as referring to the entire period of the preaching of the gospel (for them 1,000 is a symbol of completeness), while others see a literal 1,000-year period at the end of the gospel age, but still before the return of Jesus.

OVERVIEW OF REVELATION 20

Four sections. Revelation 20 has four sections. Section 1 (verses 1-3) describes the binding of Satan for 1,000 years. Section 2 (verses 4-6) describes the 1,000-year reign of the saints with the Lamb. Section 3 (verses 7-10) details the events that transpire at the end of the 1,000 years, including the final destruction of Satan and the lost. Section 4 is the vision of the judgment at the great white throne (verses 11-15).

Having noted the natural divisions, one is immediately struck by the fact that a judgment of the lost is described after they have been finally destroyed! Commentators approach this incongruity in a variety of ways, but the simplest explanation is probably the best. John does not mean us to take the various segments of these final vignettes in chronological sequence any more than we have done in the earlier visions. For example, we noted in chapters 6 and 7 that John pictures the return of Jesus followed nonchronologically with the sealing of the 144,000. This is typical apocalyptic. We ought not to be disturbed by disjunctive chronology in this chapter after having already seen examples in the previous chapters.

One thousand. One other comment must be made before we begin the exposition of the chapter as a whole, and it concerns the number 1,000. We have seen throughout this work that numbers for John are first qualitative and sometimes, but not always, quantitative as well. First, we should observe that 1,000 is 10 x 10 x 10—at last the saints' joy is complete, complete, complete as they begin their eternity with the Lord Jesus.

Plato's *Republic* has a brief passage that illustrates this qualitative notion of completeness. Socrates mentioned sinners who were "weeping and lamenting" for "a thousand years," (which he adds is 10 times a "full life of 100 years"). John's thousand years spell the end or "completeness" of the wild and agonizing history of sin. Thus the idea of 1,000, a multiple of the numeral 10, symbolizing full completeness, has a long history, one that was well established before John wrote the Apocalypse.

We have noted that John uses the number 10 in the sense of completeness on several occasions, including chapter 7 with the 144,000, chapter 9 with the 200 million horsemen, and chapter 14 with the 1,600 furlongs. Because numbers have had this qualitative sense throughout the book, to be consistent we should see a qualitative significance for 10 in Revelation 20 as well.

But does the idea of completeness exhaust the significance of the numeral 1,000? Should we see a quantitative significance as well? The expectation of the Advent in the mid-nineteenth century had been based in no small measure (at least initially) on the early Christian notion of 6,000 years of history and a seventh 1,000-year period for the Sabbath millennium. Bishop Ussher's chronology, published between 1650 and 1654, purported to pinpoint the hour, day, and year of Creation, and with some modifications, that chronology suggested to some nineteenth-century Bible students an imminent return.

After the great disappointment of 1844 (when the word "eschatology" first entered the English vocabulary), the significance of the millennium assumed increasing importance among Christians of various denominations. But there were and continue to be great differences of opinion. For example, on the basis of the prophetic day-for-a-year principle noted in chapters 11, 12, and 13, some assume that the 1,000 years will be 360,000 or 365,000 solar years.

Then how should we view the 1,000 years today? As a symbol of completeness only? As meaning 1,000 solar years? Or 360,000 or 365,000 solar years? Each student of the Apocalypse must make a personal choice.

Louis Were's hermeneutic. A few decades ago a construct was developed in an attempt to resolve the dilemma. Louis Were has suggested that we consider three settings of some prophetic passages (*The Certainty of the Third Angel's Message*, pp. 308-314). We are well acquainted with the *literal and local* applications in the times of literal Israel in which believers looked to literal local fulfillments of prophetic pronouncements. Then, according to the principle that we have applied throughout Revelation, we have seen that the literal/local is applied *spiritually and worldwide* in the age of the New Testament. Literal Israel becomes the spiritual Israel of God. We look to the temple in heaven, not on earth. What happened locally now happens across the globe. Babylon, for example, is now a worldwide force far beyond the Mesopotamian area.

But according to Were, there may be a third setting for some prophecies in which we see *a literal application once again.* After the coming of Jesus there will be one nation under God, Jesus the prince and king of all, and a literal Jerusalem to which all come and in which all worship. If Were is right, then the 1,000 years at the end of this age may be a period of solar years as measured on earth (our years are measured by the earth's rotation around the sun) in which the saints do the work described in Revelation 20.

Summary. The 1,000 years should certainly be viewed first as qualitative, a symbol of the completeness of the plan of salvation. Whether it also has a quantitative meaning, either literal time or prophetic time, is something only the future will confirm.

SATAN IS BOUND

We now begin our examination of the four sections of Revelation 20. At the end of Revelation 19 we saw Jesus revealed as the ultimate conqueror. Babylon, beast, and false prophet have been completely put down. But God cannot write *finis* to the ages of sin until Satan, the originator of the great controversy, has also been dealt with. The opening words of chapter 20 show us that this is precisely what Jesus will do next.

"And I saw an angel coming down out of heaven, having the key to the Abyss and holding in his hand a great chain.

"He seized the dragon, that ancient serpent, who is the devil, or Satan, and bound him for a thousand years. He threw him into the Abyss, and locked and sealed it over him, to keep him from deceiving the nations anymore until the thousand years were ended. After that, he must be set free for a short time" (Rev. 20:1-3).

One would not expect a detailed set of chronological facts at the climax of a series of apocalyptic visions, and we find none. But the New Testament, in various places, fills in the details of the events accompanying Jesus' second coming. First, we learn that the rejecters are slain by the brightness of the Lamb's coming and His angels (2 Thess. 1:8; 2:6-8). Second, we learn from various passages that the wicked are dealt with first; that is, they are destroyed at Jesus' return. It is only after they are slain that the accepters are caught up to meet Jesus in the air to be with Him eternally (Matt. 13:30, 49; Ps. 50:3; Jer. 25:33). But John was not in the least concerned with such details. He painted a broad, surrealistic canvas.

That the saved are taken to heaven to be with Jesus when He returns (presumably for the millennium) is supported in Scripture, but not documented in the Apocalypse itself. John's Gospel recalls Jesus' words that He would go and prepare places in heaven for His followers and return to take us to them (John 14:1-4). Paul recalled that we will be caught up from the earth to meet Jesus in the air and be with him forever (1 Thess. 4:16, 17). The series of events may be summarized as follows:

When Jesus returns:

rejecters are slain first;

accepters who are dead are resurrected;

accepters who are alive, plus the resurrected, meet Jesus in the skies;

all the redeemed are taken to their homes in heaven; and

the millennium begins.

One additional point might be added here. John writes that "the rest of the dead" did not come to life until the end of the millennium (Rev. 20:5). That statement makes it clear that only some of the dead come to life at the beginning of the millennium, and they must be the redeemed of all ages. John also notes that the resurrection at the beginning of the millennium is the "first resurrection" (verse 5). We shall refer to the "second resurrection" after discussing the events that transpire during the millennium.

In the fifth trumpet a fallen angel received the key to the "bottomless pit" and opened it, and immediately the hosts of Satan poured out to do their dastardly work. In Revelation 20 an *un*fallen angel descends from heaven, takes hold of Satan, chains him, throws him into the bottomless pit, and seals it. But John adds that the sealing would be only for 1,000 years and then Satan would be loosed for a short time.

The binding of Satan is a symbol not unlike some we use in the West today. If someone wishes to do something but through circumstances cannot, he or she might say, "My hands are tied." If there is something that a person wishes to say but feels compelled not to say, he or she might comment, "My lips are sealed." In neither case is there anything literal about the words. But they are perfectly understandable metaphors.

In the case of Satan it is quite obvious that a gargantuan set of circumstances has just occurred. All earth's inhabitants who have rejected Jesus (symbolized by Babylon, beast, and false prophet) have been annihilated. His ugly experiment on this wayward planet has come to naught, and Satan at that moment will stand, as he once did in heaven, with only the angels who sided with him in the heavenly dispute. Together, bound by the circumstances of the death of the lost at the coming of Jesus, they must sit in "lonely confinement" for the millennium while a judgment takes place.

JUDGMENT OF THE LOST

"I saw thrones on which were seated those who had been given authority to judge. And I saw the souls of those who had been beheaded because of their testimony for Jesus and because of the word of God. They had not worshiped the beast or his image and had not received his mark on their foreheads or their hands. They came to life and reigned with Christ a thousand years. (The rest of the dead did not come to life until the thousand years were ended.) This is the first resurrection."

"Then I saw a great white throne and him who was seated on it. Earth and sky fled from his presence, and there was no place for them. And I saw the dead, great and small, standing before the throne, and books were opened. Another book was opened, which is the book of life. The dead were judged according to what they had done as recorded in the books. The sea gave up the dead that were in it, and death and Hades gave up the dead that were in them, and each person was judged according to what he had done. Then death and Hades were thrown into the lake of fire. The lake of fire is the second death. If anyone's name was not found written in the book of life, he was thrown into the lake of fire" (Rev. 20:4, 5, 11-15).

The judgment of the lost that transpires during the millennium is twice described in Revelation 20, once from the perspective of the redeemed (verses 4-6) and once from God's personal perspective (verses 11-14). In the first account, John records that he saw thrones and people seated on them involved in a work of judgment. But in somewhat typical apocalyptic fashion, he does not identify the judges until the next sentence, and then as a kind of parenthetical afterthought he notes that the judges are those who had been martyred for "the testimony of Jesus." Some of them, under the fifth seal, had begged God to bring vengeance on Satan. God had replied that time would have to run its course, but He promised there would be a full accounting. During the millennium the martyrs sit in judgment on their persecutors and executioners. These are the people of whom it could truthfully be said at the close of probation that they did not worship the beast or his image, did not receive the mark of the beast on forehead or hand, and thus they live and reign with the Lamb for the millennium.

Since it is obvious that the lost are "lost" at this point, by what strange quirk could they be the subjects of judgment? Evidently God will not execute *eternal* death on any person until the redeemed have had the opportunity to investigate any case and confirm that He has acted with full justice. Here is the ultimate in divine vulnerability.

In addition, this is the *end* of the great controversy. Not only are human beings on trial, but also Satan and his angels must answer for their lies about God. So while discussing the judgment described at the beginning of the chapter (verses 4-6), we must also consider the verses at the end of the chapter (verses 11-15), which describe God as seated on His throne.

No one would ever choose to be called to stand before God in this judgment of the lost. As John expresses it: "Earth and sky fled from his presence" (verse 11). Then John notes that the dead, the small and the great, stood before this throne. Not the living, but the *dead* are on trial. They are not there in person, because they are dead—some have been slain by the brightness of the return of Jesus, and the rest remain dead from the time of their demise on earth.

John emphasizes that no lost person can escape this judgment. He states that even those who died at sea, with no traditional burial place, would be included in this judgment. And all will be judged by their deeds, their works, their actions. Ladd wrote that this is to emphasize that God's final judgment will not be "arbitrary and capricious, but based squarely upon the deeds of men" *(A Commentary on the Revelation of St. John,* p. 273).

Barclay has added: "The idea here is very simple; the idea is that a record of all men's deeds is kept by God. The symbolism is that all through life we are writing our own destiny; we are compiling a story of success or failure in the sight of God; we are acquiring a record which will bring us either honor or shame in the presence of God. Every man is the author of his own life story. It is not so much God who judges a man as it is that a man writes his own judgment" *(The Revelation of John,* vol. 2, p. 251).

The saved will not be saved by their works or deeds, but by the Lamb's works and deeds. Yet it is in daily works, or the lack of them, that *evidences* of choices and loyalties are revealed. We show by how we live on which side of the great controversy we stand. And for the lost, it is the same. To summarize—during the millennium:

- Satan and his angels are "bound" on this earth,
- the lost are all dead, and
- the redeemed are in heaven investigating and assisting in the final judgment of the lost.

THE FIFTH BEATITUDE

"Blessed and holy are those who have part in the first resurrection. The second death has no power over them, but they will be priests of God and of Christ and will reign with him for a thousand years" (verse 6). This beatitude offers three promises.

The first is that those who are raised to eternal life at the coming of Jesus, those who are raised in this first resurrection, will never experience what John terms "the second death." We all die once (except those few who will be alive at the end of this age and go to heaven without seeing death, but they are exceptions). We die the first time because of Adam's sin. In the words of Paul: "In Adam all die" (1 Cor. 15:22). Adam and Eve's act of rebellion brought the sentence of death on themselves and all their progeny. But Paul continues: "So in Christ all will be made alive." We are all sentenced to die, but Jesus' triumphant death guarantees for everyone a resurrection from that first death.

The second promise that comes to those who rise in the first resurrection is that they will be priests of God. In the days of the Old Testament sanctuary the priests were honored guests, so to speak, in God's house. Although only one tribe walked and worked in this sacred atmosphere, it will not be this way in heaven. When Jesus redeems us from the presence of sin at His return, as His priests we will all work and walk in His presence forever.

There is also a present meaning for the second promise of this beatitude. The Latin word for priest comes from *pontifex* and means "a bridge builder." Today all who accept Jesus act as bridge builders for the lost. In some way each of us can be a bridge who offers to those who have yet to experience it the catharsis of forgiveness and the regeneration that eliminates guilt, all through a personal encounter with Jesus.

The third promise of the beatitude is that we will reign with Jesus. He is king, and as members of His family we also are royalty. As princes and princesses we will reign in heaven with our Father during the millennium and forever. This notion of the reigning of the saints appears first in Revelation 5:10 in the song of the elders and the four living creatures. There it states that the redeemed will reign on the earth. Revelation 20:6 adds, as just noted, that the redeemed will reign in heaven, and Revelation 22:5 adds that their reign will last forever and ever.

Wordsworth noted that the Alexandrine manuscript has the word "reigning" in Revelation 20:4 in the present tense—"they are reigning." This would fit nicely with the assertion in Ephesians that in a sense "God raised us up with Christ and seated us with him in the heavenly realms in Christ Jesus, in order that in the coming ages he might show the incomparable riches of his grace" (Eph. 2:6, 7).

AT THE CLOSE OF THE MILLENNIUM

Revelation 20:7-10 details the end of the controversy with Satan when he receives his eternal judgment. The passage is cryptically short. It seems as if John just wanted to say it and finish with it, then press on to paint the details of the pictures of the New Jerusalem and the bliss of eternal togetherness with Jesus.

"When the thousand years are over, Satan will be released from his prison and will go out to deceive the nations in the four corners of the earth—Gog and Magog—to gather them for battle. In number they are like the sand on the seashore. They marched across the breadth of the earth and surrounded the camp of God's people, the city he loves. But fire came down from heaven and devoured them. And the devil, who deceived them, was thrown into the lake of burning sulfur, where the beast and the false prophet had been thrown. They will be tormented day and night for ever and ever" (Rev. 20:7-10).

John states that at the end of the millennium Satan will be unsealed or released from his prison (verse 7). This confirms the words of verse

3 that Satan's "chaining" will last for just the millennium, and then he will be released for a short time. It was observed earlier that it is the death of the rejecters of God's love that causes Satan's binding. For the first time in his connection with the earth he will have no one to tempt, no one to model his character of rebellion. It is only the reversal of the circumstances that bound Satan that can release him, and that means a resurrection. Again, to quote John, "the rest of the dead [i.e., the wicked dead who were not raised at the beginning of the millennium in the first resurrection] did not come to life until the thousand years were ended" (verse 5).

The second resurrection is the resurrection of the lost. They are raised so that they can answer for their own choices. During the millennium it will be confirmed beyond any doubt that they chose not to accept Jesus and thus have sentenced themselves to eternal death in keeping with God's warning that "the wages of sin is death" (Rom. 6:23). The judgment at the great white throne does not make any arbitrary decisions. It simply recognizes each person's decision about Jesus.

In his Gospel, John quotes the words of Jesus: "Do not be amazed at this, for a time is coming when all who are in their graves will hear his voice and come out—those who have done good will rise to live, and those who have done evil will rise to be condemned" (John 5:28, 29).

It is only in the Apocalypse that we learn that these two resurrections are a millennium apart. But that the first is for the saved and the second exclusively for the lost is plain from Jesus' statement.

There is an element of justice here that we might miss if we do not pause to consider it. God will not bring any person into the worship atmosphere of the New Jerusalem against that person's free will. Only those who choose such a life enjoy it. Take people who love sin and ask them to attend church, prayer meetings, and Bible study groups, and they are most uncomfortable. The child of Satan is offended by the joys of the Christian, just as the child of God is increasingly offended by sin. God would not do willing rebels a service by placing them in the holy atmosphere of worship in heaven.

At the second resurrection the lost of every age will be living at one time. The earth will be teeming with uncounted millions of people. At that sight Satan will be filled with a rage that cannot be measured. The lost reach to the "four corners of the earth," and they number as "the sand on the seashore" (Rev. 20:8). We can only guess at Satan's plans, because John skips over the events with such rapidity that there is virtually no detail. But evidently Satan suggests to his followers that they take the New Jerusalem by force, since they vastly outnumber the redeemed.

John moves with such short staccato phrases that he omits to say that the New Jerusalem will descend from heaven at the end of the millennium in fulfillment of the words of Zechariah 14:4, 5. It is only in the next chapter that he describes it: "I saw the Holy City, the new Jerusalem, coming down out of heaven from God, prepared as a bride beautifully dressed for her husband. And I heard a loud voice from the throne saying, 'Now the dwelling of God is with men, and he will live with them. They will be his people, and God himself will be with them and be their God'" (Rev. 21:2, 3).

GOG AND MAGOG

At the sight of the magnificent city, Satan will marshal his worldwide army and send them marching toward "the camp of God's people, the city he loves" (Rev. 20:9). This description is based in part on the words of Ezekiel 38 and 39, as mentioned in the latter part of the exposition of Revelation 19. It is for this reason that John likens the forces of the lost to Gog and Magog.

Ezell ably commented on this literary borrowing: "At this point we would do well to see how John has adapted the two sections of Ezekiel which are central to his message in Revelation 19 and 20. . . . The first passage of central importance in John's vision is Ezekiel 39:17-20. This section describes the Lord telling Ezekiel to call forth the birds and beasts of the field to feast upon the dead armies of Gog. This is followed by a description of God setting His glory among the nations. This section in Ezekiel provides the allusion to the feast of the birds in Revelation 19:17-21. Ezekiel 38:14-16 speaks of the invasion of Gog coming upon the people of Israel *after* they were in the land of promise. This passage is alluded to in Revelation 20:7, 8" (*Revelations on Revelation*, p. 92).

It has been observed that no historical character called Gog fits the passage and no place called Magog is known, and this constitutes something of a puzzle to exegetes.* Some have seen Magog as a code name or cipher for Babylon, because although Ezekiel named so many of the great enemies of Israel in his earlier chapters, there is just one major exception—Babylon.

That Gog might be a code name or cipher for Babylon in Revelation is an intriguing possibility, because this is the Bible's last reference to Satan and sinners, the kingdom that throughout Revelation has been referenced by the name *Babylon*.

In two sentences John describes the end of the controversy: "They marched across the breadth of the earth and surrounded the camp of God's people, the city he loves. But fire came down from heaven and devoured them. And the devil, who deceived them, was thrown into the lake of burning sulfur, where the beast and the false prophet had been thrown. They will be tormented day and night for ever and ever" (verses 9, 10).

Earlier we discussed the meaning of the Hebrew expression "for ever" and saw that we must consider the context to determine the meaning. In Revelation 20 we would assume the meaning also to be "as long as life lasts" and "until God's purposes have been accomplished." The lake of fire is designed to eliminate from the earth every trace of sin in preparation for the re-creation in which Jesus will restore the Eden once lost through sin.

When the fires burn out, we will shake our heads in a mixture of sorrow and great joy—sorrow that so many have not stood with Jesus, and joy that Satan's great experiment in rebellion has been put down and that we can enter eternity secure and at peace. At last we will be with Jesus and each other face-to-face in a union of love that will never be disrupted, because "trouble will not come a second time" (Nahum 1:9).

---

* Some exegetes apply Gog to Antiochus IV as a type of the future antichrist.

Outline

1. Introduction to Revelation 21, 22
   Suggestion of a chiasm
   Use of numerals 7 and 12

2. New heaven and new earth

3. The Holy City

4. Tree and river and life

5. Final invitations

CHAPTER TWENTY

HOME AT LAST

H ome at last"—that is the theme on which John ends his apocalyptic version of the great conflict. Under the inspiration of the Holy Spirit, the last two chapters of his book form the most sublime anthem.

INTRODUCTION TO REVELATION 21 AND 22

These last two chapters contain some important elements that we should note at the outset. First, the accent at the climax is where it should be—on Jesus the Lamb. Here John names the Lamb 7 times, because in these two chapters the eternal Sabbath rest begins. Then we observe an extensive use of the numeral 12, a predictable symbolic element in describing the eternal kingdom of glory, now a reality.

These two final chapters divide themselves into four major sections. In Revelation 21:1-9 John describes the new heaven and earth. In Revelation 21:10-27 he describes the New Jerusalem. In Revelation 22:1-9 we read of the glory of the river of life and the tree of life, elements from the original Eden. And the book closes with intensely personal invitations to accept Jesus as Lord and Saviour, a fitting apocalyptic version of the appeals at the end of the Olivet sermon. After the horrendous chapters detailing the annihilation of the opposition, this is nothing but bliss.

NEW HEAVEN, NEW EARTH

"Then I saw a new heaven and a new earth, for the first heaven and the first earth had passed away, and there was no longer any sea. I saw the Holy City, the new Jerusalem, coming down out of heaven from God, prepared as a bride beautifully dressed for her husband. And I heard a loud voice from the throne saying, 'Now the dwelling of God is with men, and he will live with them. They will be his people, and God himself will be with them and be their God. He will wipe every tear from their eyes. There will be no more death or mourning or crying or pain, for the old order of things has passed away.'

"He who was seated on the throne said, 'I am making everything new!' Then he said, 'Write this down, for these words are trustworthy and true.'

"He said to me: 'It is done. I am the Alpha and the Omega, the Beginning and the End. To him who is thirsty I will give to drink without cost from the spring of the water of life. He who overcomes will inherit all this, and I will be his God and he will be my son. But the cowardly, the unbelieving, the vile, the murderers, the sexually immoral, those who practice magic arts, the idolaters and all liars—their place will be in the fiery lake of burning sulfur. This is the second death.'

"One of the seven angels who had the seven bowls full of the seven last plagues came and said to me, 'Come, I will show you the bride, the wife of the Lamb'" (Rev. 21:1-9).

The climax of the Apocalypse begins, predictably, with words from the Olivet address. Jesus had foretold, "Heaven and earth will pass away" (Matt. 24:35), and here we read the fulfillment: "The first heaven and the first earth had passed away" (Rev. 21:1). All that has been contaminated with sin must be replaced. The crust of this earth and the atmosphere constantly befouled by our industries will be replaced. Then the earth will be as verdant as the original Eden, and the sky above more pure than any we have experienced. John adds that in this re-creation there will not be any sea. Barclay commented: "The sea is always an enemy. The Egyptians saw the seas as the power which swallowed up the waters of the Nile, and left the fields sterile and barren and unfruitful for the want of water. In the old myths and legends the sea is an enemy, hostile to man, container of the forces of chaos and destruction. . . .

"*The Sybilline Oracles* (5.447) say that in the last time the sea will be dried up. *The Ascension of Moses* (10.6) says the sea will return into the abyss. In Jewish dream the end of the sea is the end of a power and a force hostile to God and to man" *(The Revelation of John,* vol. 2, pp. 254, 255).

The sea is the first of seven evils John names, which in this new heaven and new earth state will cease to exist as eternal Sabbath rest begins. The other six are death, mourning, weeping, pain, curse, and night. The elimination of the great seas, which today cover three quarters of the earth's surface and separate people from each other, does not imply the elimination of all rivers, streams, and lakes. And when one considers the Great Lakes of America and Canada, such bodies of water can be gigantic in size and surpassing in beauty.

The sight of the New Jerusalem left John grasping for adequate words. As one who must have attended many Eastern weddings, the metaphor came that the city was "prepared as a bride beautifully dressed for her husband" (verse 2).

One of the most difficult questions about the description of the New Jerusalem is How much of what John states is to be taken symbolically, and how much is literal? For example, what purpose would be served by God building a wall around the city in a perfect world without conflict and without the slightest threat of danger? And what purpose would be served by God spreading gold on every thoroughfare?

We have no complete answers. Perhaps much of this is to be accepted symbolically. Ladd said: "The details of the description of the holy city are altogether symbolic terms in describing the redeemed church" *(A Commentary on the Revelation of St. John,* pp. 276, 277).

But then again, John is describing the era when literal terminology may be appropriate again, a point made in connection with the millennium. By faith we are looking for "a city . . . whose builder and maker is God," as has been the case with the line of believers stretching back to patriarchal times (Heb. 11:10, KJV). There is to be a reality, and just as Adam and Eve could not have known the slightest disappointment in what they found at their creation, neither will we. But we will have to wait until the end to know how literal these descriptions turn out to be. It is certain that no matter how graphically John may have painted the picture, with our limited minds we cannot even image how magnificent it will be.

When the New Jerusalem settles on this earth with the Lamb in the midst surrounded by the redeemed, they will experience literally what the ancient tabernacle had symbolized through the *shekinah* in the Most Holy Place. For centuries that radiant glow hovered above the mercy seat of the ark of the covenant, showing that God dwelt with His people, abiding in that humble house made with human hands. But after He returns, "the dwelling of God is with men, and he will live with them" (Rev. 21:3).

This is the transition moment in eternity. The cross of Jesus is the hinge of time, and that sacrifice purchased the right to this transcendent transition. From now on there will be no more tears, death, mourning, or pain. All those experiences have "passed away" (verse 4). The form of the verb suggests that this is something which happens suddenly, abruptly. As we see death disappearing in the smoke of the lake of fire, so also we see the great reversal of the curse on the first Eden.

At this point in the Apocalypse we hear the voice of God the Father. Jesus the Lamb has spoken often, but now the Father joins the Son in proclaiming: "I am making everything new!" (verse 5). After those words God makes an earnest appeal. As the First and Last, the Beginning and the End, as Author and Finisher of our faith, God offers us the water of life "without cost."

Who could refuse such an invitation? Unhappily, many will, and God gives the list, which begins with "the cowardly." Far more people will miss heaven for this reason than for murder and immorality. In John's day courage had to be displayed. In the shadow of the might of Rome and its misunderstanding of the Christian church, one needed courage to stand for conviction. And in the coming final conflict, courage will be just as important.

THE HOLY CITY

"And he carried me away in the Spirit to a mountain great and high, and showed me the Holy City, Jerusalem, coming down out of heaven from God. It shone with the glory of God, and its brilliance was like that of a very precious jewel, like a jasper, clear as crystal. It had a great, high wall with twelve gates, and with twelve angels at the gates. On the gates were written the names of the twelve tribes of Israel. There were three gates on the east, three on the north, three on the south and three on the west. The wall of the city had twelve foundations, and on them were the names of the twelve apostles of the Lamb.

"The angel who talked with me had a measuring rod of gold to measure the city, its gates and its walls. The city was laid out like a square, as long as it was wide. He measured the city with the rod and found it to be 12,000 stadia in length, and as wide and high as it is long. He measured its wall and it was 144 cubits thick, by man's measurement, which the angel was using. The wall was made of jasper, and the city of pure gold, as pure as glass. The foundations of the city walls were decorated with every kind of precious stone. The first foundation was jasper, the second sapphire, the third chalcedony, the fourth emerald, the fifth sardonyx, the sixth carnelian, the seventh chrysolite, the eighth beryl, the ninth topaz, the tenth chrysoprase, the eleventh jacinth, and the twelfth amethyst. The twelve gates were twelve pearls, each gate made of a single pearl. The great street of the city was of pure gold, like transparent glass.

"I did not see a temple in the city, because the Lord God Almighty and the Lamb are its temple. The city does not need the sun or the moon to shine on it, for the glory of God gives it light, and the Lamb is its lamp. The nations will walk by its light, and the kings of the earth will bring their splendor into it. On no day will its gates ever be shut, for there will be no night there. The glory and honor of the nations will be brought into it. Nothing impure will ever enter it, nor will anyone who does what is shameful or deceitful, but only those whose names are written in the Lamb's book of life" (verses 10-27).

The second main section of the climax to the Apocalypse describes the New Jerusalem. And unpredictably, it is one of the angels with the seven last plagues who has the privilege of showing John "the bride, the wife of the Lamb" (verse 9). We can find encouragement in this. We sometimes feel that others always get the breaks, while we are left to do what everyone else chooses not to do. But time will right such problems. Would any angel choose to be the carrier of a plague that devastates the earth? Yet to one of these same angels came the joy of being John's personal escort, showing him the Holy City.

God's appointed angel chose a place to view the New Jerusalem that would show it to its best advantage. He took John to "a mountain great and high," from which he watched, spellbound, "the glory of God" (verses 10, 11). At last the kingdom of glory becomes reality, and to celebrate that kingdom John launches into the repeated use of the symbolic number 12, using it 12 times. He names 12 gates (verse 12), 12 angels (verse 12), 12 tribes (verse 12), 12 foundation stones (verse 14), 12 names (verse 14), 12 apostles (verse 14), 12 x 1,000 furlongs (verse 16), 12 x itself cubits (verse 17), 12 foundation stones (verses 19, 20), 12 gates (verse 21), 12 pearls (verse 21), and 12 kinds of fruit (Rev. 22:2).

In this description we see the sharpest contrasts between the bride and the harlot, Jerusalem and Babylon, Holy City and great city, lofty mountain and wilderness, Lamb and beast, faithfulness and faithlessness.

The first part of the city on which John comments is the wall, and as has already been observed, this is not needed in a perfect world. Walls are for protection, safety, and security. Thus this wall reminds us that in the presence of the Lamb we have eternal safety and security. As Isaiah wrote: "In that day this song will be sung in the land of Judah: We have a strong city; God makes salvation its walls and ramparts" (Isa. 26:1).

John sees 12 gates, three on each of the four compass points, to show that the church has been gathered in unity into the kingdom from all the world. The names of the 12 tribes and the 12 apostles celebrate the united church of the Old and New Testaments, and remind us that the church is built on prophets and apostles, with the Lamb as the chief cornerstone (Eph. 2:20).

The 12 foundations are precious stones, reminding us of the 12 stones in the breastplate of the high priest. Throughout history Jesus, our High Priest, has carried His people in His heart. These stones are also known as the 12 signs of the pagan zodiac, but John lists them in the reverse order, perhaps to show that God has overthrown paganism.

The measurements of the city, we must assume, are symbolic. The length, breadth, and height of this city are said to be equal, and all are multiples of 12. John describes the city in terms of the Most Holy Place, a perfect cube. The original room, some 17 feet long, high, and wide, which "contained" the presence of God, is now expanded beyond comprehension to a city of the redeemed, basking in the literal *shekinah*—the Lamb Himself.

In Revelation 11 John received a rod with which to measure the temple and the altar. In that passage we saw a work of preservation parallel to the work of the sealing in Revelation 7. As we come to the climax, not John but an angel receives a rod with which to measure everything—gates, walls, and city. Here is the symbol of the preservation of the redeemed.

When describing the city, John chooses a word for "gates" that is used in the New Testament mostly in connection with a house (Acts 10:17; 12:13, 14; Luke 16:20), but this city is the home of the saved, the Most Holy Place of the Lamb, so John speaks of the entrances as the doors of a home.*

But what are we to understand about a city gate fashioned from a single pearl? Pearls come from oysters. A single grain of irritation is turned into an item of surpassing beauty. Similarly, in this life the saved take the irritations and trials designed to discourage, and through the power of the Holy Spirit use them to develop characters of beauty. This is the heart meaning. But of the literal, who can know?

Streets of gold are also an interesting feature of the description. Perhaps the most obvious intent of the description is that the most precious of all metals, the possession of the rich and a foundation of the international monetary system, will not be stored in vaults or reserved for the few in the hereafter. What in this life is so precious will be so common as to be appropriate for the paving of streets.

There is no temple in God's Jerusalem. Throughout history the temple has been the place to worship the invisible God. But hereafter, as it was in Eden, we will worship face-to-face in the temple of the Creator's creation.

Barclay commented: "Here there is a symbolism which is plain for all to see. Where God is, the church is; where the presence of Christ is, there is the church. In the words of the old Latin tag: *Ubi Christus, ibi ecclesia*. Buildings do not make a church; liturgy does not make a church; no form of government makes a church; no method of ordination to the ministry makes a church. The one thing which makes a church is the presence of God and of Jesus Christ. Without that there can be no such thing as a church" (vol. 2, pp. 275, 276).

RIVER AND TREE OF LIFE

"Then the angel showed me the river of the water of life, as clear as crystal, flowing from the throne of God and of the Lamb down the middle of the great street of the city. On each side of the river stood the tree of life, bearing twelve crops of fruit, yielding its fruit every month. And the leaves of the tree are for the healing of the nations. No longer will there be any curse. The throne of God and of the Lamb will be in the city, and his servants will serve him. They will see his face, and his name will be on their foreheads. There will be no more night. They will not need the light of a lamp or the light of the sun, for the Lord God will give them light. And they will reign for ever and ever" (Rev. 22:1-5).

John reserves his last description for the river of life and tree of life, because eternity is about life. Wordsworth has made an apt comment comparing Eden's tree with the New Jerusalem's: "The Book of Genesis reveals Almighty God, the Creator of all things very good; Adam, formed from the earth; Eve, taken from his side; the Serpent in Paradise; Man tempted, and a curse pronounced on him for disobedience in eating the fruit of the forbidden tree; and driven from Eden; and the way of the Tree of Life guarded by a flaming sword; and the promise made in mercy, that the seed of the Woman should bruise the Serpent's head.

"Pass now from the first chapters of Genesis to the last of the Apocalypse. The same God is revealed, seated on His throne; Heaven and Earth adore Him: Man also is there; Adam is there in Christ, the Second Adam; Eve also is there, in the Bride of the Second Adam, the Church; Paradise is also there, not lost, but regained, and the Tree of Life, no longer fenced with a flaming brand, but open to all, *for the healing of the nations*. And there 'is no more curse'" *(The New Testament of Our Lord*, vol. 2, p. 275).

The way John sees it, the tree grows on both sides of the river. Is this grove of trees on each side of the river of life an apocalyptic version of God's provisions for the life to come? This appears to be drawn from Ezekiel's vision: "Fruit trees of all kinds will grow on both banks of the river" (Eze. 47:12). And the usual process of nature, of trees producing one kind of fruit a year, is transformed, because this restored "tree" produces 12 different kinds of fruit, one during each month of the year. And even the leaves of the trees are nutritious, for "the healing of the nations" (Rev. 22:2). This does not imply sickness. Rather, it symbolizes God's endless provision for the redeemed; though once doomed to die, they now enjoy eternal life and health.

It is interesting that centuries before John, Homer wrote of a garden in the palace of King Alcinous in which pears, pomegranates, olives, apples, figs, and grapes grew through every season, and whenever a piece of fruit was picked, another immediately grew to take its place. The description has some interesting parallels to John's garden.

FINAL INVITATIONS

"The angel said to me, 'These words are trustworthy and true. The Lord, the God of the spirits of the prophets, sent his angel to show his servants the things that must soon take place.'

"'Behold, I am coming soon! Blessed is he who keeps the words of the prophecy in this book.'

"I, John, am the one who heard and saw these things. And when I had heard and seen them, I fell down to worship at the feet of the angel who had been showing them to me. But he said to me, 'Do not do it! I am a fellow servant with you and with your brothers the prophets and of all who keep the words of this book. Worship God!'

"Then he told me, 'Do not seal up the words of the prophecy of this book, because the time is near. Let him who does wrong continue to do wrong; let him who is vile continue to be vile; let him who does right continue to do right; and let him who is holy continue to be holy.'

"'Behold, I am coming soon! My reward is with me, and I will give to everyone according to what he has done. I am the Alpha and the Omega, the First and the Last, the Beginning and the End. Blessed are those who wash their robes, that they may have the right to the tree of life and may go through the gates into the city. Outside are the dogs, those who practice magic arts, the sexually immoral, the murderers, the idolaters and everyone who loves and practices falsehood.

"'I, Jesus, have sent my angel to give you this testimony for the churches. I am the Root and the Offspring of David, and the bright Morning Star.'

"The Spirit and the bride say, 'Come!' And let him who hears say, 'Come!' Whoever is thirsty, let him come; and whoever wishes, let him take the free gift of the water of life.

"I warn everyone who hears the words of the prophecy of this book: If anyone adds anything to them, God will add to him the plagues described in this book. And if anyone takes words away from this book of prophecy, God will take away from him his share in the tree of life and in the holy city, which are described in this book.

"He who testifies to these things says, 'Yes, I am coming soon.' Amen. Come, Lord Jesus.

"The grace of the Lord Jesus be with God's people. Amen" (verses 6-21).

The postlude of the Apocalypse contains a rich montage of speakers. For example, in verses 6 through 9 we meet at least three. First, we hear from one of the angels who has been instructing John through the series of visions. Then Jesus speaks, personally announcing His imminent return. This is followed by some comments and appeals from John himself. As a sign of authenticity the apostle writes: "I, John, am the one who heard and saw these things" (verse 8).

The concluding word comes from Jesus, and it is appropriate that

He should have the final major comment, because it is a book about Him and from Him. His thrust lies in two areas: first, the imminence of His return: "Behold, I am coming soon" (verse 7); "Behold, I am coming soon! My reward is with me, and I will give to everyone according to what he has done" (verse 12); and "Yes, I am coming soon" (verse 20).

Second, hard on the heels of Jesus' triple announcement of His return, is the triple invitation to be part of the kingdom when He returns. "The Spirit and the bride say, 'Come!' And let him who hears say, 'Come!' Whoever is thirsty, let him come; and whoever wishes, let him take the free gift of the water of life" (verse 17).

At the end of the Olivet address Jesus described the two categories of people living at the end of history as sheep and goats. Each person will be settled into a course that cannot be changed: one with the seal of the Lord's character, the other with the mark of Satan's character. In recognition of personal choices, Jesus will say at the close of probation: "Let him who does wrong continue to do wrong; let him who is vile continue to be vile; let him who does right continue to do right; and let him who is holy continue to be holy" (verse 11).

In the final sentences of his book John comments on those who are going through to the kingdom of the Lamb. In the King James Version, we read that the saved will be those who have kept His commandments, and this parallels the thought expressed in Revelation 14:12. But this is not the preferred reading, as most modern translations attest. Now more commonly we read: "Blessed are those who wash their robes, that they may have the right to the tree of life" (verse 14). Barclay has suggested a reason for this difference: "In Greek the two phrases would be very like each other. *Those who have washed their robes* is *hoi plunōntes tas stolas,* and *those that do His commandments* is *hoi poiountes tas entolas.* In the early Greek manuscripts all the words are written entirely in capital letters, and there is no space left between the words. If we set down the two phrases in English capital letters we see how closely they resemble each other:

HOIPLUNONTESTASSTOLAS
HOIPOIOUNTESTASENTOLAS

"'Those who have washed their robes' is the reading of the best manuscripts, and it is easy to see how a scribe could make a mistake in copying, and could substitute the more ordinary and usual phrase" (vol. 2, pp. 289, 290).

Morris added: "There is a sense in which the saved are washed once and for all. . . . But we so easily defile ourselves day by day as we live in the pressures of this world, that it is necessary for Christ's own to be cleansed continually (1 John i. 7). We are reminded of the soiled robes of those in the church of Sardis. John brings out the effect of the washing in terms of two pieces of imagery he has already used: those who wash in this way *have right to the tree of life* (cf. verse 2), and they *may enter in through the gates into the city* (cf. xxi. 27)" *(The Revelation of St. John*, p. 260).

Joyfully John then pens the last words: "The grace of the Lord Jesus be with God's people. Amen" (verse 21). How fitting that the last written words from the aged apostle should be about grace! And because we have seen Jesus through every chapter and every vision, we too should close the pages of the Apocalypse breathing words of praise for the grace of the Lamb, who has purchased us, sustained us, and will protect us until He can glorify us within the secure walls of His love in our eternal home.

> "Through many dangers, toils, and snares,
> 　I have already come;
> 'Tis grace hath brought me safe thus far,
> 　And grace will lead me home" (John Newton). ●

---

* Plutarch used the same word to describe the entrances of temples and palaces. In New Testament times the gate was separated from the house by a courtyard.